# Lead with Me

*Lead with Me*, Second Edition, provides courageous principals with the tools for partnering with teachers in the student learning and improvement process. This practical guide explains the skills teacher leaders need and offers advice for principals who wish to engage teachers in learning these skills. Packed with stories and examples from educators in the field, this second edition explores how to:

- build mutual trust and accountability with teachers and faculty
- encourage and facilitate professional development
- carefully manage the distribution of power and authority by involving faculty members in decision-making

The revised second edition provides a variety of helpful tools—PowerPoint presentations, reflection questions, activities for professional learning sessions, and annotated lists of additional resources—that can be downloaded as eResources: www.routledge.com/9781138785595

**Anita Pankake** is an independent dissertation editor and coach. She was formerly Professor and Director of the Doctoral program in Educational Leadership at the University of Texas Pan American. Prior to her work in higher education she was a teacher, team leader, assistant principal, and principal.

**Jesus Abrego, Jr.** is Associate Professor of Educational Leadership at the University of Texas Rio Grande Valley. He was a teacher, administrator in the Texas Education Agency, high-school assistant principal, and middle-school principal before moving to the university.

# Other EYE ON EDUCATION
## Books Available from Routledge

(www.routledge.com/eyeoneducation)

*Ten Steps for Genuine Leadership in Schools*
David M. Fultz

*College for Every Student: A Practitioner's Guide to Building College and Career Readiness*
Rick Dalton and Edward P. St. John

*Leading Learning for ELL Students: Strategies for Success*
Catherine Beck and Heidi Pace

*Leadership in America's Best Urban Schools*
Joseph F. Johnson, Jr., Cynthia L. Uline, and Lynne G. Perez

*The Power of Conversation: Transforming Principals into Great Leaders*
Barbara Kohm

*First Aid for Teacher Burnout: How You Can Find Peace and Success*
Jenny G. Rankin

*What Successful Principals Do! 199 Tips for Principals, Second Edition*
Franzy Fleck

*The Revitalized Tutoring Center: A Guide to Transforming School Culture*
Jeremy Koselak and Brad Lyall

*7 Ways to Transform the Lives of Wounded Students*
Joe Hendershott

*School Leadership through the Seasons: A Guide to Staying Focused and Getting Results All Year*
Ann T. Mausbach and Kimberly Morrison

*Distributed Leadership in Schools: A Practical Guide for Learning and Improvement*
John A. DeFlaminis, Mustafa Abdul-Jabbar, and Eric Yoak

*The Leader's Guide to Working with Underperforming Teachers: Overcoming Marginal Teaching and Getting Results*
Sally Zepeda

*Five Critical Leadership Practices: The Secret to High-Performing Schools*
Ruth C. Ash and Pat H. Hodge

*Strategies for Developing and Supporting School Leaders: Stepping Stones to Great Leadership*
Karen L. Sanzo

# Lead with Me
# A Principal's Guide to Teacher Leadership

Second Edition

Anita Pankake and Jesus Abrego, Jr.

NEW YORK AND LONDON

First published 2017
by Routledge
711 Third Avenue, New York, NY 10017

and by Routledge
2 Park Square, Milton Park, Abingdon, Oxon, OX14 4RN

*Routledge is an imprint of the Taylor & Francis Group, an informa business*

© 2017 Taylor & Francis

The right of Anita Pankake and Jesus Abrego, Jr. to be identified as authors of this work has been asserted by them in accordance with sections 77 and 78 of the Copyright, Designs and Patents Act 1988.

All rights reserved. No part of this book may be reprinted or reproduced or utilised in any form or by any electronic, mechanical, or other means, now known or hereafter invented, including photocopying and recording, or in any information storage or retrieval system, without permission in writing from the publishers.

*Trademark notice*: Product or corporate names may be trademarks or registered trademarks, and are used only for identification and explanation without intent to infringe.

*Library of Congress Cataloging-in-Publication Data*
Names: Pankake, Anita M., 1947– author. | Abrego, Chuey, author.
Title: Lead with me : a principal's guide to teacher leadership / by Anita Pankake and Chuey Abrego.
Description: [Second edition] | New York : Routledge, 2017. | Previous edition published: Larchmont, N.Y. : Eye on Education, c2006, by Gayle Moller and Anita Pankake. | Includes bibliographical references and index.
Identifiers: LCCN 2016053629 | ISBN 9781138785588 (Paperback) | ISBN 9781138785595 (Hardback) | ISBN 9781315767734 (eBook)
Subjects: LCSH: Teacher participation in administration. | Teacher-principal relationships. | Educational leadership.
Classification: LCC LB2806.45 .M65 2017 | DDC 371.1/06—dc23
LC record available at https://lccn.loc.gov/2016053629

ISBN: 978-1-138-78558-8 (hbk)
ISBN: 978-1-138-78559-5 (pbk)
ISBN: 978-1-315-76773-4 (ebk)

Typeset in Palatino LT Std
by Apex CoVantage, LLC

Visit the eResource website: www.routledge.com/9781138785595

# Dedication

For my part, this book is dedicated to Dr. David W. Pankake, my husband, my mentor, and my most admired educator. As I shared in another of my works, David has been "the wind beneath my wings" for all of my professional career, and he remains my model for life-long learning. I can only hope to be so well read and knowledgeable about issues of the past and present as he is at 89 years of age. His penchant for wanting to "know more" continues to amaze me. I do not know how much more time together God will grant us, but I want to work hard to make each and every moment full, fun, and memorable.

Anita Pankake

I dedicate *Lead with Me* to my parents and first teachers, Lupita and Jesus S. Abrego. I recall Mommy helping me with my homework, while Papi taught math on the front porch on a chalkboard, setting high standards and encouraging success.

Jesus "Chuey" Abrego, Jr.

# Contents

| | |
|---|---|
| Meet the Authors | ix |
| Preface | xiii |
| Acknowledgments | xvi |
| eResources | xvii |

*Part 1: Taking Responsibility for Intentional Leadership*    1

**1: Ushering In a New View of Leading and Learning**    5
- Why We Should Be Concerned    5
- Shifting Scope of Principal Responsibilities    7
- Principles for Promoting, Building, and Sustaining Quality Teacher Leadership    9
- Intentional Leadership Is Required    13
- Summary    15

**2: Investigating the Vision, the Roles, and the Reasons**    17
- The MMS Efforts Continue: What's Next for Theresa?    23
- What Are Teacher Leader Roles?    25
- Teacher Leadership from Multiple Perspectives    29
- What Makes Teacher Leadership Essential?    29
- Summary    34

**3: Developing a Culture of Continuous Improvement**    36
- A History of Change    38
- Themes Common to the Change Process    38
- Adult Growth and Development    42
- Teaching Career    47
- Personal Issues    50
- Philosophy of Teaching and Learning    51
- Preparing Others    51
- Making the Long-Term Commitment: Advice for Staying on Target    53
- Summary    55

*Part 2: Putting the Principles into Action*    57

**4: Building Positive Relationships**    61
- Investing in Teacher Leadership to Build Human and Social Capital    62
- Self-Study: Potential for Increasing Human and Social Capital    63
- Summary    80

**5: Distributing Power and Authority**    83
- Reasons to Distribute Power and Authority    84
- Self-Study: Beliefs About Distributed Power and Authority    85

|  |  |  |
|---|---|---|
|  | Acting to Distribute Power and Authority | 89 |
|  | Structures to Facilitate the Distribution of Power and Authority | 94 |
|  | Summary | 98 |
| 6: | **Aligning Teacher Leadership with Professional Learning** | **100** |
|  | Thinking Differently About Professional Learning | 101 |
|  | Self-Study: Experiences with Professional Learning | 103 |
|  | Structures for Professional Learning | 105 |
|  | A Comprehensive Professional Leading and Learning Model | 111 |
|  | Reluctant Teacher Learners | 115 |
|  | Summary | 118 |

*Part 3: Supporting and Sustaining Teacher Leadership* — 121

| 7: | **Creating a Context of Support for Teacher Leaders** | **125** |
|---|---|---|
|  | Tensions Between Principals and Teacher Leaders | 126 |
|  | Teacher Leader Roles and Functions | 127 |
|  | Teacher Leadership Skills Development | 134 |
|  | Summary | 144 |
| 8: | **Sustaining Teacher Leading and Learning** | **146** |
|  | Jay's Intentional Leadership: Connecting to the Framework for Intentional Leadership | 151 |
|  | Theresa's Intentional Leadership: Connecting to the Framework for Intentional Leadership | 155 |
|  | Markham Middle School and Predictable Disruptors | 158 |
|  | Theresa Manages Her Disruptors | 161 |
|  | Summary | 162 |

**Afterword** — 163
**Bibliography** — 164

# Meet the Authors

## Our Own Teacher Leadership Stories

It seems fitting to begin by sharing our own teacher leadership stories—our personal histories and experiences as teacher leaders. We both have spent our careers working, teaching, training, and leading as teachers and alongside teachers. We believe the narratives below reveal how being a teacher leader is often something you do without necessarily being aware you are doing it. Over the years we have worked with teacher leaders, we find this is not an uncommon phenomenon.

## Anita Pankake: *Opportunities Abound*

I did not begin college thinking I would end up being a teacher and I did not become a teacher thinking I would end up as a school administrator. In a way, I hate to admit that, since it sounds more serendipitous than rationally planned. But, by this stage of life, I have come to believe we can plan all we like, but in many cases opportunities and people come into our lives that we could never have planned for and take us in directions we would not have considered on our own. My first teaching job was as a kindergarten teacher. My college preparation was in elementary education with an emphasis in early childhood, so teaching kindergarten was a perfect assignment for me.

Prior to the opening of school that year, I was discovering all of the ins and outs of my new school, attending the new faculty orientations, and meeting colleagues with whom I would be working for the coming year and hopefully beyond. While preparing my classroom for the first-day arrival of my students, a central office administrator stopped by. I recall, vividly, attaching construction paper grapes and bananas with students' names on them to my classroom door with large letters reading: Welcome to the Bunch!!

The visit from this central office administrator set in motion an opportunity to work with a large group of kindergarten teachers in the school district on kindergarten curriculum. I enjoyed released time for this project, visits to almost every school in the district and friendships with several of my kindergarten teacher peers. Wow, what a first-year experience! One of the major things I learned during this time was that not everyone was as welcoming in these teacher leadership opportunities for me as I was! Some of my teacher colleagues did not appreciate that "the new kid" seemed to be playing a starring role in a world they had occupied for some time. This situation caused me to have mixed feelings about the wonderful things I was learning and people I was meeting; at the same time, there was great resentment and cool-to-cold interactions with individuals I had anticipated would be my colleagues. In many ways, I felt I was being punished for doing good work. As I think about it now, I see that this was my first experience with being a teacher leader.

For my third year, I transferred to another elementary school with a reputation for innovative programs. I was hired in on a primary team and during my second year at that school was appointed team leader of a 4th–6th-grade team.

In my fifth year of teaching, with my master's degree completed and my administrative certificate in hand, I began applying for principalships. I had numerous interviews, but no offers. I suppose being 26 years old, female, and only 5 years of teaching might have had something to do with not being selected. This was sort of a downer given my grand start with the curriculum work, my move to a highly innovative (for the time) elementary school and appointment as a team leader in that school. Looking back, this would have been a perfect time to savor all that I had done and allow some of my experiences to mature internally, to transform from learning to wisdom. But, I was young and absolutely sure I could conquer the world, given the chance.

Eventually, I secured a position in which I was half-time teacher/half-time assistant principal. This was one of the most challenging jobs I have ever had. Having two half-time jobs really ends up becoming 1.5 to 2 full-time jobs. As I reflect, it was an excellent way to transition from being a full-time teacher to engaging with a variety of administrative responsibilities. My immediate supervisor was good to me and very forgiving of my inexperience. From here I moved into a full-time assistant principalship and on to a principalship in a large elementary school.

I really had a lot of opportunities early in my career. Thankfully, I also had some wonderful mentors at every point along the way. Because so much came so fast, I think without these supportive individuals, I might have drowned. As it was, these early experiences helped me in my career in both public schools and higher education to look for leaders in every aspect of those organizations. I regret not having been smarter about the concepts we share in this book. While I think my work was good, I know it could have been better, especially with a deeper knowledge of self, others, and organizations.

**Anita Pankake** attended Indiana State University in Terre Haute, Indiana, for her bachelor's and master's degrees; she attained her EdD at Loyola University–Chicago. She has worked for 13 years as an elementary teacher, team leader, assistant principal, and principal in public schools in Indiana and Illinois. She retired after 27 years in higher education working in universities in Texas, Illinois, and Kansas. She has remained active in the field through adjunct work with The University of Nebraska, through writing for publication, and as an independent consultant and dissertation editor/coach. She and her husband, David, along with their little dog, Scruffy, live in San Antonio, Texas. Anita enjoys various crafts, especially knitting and quilting. She is an avid reader and belongs to a local book discussion group.

# Jesus "Chuey" Abrego, Jr.: Caught in the Middle

I began my teaching career at a middle school mid-year—interviewed with the principal on a Friday and began my work as a science teacher the following Monday. It was my first teaching job right after graduation; I was ecstatic to have a job! However, my friends suggested that I should wait. They stressed that taking on a teaching position during the middle of the year would be difficult and challenging. Nonetheless, I was too excited to listen to family and friends or understand the various challenges that I would be facing as a first-year teacher. Besides I was a certified teacher. I was ready to take on the classroom! What did they know?

Excited to begin my tenure as a science teacher, I spent the weekend shopping for school supplies at the local Wal-Mart. This was my first "real" job, so I had to borrow a few dollars to get my room ready for Monday. I spent $100 of my mother's money (my mother has reminded me often that I had to borrow funds). I purchased a box of yellow chalk, pencils, reams of paper, writing pads, a stapler, and other materials to help me get through the semester.

I believed, at the time, I was ready for my first day. In retrospect, I had no sense or idea of what I should have expected on Monday or how I would begin my week. I was a certified teacher, but all my experiences had taken place under guidance of a university supervisor. I received support and direction from beginning to end through my practicum. However, this setting was different. I would be the official teacher of record. It was my classroom! I would be making all the decisions without having to go through a supervisor . . . or least I thought that's how it worked.

As I walked onto the campus Monday morning, I realized I didn't know anyone there. The principal hadn't introduced me to any of the faculty, even the science faculty. Perhaps the fact that the principal interviewed me without any input from other faculty contributed to my apprehension. I realized at the moment I entered the main office to sign in that I was a complete stranger!

In my preparation to become a science teacher, most, if not all, of my work followed an organized process with clear guidance. I assumed that in my new setting the principal and teachers would provide direction and a sense of order for me. To my surprise, my week was chaotic. No one came to my aid. The staff thought I was the substitute teacher. And the kids asked what had happened to their previous teacher. Not one person on campus knew what was happening to me or my students. I was not prepared for my first week and I wasn't sure who or how to ask for help. Regardless, after I had only taught for a few weeks, the science faculty voted unanimously that I should serve as chair of the science department—I happily accepted. How exciting! I was now in charge of helping other teachers!! Only 2 months on the job, and I was already the department leader!

I survived my first semester. But, the experience left an impression I would never forget!

I began the following year as the new department head and still a relatively new teacher. To my surprise a new science teacher had been hired over the summer. She seemed passionate, but had similar concerns and questions about her role, discipline, curriculum, and overall fit within the campus. I had only been at the campus for 6 months, but gave my advice freely and without really understanding my own role as a teacher and department head. We became a team of two misfits and a real force for change.

Since then, Anita and Jesus have enjoyed and sometimes endured numerous growth experiences and career opportunities.

**Jesus "Chuey" Abrego, Jr.** attended the University of Texas Pan American–Edinburg (at the Brownsville campus) in Brownsville, Texas, for his bachelor's degree. He completed his master's degree at Texas State University in San Marcos, Texas, and attained his EdD at the University of Texas Pan American–Edinburg. He has worked as a middle-school science teacher, department head, in numerous capacities for the state department of education, inner-city urban high-school assistant principal, and middle-school principal in Texas. He is currently an Associate Professor in the department of Organization and School Leadership with the College of Education and P-16 Integration at the University of Texas Rio Grande Valley. His research interests focus on professional learning communities and teacher leadership. He and his wife, Michelle, along with their daughter, Hannah, live in Rancho Viejo, Texas. They also have two dogs, Taco and Patticake. Chuey enjoys spending time with his family.

# Preface

## Overview of the Book

The first edition of this book aimed to assist hard-working principals who want to see improvement in student learning, believe that teachers can be their partners in this goal, and are willing to put aside the traditional leadership thinking of the past and move toward a new way of leading, a way that has gained increased attention and acceptance, but still is not the norm. These are the courageous principals who want to build trust among the adults so that all teachers can be involved in making decisions about teacher and student learning. While principals may not always be the sources of change, they most certainly must be advocates for it. If principals can be supported in their work to lead in a new way, there is the likelihood that school change will start, grow, and stay over time.

This second edition remains organized in a way that recognizes the busy lives of principals. We know principals must snatch opportunities for their own professional renewal while dealing with a multitude of school issues. We retained the purposeful repetition of ideas throughout the book. We believe returning to the key ideas in our framework enhances the possibility the reader will understand the connections between chapters. It also allows the chapters to be read out of sequence without losing the big picture. Consequently, as you read, if you occasionally ask, "Didn't they say that earlier?", that is good—very much what we intended.

The book has three parts. This division was not arbitrary; the parts are designed to make the book user friendly. As we worked on this edition, many conversations were held about the need for more sections or fewer sections; if there should be more components in the framework or whether it was okay as is. Much time was spent on how to include new things without eliminating what is already so good. We have worked hard to improve and update the work without losing the solid core of the first edition.

Our preference would be for every reader to start at the beginning and read through the entire book in sequence. However, the book's organization continues to allow for other methods. We believe it is essential for everyone to read Part 1; this section contains the foundational information on which the remaining chapters are built. In Chapter 1, readers will explore the principles on which the suggested practices that follow are based. Chapter 2 starts with a description of Markham Middle School, where teacher leadership is well developed and influences the core operations of the school. A new component is a chronicling of one teacher's journey into a formal leadership position at MMS and Jay's, MMS principal, and planning as he gets closer and closer to retirement. Theresa's emerging story appears at the beginning of each chapter. Her development as a teacher leader in this formal role has allowed us to "film live," rather than just look back. Our decision to include Theresa's story in this edition was based on a desire to look deeper into the teacher leadership development phenomenon. We met Theresa in the first edition as the individual telling the story of Markham Middle School's development as a learning community, of Jay's actions as a school leader with a new view of leadership as an organizational quality rather than a position, and of her own reflections about both herself and her colleagues' journey toward recognizing themselves as leaders. In this second edition, Theresa remains reflective, but also decides to seize the opportunity to increase her influence as a leader beyond her team to curriculum and instruction issues affecting the entire school. Readers witness this new chapter in Theresa's leadership journey as it unfolds. Jay's story in this edition links the past of MMS and its future. We have retained the original story of MMS, but have added crucial but often forgotten components in change, those of sustainability and leadership succession. Jay not only remembers the past but also looks toward the time when he will no longer be principal at MMS.

Following the school vignettes, *teacher leadership* is defined, characteristics of teacher leaders are described, and a list of reasons for building and sustaining teacher leadership is shared. Chapter 3 includes information about the change process and readiness strategies required for moving toward full implementation of this new way of leading and learning.

The chapters in Part 2 focus on the principles that form the framework for the book: building positive relationships, distributing power and authority, and aligning teacher leadership and teacher learning. Here, readers may choose to read the chapters in sequence or select what seems most relevant for their situation.

Part 3 focuses on the principal's actions needed to assure the ongoing development of teacher leadership. In Chapter 7 we address the special learning needs of teacher leaders, including leadership skills that may not have been a part of their professional preparation. Additionally, this chapter emphasizes the special relationships that must develop between principals and teacher leaders. These relationships include mutual trust, mentoring, and accountability. Chapter 8 revisits Markham Middle School, 7 years later, as the development of teacher leadership continues not only at the school but also throughout the school system. It is here that we review not only what has been accomplished at MMS, but also what Jay and his MMS teacher leaders have done and plan to do to maintain and sustain the good work for their students. We describe important actions needed to ensure that teacher leadership continues as a key component of achieving the school's vision of student learning, even in the face of formal leadership changes and other predictable disruptors. Theresa also reviews her first year focusing on each of the three framework principles. We also give more emphasis to leadership succession as a planned activity, not a serendipitous one.

Following this chapter is an Afterword consisting of a letter from Jay, the principal of Markham Middle School, with a P.S. from Theresa. Both Jay and Theresa challenge other principals and teacher leaders to usher in this new way of leading and learning.

## Special Features

Voices from the Field: Throughout the book, to strengthen ideas and recommendations, we draw on teacher leader and principal voices through direct quotes that are set off in shaded boxes. These messages from people in the field remind the reader about the importance and reality of this work.

Additional Resources and Tools: In this edition, we provide resources and practical tools that can be used by school leaders individually or with others in the school. The resource lists have been updated. These lists contain both printed and online resources that supplement, complement, or extend the material presented in the chapter.

Tools for each chapter are available in the eResources online. Most all tools from the first edition have been retained and a few new items have been developed specifically to enhance and reinforce concepts in this new edition. The tools are labeled by name and by chapter number and sequence of presentation in the chapter (1.1, 1.2, etc.)

Updated References: Myriad pieces of writing and research on topics related to teacher leadership have appeared over the last decade. We have attempted to include many of these as updates to our references throughout the book. However, we have also retained some of the works of note upon which many of the more recent ones have built. We believe we offer a balanced combination of foundational materials and recent trends in our presentation. A full list of all references used is included at the end of the book.

PowerPoints and Focused Activities: As additional elements in our eResources, we provide prepared PowerPoint presentations for each chapter, along with some additional information and activities for leaders of professional learning and instructors in principal preparation programs. We offer some suggestions on ways these activities might be used, but are confident that new and more creative ways to make use of these will be found.

We applaud those courageous principals and other leaders who will embrace and act on the ideas presented in this book. Their efforts to put these ideas into practice will enrich schools with increased learning for both adults and students.

*Anita & Jesus ("Chuey")*

# Acknowledgments

Many colleagues, friends, and family members deserve our sincere appreciation for their patience and continuing encouragement of our work in writing this book. First we acknowledge the support of our professional colleagues. Significant contributions to this book are quotes from accomplished teacher leaders and administrators in the United States and Canada. We thank each for their willingness to share. We also want to thank Jaime Lopez from Harlingen, TX and Braden Welborn and Nancy Gardner from the Center for Teaching Quality (CTQ) in Chapel Hill, North Carolina (www.teachingquality.org) for their help in identifying and securing these voices from the field. The initial graphic representation of the Intentional Leadership Model took form with the technical talents of Ramiro Lazano and Angelo Morsello. There is a SUPER special "thank you" to Heather Jarrow, our publisher, who remained positive regardless of the number of times we promised a final manuscript but failed to deliver.

Most importantly, though, is our heartfelt gratitude for the support of our spouses David Pankake and Michelle H. Abrego, who waited patiently on the sidelines while we were consumed with this work. David and Michelle are our best friends and both are truly gifted educators.

Acknowledgments would not be complete without expressing our debt of gratitude to Dr. Gayle Moller. Her partnership in developing the first edition of *Lead with Me* was an unbelievable learning experience and collegial interaction that I, Anita, will always cherish. Obviously, the second edition would not have been possible without the strong foundation set in that original document. Jesus and I have performed significant remodeling to the original work, including changing language, updating some references and locating new ones, creating some special support materials for use with groups, found new technology links to enhance readers' sources of current information, and taken some different perspectives here and there. All of these we see as improvements, but we fully recognize the strong base upon which these improvements are made. Thank you Gayle; we hope you are pleased with the results of our work.

# eResources

Resources to complement this book can be downloaded, printed, used to copy/paste text, and/or manipulated to suit your individualized use. You can access these downloads by visiting the book product page on our website: www.routledge.com/9781138785595. Then click on the tab that reads "eResources" and then select the file(s) you need. The file(s) will download directly to your computer.

- Part I Overview PowerPoint
- Chapter One
  - Chapter Overview PowerPoint
  - Online Resources
  - Reflection Questions
- Chapter Two
  - Chapter Overview PowerPoint
  - Online Resources
  - Reflection Questions
- Chapter Three
  - Tool 3.1: Working with the Administrative Staff
  - Tool 3.2: Working with the Administrative Staff
  - Chapter Overview PowerPoint
  - Online Resources
  - Reflection Questions
- Part II Overview PowerPoint
- Chapter Four
  - Tool 4.1: Common Characteristics of Teacher Leaders
  - Tool 4.2: Teacher Leader Information
  - Tool 4.3: Develop a Sociogram
  - Tool 4.4: Suggestions for Recognizing Teachers
  - Tool 4.5: Teacher Leadership Myth Busters

- Chapter Overview PowerPoint
- Online Resources
- Reflection Questions
♦ Chapter Five
  - Tool 5.1: A Guided Reflection
  - Tool 5.2: Creating a Personal Vision Statement
  - Tool 5.3: Decision-Making Chart
  - Tool 5.4: Project Delegation Form
  - Tool 5.5: School Structures Inventory
  - Chapter Overview PowerPoint
  - Online Resources
  - Reflection Questions
♦ Chapter Six
  - Tool 6.1: Assessing Supportive Conditions for Professional Learning
  - Tool 6.2: Inventory of Professional Learning Formats
  - Tool 6.3: Reluctant Teacher Learners
  - Chapter Overview PowerPoint
  - Online Resources
  - Reflection Questions
♦ Part III Overview PowerPoint
♦ Chapter Seven
  - Tool 7.1: Personal–Professional Balance
  - Tool 7.2: Building Consensus
  - Chapter Overview PowerPoint
  - Online Resources
  - Reflection Questions
♦ Chapter Eight
  - Chapter Overview PowerPoint
  - Reflection Questions
♦ Letter Examples
♦ Letter Use Directions
♦ Sociogram Activity

- ♦ Sociogram 1
- ♦ Sociogram 2
- ♦ Sociogram 3
♦ Team Rescue PowerPoint
♦ What Is Teacher Leadership Activity?

# Part 1: Taking Responsibility for Intentional Leadership

# Intentional Leadership

- Relationships
- Teacher Leadership
- Distributed Power & Authority
- Professional Learning

# Part 1
# Taking Responsibility for Intentional Leadership

The Framework for Intentional Leadership, located on the opposite page, is a graphic interpretation of the principal leadership promoted in the first and now second editions of this book. Within the figure are circles representing the principles on which the original work is based: building positive relationships, distributing power and authority, and aligning teacher leadership and professional learning. When these three conditions converge, teacher leadership emerges and thrives, as denoted in the overlap of the circles. A portion of each of these three circles stands alone, indicating that some concepts and activities within the area are unique to that principle. Additionally, a portion of each of the three circles overlaps with the others. This overlapping indicates the interdependency of many of the concepts and activities in all three circles. None of this will happen, however, without the principal's purposeful actions in each of the three inner circles. Intentional leadership is on the outside of the graphic, in order to represent how it drives the development of teacher leadership.

Part 1 consists of three chapters that provide the knowledge base needed to make the best use of the recommended actions proposed in the other parts of the book. In Chapter 1, "Ushering In a New View of Leading and Learning," the rationale for the Framework for Intentional Leadership is presented. In Chapter 2, "Investigating the Vision, the Roles, and the Reasons," the Markham Middle School (MMS) vignette, used in the first edition, describes a school where teacher leadership is well developed and, thus, clarifies the vision. We have added a scenario intended to update and extend the original MMS story. The focus remains on Markham Middle School (MMS) but shifts to Theresa's continuing development as both a teacher leader and a developer and supporter of teacher leaders. This is followed by definitions of teacher leadership, and descriptions of those who emerge as teacher leaders, the roles they take, and the benefits of teacher leadership to individual teachers, the school, and the principal. Chapter 3, "Developing a Culture of Continuous Improvement," begins with a scenario chronicling Theresa's teacher leadership journey and provides an overview of the complexity of introducing change in a school culture due to the diversity of individual teachers' reactions. The principal is offered interventions to consider for dealing with this diversity of reactions.

# 1 Ushering In a New View of Leading and Learning

"Although some teacher leaders may seek administrative roles, most teachers in leadership roles do not view these opportunities as steps up the ladder to the administrative ranks. These teachers want to remain close to students and are willing to assume leadership roles that will affect decisions related to their daily practice with those students."
Katzenmeyer & Moller in *Awakening the Sleeping Giant*

Whereas the old models of leadership may have encouraged building the capacity of a single person, specifically the campus principal, the problems facing education today require principals and teacher leaders to work side by side as a community of practitioners.

What is teacher leadership? How is it defined? Why is teacher leadership important in a school? Are teachers comfortable talking about teacher leadership with other teachers and campus administrators? What role does a principal play in developing and supporting teacher leadership? How does a typical campus go about identifying, building capacity of and supporting teacher leaders? What actions or specific strategies can a principal carry out across the campus in order to enable teachers to lead? These and other questions are answered in this second edition of *Lead with Me*.

The initial hard work in *Lead with Me* by Moller and Pankake published in 2006 focused on the premise that teacher leadership plays an integral part in a successful campus, and is best supported when principals are deliberate in their efforts in creating the right conditions so that shared leadership flourishes.

The second edition continues to acknowledge that Intentional Leadership in managing and leading a school is not just the work of one person, namely the principal. The principal is the person at the top of the hierarchy in most schools. He or she directs and evaluates the work of the faculty and staff in all facets of the school's mission. Historically, the principal was responsible for management responsibilities, maintaining order, hiring teachers, working with the community, and addressing any unanticipated problems that only the principal could resolve.

## Why We Should Be Concerned

While these expectations still exist, over the past decade there have been the added burdens of grade retention, issues related to poverty, international comparisons of student achievement, high-stakes testing, gangs, high school graduation rates, increased numbers of special interest groups—especially English Language Learners (ELLs), issues with lack of preparation for universities and college, expanded local, state and federal regulations, and heightened parent demands. Additionally, the principal must be the liaison for school system demands, the instructional leader, and an innovator in operations. Every element of the organization appears to be dependent on the strengths and talents of this single individual.

Most principals struggle to meet these ever-expanding expectations. Data from 500 principals interviewed in *The 29th Annual Met Life Survey of the American Teacher* (MetLife, 2012) reported 75 percent of the principals polled felt the job is too complex, with nearly half, 48 percent, reporting they were under great stress. Unfortunately, many leave the position, resulting in recurring turnover and a shortage of highly qualified principals. They are not being replaced because teacher leaders recognize the undesirability of these administrative roles. In the same MetLife survey (2012), 69 percent of the teachers asked were not at all interested in becoming a principal.

Long gone, however, are the days of a single hero leading the charge. Instead, schools in the twenty-first century deal with complex issues and challenging problems requiring a bolder approach to problem solving. Schools require a community of practitioners focused on shared leadership to create opportunities for teachers and principals to engage collaboratively and collectively as learners and leaders of the school. Thus intentional leadership encourages purposeful collaboration and the redesign of the educational environment into a learning community. However, before teachers and principals can do this work, they must redesign and reculture schools with regards to attitudes and perceptions about shared leadership and teacher leadership. Creating and implementing structures that encourage a team to collaborate, share leadership, and improve relationships are the critical challenges of intentional leadership for both principals and teachers.

The time has come for a change in the way we structure school leadership. Currently, the structure is not working effectively for principals, teachers, or students. Rather than trying to do it all, principals should follow the precept that "good principals are more hero-makers than heroes" (Barth, 2001, p. 448). We believe principals can intentionally support these "heroes," or teacher leaders, to help move schools beyond this current leadership quandary. This, however, will happen only if they begin viewing leadership as more than just a few people in formal roles.

This new leadership structure emerges within a community of learners focused on the moral purpose of schooling which is improved student learning. While a principal's attention to this work could certainly be grounded in a variety of goals, such as reducing the work overload, preventing chaotic interactions or many others, the most important aspect of everyone's efforts at the school is to ensure a sustained focus on the school's vision for student learning. Consequently, the improvement of teaching and learning in schools cannot be left to chance, but rather, requires that principals' actions focus on meeting this goal. Whatever the motive for seeking the principalship, the primary responsibility, once in the position, should be providing leadership that builds an ongoing commitment to continuous improvement of teaching that results in increased learning for all students.

In this chapter, we explore the expanding instructional leadership responsibilities of principals and discuss how teacher leaders are essential to success in achieving accountability for the learning of all students. Then, we present three principles that support a framework for principals' actions. Finally, we put forward the major premise of the book: principals can learn to be intentional in their leadership to promote, build, and sustain teachers' leading and learning which will ultimately affect student learning.

## Shifting Scope of Principal Responsibilities

The main difference between highly effective and less effective principals is that the former are actively involved in curricular and instructional issues and the latter spend most of their time on organizational maintenance and student discipline (Cotton, 2003). Additionally, effective principals really don't work any harder than less effective ones, they just work smarter. Essential to working smarter is encouraging and enlisting teachers' leadership as a means of leveraging their own (Ackerman & Mackenzie, 2007). Too often, principals can become consumed with issues not directly related to instruction. However, to be successful, principals must make students' learning needs the top priority.

### From the Field

Ensuring that every student achieves such targets and has such experiences in our schools is beyond the scope of any one individual working in a school building. Even the best building principal, if working in isolation, will find such goals nearly impossible to achieve and sustain.

Brad Hurst<br>
10th–12th-grade Science<br>
Grimes, Iowa

Historically, the principalship role responsibilities have evolved more toward indirect support for the teaching and learning process rather than direct involvement in that process. One consequence of this is the lack of opportunities for principals and teachers to work together, often resulting in adversarial roles. Now, with the increased emphasis on accountability for student learning, bridges must be built between the administrative and the instructional functions. Effective principals and teacher leaders are the pioneers in these developing but fragile relationships.

We have created Venn diagrams to represent principal leadership and teacher leadership in varying relationships. When little or no overlap between teacher leadership and principal leadership exists, the two circles of the diagram barely touch (Figure 1.1), indicating both classroom activities and school operations are functioning but there is no overlap between the two entities—principals manage school-wide issues, and teachers take care of their individual classrooms. This situation sometimes occurs when well-meaning principals try to protect teachers' time by doing as much as possible alone so teachers are not burdened. It also happens when principals do not know how to collaborate, or fear the risks inherent in such interactions.

When principals increase the time they spend on instructional activities and teachers participate in leadership responsibilities, the two circles begin to overlap (Figure 1.2). This indicates both principal and teachers are beginning to view instructional and management issues as closely related. Teachers' classroom leadership experiences may bring an important perspective to the decisions and activities

Figure 1.1. **No Interdependence**

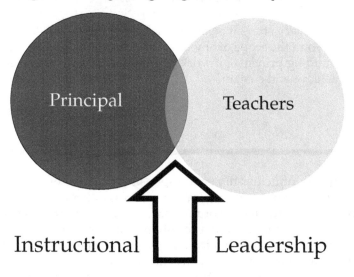

Figure 1.2. **Beginning Stages of Interdependence**

being initiated at the school level. In *Cage-Busting Teacher*, Hess (2015) claimed that teachers find ways, inside or outside their classrooms, to bring all their ideas and experience to bear. Thus, it makes sense that principals help create environments that provide teachers opportunities to grow, learn, and lead without having to leave the classroom or their school. As success with individual projects and processes reveals the positive impact teacher leadership can have, and as school-wide issues and programs move into classrooms, the amount of coordination and collaboration between teacher leaders and principals increases.

When implemented, a range of 30 to 50 percent overlap of the two entities—administrative leadership and teacher leadership—exists (Figure 1.3). Placing an upper limit of 50 percent is purposeful. More than 50 percent overlap might intrude on the teachers' energy and time needed to focus on their fundamental work of instructing students.

Figure 1.3. **Principal and Teacher Leadership Interdependence**

Principals must both address day-to-day demands and provide leadership for instructional improvement. Consequently, they are faced with three options:

- *Do everything themselves or with a few teachers they select.* The impracticality of doing everything alone becomes evident as the principal's responsibilities expand. Working with only a few selected teachers establishes a kind of elitism and can create the illusion that there are "insiders" who influence the principal. This discourages other teachers who might lead.
- *Sit back and let leadership occur in a chaotic manner.* Letting leadership emerge haphazardly may result in dysfunctional teacher leadership creating a toxic school culture.
- *Intentionally plan and facilitate the process of collaborative leadership.* Effective principals are intentional in their efforts to build collaborative leadership. Teacher leaders influence others; therefore, we advocate principals exercise intentional leadership to ensure teacher leadership is focused on student learning.

We suggest that principals not hold "leadership rights," but be responsible for creating opportunities for teachers to lead and learn. This is not a quick-fix program; instead, developing teacher leadership demands high energy and devoted time over an extended period. None of this happens, however, unless the formal leader, the principal, is *intentional* about facilitating the effort.

We want to point out that teachers' perspectives regarding leadership in the school must also change. Teachers must believe they can be or realize they already are leaders in the school.

Next we describe three related principles that, when coupled with the principal's intent, can result in effective teacher leadership.

## Principles for Promoting, Building, and Sustaining Quality Teacher Leadership

The guiding principles we offer provide the framework for this book. Building positive relationships, distributing power and authority, and aligning teacher leadership with teacher learning focus the principal's actions on increased teacher leading and learning.

## Principle #1: Leadership Through Relationships

*To promote, build, and sustain quality teacher leadership, positive relationships are essential.* Relationships are primary in determining how effective a principal will be. A relationship-motivated leader focuses on developing close interpersonal relationships throughout the organization. Group members in these organizations have a high degree of confidence in and loyalty for their leader. The atmosphere is generally positive with teachers trusting, liking, and getting along with the leader (in our case, the principal or teacher leader) (Northouse, 2013). Donaldson (2001) summed it up nicely: "Leadership is a *relational*, not an individual phenomenon" (pp. 5–6).

Principals have formal power and authority to lead a school, but their effectiveness as leaders depends on the willingness of people to follow. Leadership can surface in unpredictable ways. Some principals have the false impression they are leading, when in fact powerful teachers with social networks operate more effectively to spread their influence throughout the school, sometimes producing undesirable results. Principals may blame teacher cliques, the "old guard," or community politics. Sadly, principals often learn about these relationship landmines from on-the-job experience.

Because principals learned in graduate courses about their legal, ethical, and fiscal responsibilities, they realize it takes courage to share leadership. As a result, many principals retreat from building these relationships and thus prevent schools from moving toward a new model of leadership.

Lambert (2002) suggested that "leadership is beyond person and role and embedded in the patterns of relationships" (p. 42). Channeling this leadership depends on the principal's ability to build relationships both inside and outside the school. Principals must acknowledge negative leadership structures, build on existing positive leadership networks, establish new leadership structures, and, possibly, dismantle dysfunctional groups in order to move the school toward a shared vision focused on student learning.

When the principal commits to this particular concept of leadership, the real work begins. Just as principals can be hesitant to share leadership, many teachers are reluctant to take on leadership responsibilities. They may not have the self-confidence or they may be hesitant based on previous leadership experiences where they felt manipulated or not supported. This can mean principals need to extend multiple invitations before trust is developed and teachers believe they will have the necessary power and authority to lead. Other teachers may be reluctant because they do not see leadership roles connected to what they care about in their work. Regardless of why teachers hesitate to lead, the best predictor of success for engaging teachers in leadership activity is the strength of the positive relationships between the principal and the teachers (Smylie & Brownlee-Conyers, 1992).

The essence of teacher leadership is relationships—administrator to teacher, teacher to teacher, teacher to student, administrator and teacher to community. No other responsibility is more difficult for a principal than harmonizing existing, new, and potential relationships in an organization. As teacher leaders seek to influence other teachers, they will depend on the principal to help safeguard their relationships with those they hope to influence.

Positive relationships are the foundation on which principals gain confidence to distribute power and authority. The risks principals fear in letting go of their formal control of decisions are most frequently based on the actual or perceived tenuous relationships throughout the school. According to Wahlstrom and Seashore Louis (2008):

> Sharing leadership may have its greatest impact by reducing teacher isolation and increasing commitment to the common good. Experiencing informal influence and feedback through professional discussions encourages a focus on shared practices and goals, and it may foster organizational innovation.
>
> (p. 30)

## Principle #2: Leadership Requires Distributed Power and Authority

*To promote, build, and sustain quality teacher leadership requires authentic distribution of power and authority.* The high-energy, unusually talented principal may seem ideal for a school needing change; however, principals with these characteristics are exceptions, if they exist at all. Collins (2001), in his study of companies with long-term high performance, found that charismatic leaders were a liability for sustaining improvement. If there is not a critical mass of teacher leaders to continue the improvement efforts, the changes achieved often dissolve after the principal leaves the school.

### From the Field

They [central office leaders] are receptive to allowing us to make decisions. On campus we have cadres also. Every teacher is part of a cadre and . . . the lead teacher will meet with the principal, and they make decisions about campus things.

Sharon Raye
Elementary Teacher
Harlingen, TX

Changing from the single-leader model requires the distribution of power and authority. Principals have authority vested by school system policies, and by virtue of this authority, they have power. Principals who view their power and authority as tools for expanding leadership are in the forefront in leading today's schools. The principal must move from retaining power *over* others, which is based on rules, to giving power *to* others, which is goal directed (Sergiovanni, 2000). These principals know their own power can expand if they share it. Acting on the belief that distributing power can lead to more effective organizational results has risks, but it can also generate unlimited opportunities for the school.

Teachers cannot be empowered without the opportunity and a willingness to accept and exercise that power. The majority of teachers want to do what is best for students, and this is easier to do when they work in a supportive culture. Therefore, a primary role of the principal is to develop a school culture where teachers are authentically engaged in leadership and where diverse perspectives are welcomed. This is another reason to move away from the hero leader and build a more democratic school community. Curriculum standards commonly require teachers to instruct students about democracy; however, students often see that teachers do not have a role in school decision-making, and, in turn, many teachers do not offer students opportunities to make decisions in their classrooms. While teachers are asked to build inclusive classrooms, they are often not included in essential decision-making in the school.

Moving toward this new way of leading does not mean principals relinquish responsibility. On the contrary, this new way of leading requires more attention from the principal. The principal must provide support for teacher leading and learning with an expectation that teachers will improve their performance and fulfill their leadership commitments. Elmore (2002) reinforced this perspective by asserting that the responsibility for improved teaching practice is a reciprocal responsibility between the principal and the teachers. He points out that if principals expect changes in instruction, they must provide opportunities for teachers to build their capacity for these changes. In turn, if principals invest in the necessary supportive conditions, then teachers have a responsibility to use the new knowledge and skills in their teaching. Simultaneously, the principal implements structures that promote the success of teacher leaders.

The distribution of formal power and authority demands courage from the principal, who must trust that others will fulfill their responsibilities. This requires a firm expectation for reciprocity. This combined leadership of the principal and the teachers can result in changes that no one person could ever initiate and sustain, or even envision. Principals must decide if they are willing to distribute power and authority in developing teacher leadership. Hopefully, principals believe in the benefits of such distribution, but we realize there may be variations in the intensity of this belief. Probably a few people believe this is absolutely true, while others may be a bit more conservative believing it is possible, but risky. There are also principals who do not deny there are possibilities but demand, "Show me, and I may become a believer." We are confident the information offered in this book coupled with a willingness to use the suggested strategies will strengthen principals' confidence and capabilities in working with teacher leaders.

Ackerman and Mackenzie (2007) made the important point that "the concept of shared leadership in schools goes to the heart of the principal–teacher relationship" (p. 32). Working to build relationships and then creating structures to distribute power and authority are necessary conditions for professional learning to thrive. Sometimes it is difficult to know what comes first: Do teachers become accomplished as a result of participation in quality professional learning or through their activities as teacher leaders? Regardless of the impetus, teachers' leading and learning are the building blocks for school reform.

## Principle #3: Leadership for Professional Learning

*To promote, build, and sustain quality teacher leadership, principals must align teacher leadership with professional learning.* If we want teacher leadership to improve student learning, then the focus of the leadership must be teacher learning. Leading and learning are symbiotic. An important role of principals is to ensure teachers and other adults, including themselves, learn how to best teach all students. The responsibility moves beyond a single teacher's classroom to a collective responsibility for all students.

According to Hirsh and Hord (2012), "the most significant factor in whether students learn well is quality teaching" (p. 25). Changing demographics and increased pressure to ensure learning for all student populations present a steep curve in the demand for continuous teacher learning. Sykes (1999) stated, "The improvement of American education relies centrally on the development of a highly qualified teacher workforce imbued with the knowledge, skills, and dispositions to encourage exceptional learning in all the nation's students" (p. xv). At no other time in the history of our profession has teacher development been in the spotlight as it is now. The good news is we have significant knowledge about how teachers can learn to improve their work with students. The unfortunate news is having the knowledge and using it in practice are often not the same. Even as legislators mandate quality professional development opportunities for teachers, there are too few schools or school systems where this type of professional learning exists.

Current cognitive theories advocate a constructivist approach in which students construct their own meaning and make sense of their world. Students must have and use critical-thinking skills to face a world that is increasingly nonlinear and unpredictable. Teachers must be better equipped to help students master these skills. However, if teachers do not experience constructivist learning, using these strategies to teach their students may be difficult.

Teaching and learning today demand the involvement of teachers in determining their own learning needs based on student data. This is best done within established professional learning communities where everyone can learn together. Effective teaching strategies, based on these data, must be learned and, most importantly, implemented through job-embedded, just-in-time collective learning. To build this level of professional learning, principals must shift from being in control to being supportive of developing a community of learners. When this community becomes "self-organizing," the reliance on formal leaders, such as the principal, to continue school improvement decreases. Depending only on the principal to do this is unrealistic. Teacher leaders can initiate the discussions that move everyone toward the shared vision for student learning. Certainly, principals can begin the work, but in the long term, it is a critical mass of teacher leaders who will keep the conversations alive.

## Intentional Leadership Is Required

This book's central premise is that building positive relationships, authentically distributing power and authority, and aligning teacher leadership with teacher learning (professional learning) cannot happen without principals intentionally leading the process. This requires principals to provide resources, manage school operations, and support staff for the purpose of improving student learning.

The Framework for Intentional Leadership (Figure 1.4) illustrates the interrelationship of the three basic principles and how the principal's intentional leadership drives them. Principals cannot ignore or even delegate this responsibility, especially early on, because as the formal leaders, their actions signal the importance and commitment to this new way of leading and learning.

As principals consider their readiness for teacher leadership, the rubric in Figure 1.5 can help them determine their current levels of skills. Later we use this rubric in further exploration of the three principles. The hope is that principals will move from being unsure and unskilled to becoming leaders of teacher leaders.

Figure 1.4. **Framework for Intentional Leadership**

Figure 1.5. **Readiness for Teacher Leadership Rubric for Principals**

| Quality Teacher Leadership Requires the Following Principles Be in Place: ||
|---|---|
| *Relationships:* **Essential positive relationships** ||
| Unsure and Unskilled | Teachers are known to the principal and to each other; some self-selected groups are intact. Everyone is cordial, but limited in his or her interactions with others. |
| Moving Along | The principal knows teachers' talents, skills, and interests, as well as their social networks; the number of purposefully established groups has increased and most teachers are participating in one or more school structures. |
| Leading Teacher Leaders | Teachers' talents, skills, and interests, as well as their social networks, are known to the principal and to other teachers; groups are established voluntarily, by invitation, and by assignment; the principal, teacher leaders, and teachers themselves take the initiative to link individuals in realizing the school vision. |

Figure 1.5. **Continued**

| *Power and Authority:* Authentic distribution of power and authority | |
|---|---|
| Unsure and Unskilled | Principal does not trust teachers to lead and be accountable. May have one or two individuals with whom issues are discussed and some projects delegated, but only with close supervision. |
| Moving Along | Principal is beginning to trust a select group of teachers to lead and be accountable. The teacher leaders are generally those individuals in formal leadership roles in the school. |
| Leading Teacher Leaders | Principal has confidence that most teachers will lead and be accountable. |
| *Professional Learning:* Alignment of teacher leadership with professional learning | |
| Unsure and Unskilled | Professional learning opportunities are available, but may or may not be related to the school's vision or aligned with individual teacher needs. |
| Moving Along | A school vision has been developed and decisions regarding professional learning evolve from the vision. Teacher leaders are directly involved in determining what many of these learning opportunities will be. |
| Leading Teacher Leaders | All professional learning opportunities are aligned with the school's vision and the individuals' job needs; a variety of learning formats are employed for delivery of learning; everyone in the school is involved in continuous learning. Teacher leaders have improved their leadership skills through specific professional learning opportunities. |

# Summary

One person leading all aspects of a school campus is unrealistic. Continuous improvement at a school or district isn't about one person making a difference but instead involves a team's effort toward improvement. More importantly, this narrow view of leadership as a one person operation, like a knight in shining armor in a mythic tale, fails to empower and encourage members of the school community to take on leadership roles in various areas across a school—roles that require teachers to be involved and part of the decision-making process, which helps sustain the "health of a school" (Ackerman & Mackenzie, 2007, p. 11).

Collaboration for improvement requires leadership that encourages greater capacity in the organization for better results (Fullan, 2001). Thus, we need individuals in a variety of leadership roles to advocate for a "bold brand of teacher leadership" (Berry, Byrd, & Wieder, 2013), which focuses on building a collaborative culture that supports the different roles that exist for teacher leaders.

Continuing to believe the principal alone can expertly accomplish an impossible set of expectations, including instructional leadership, may well be the death knell of the position itself. Principals must move from center stage to the new role of coach. Scherer (2002) contrasted the metaphors of directing a band and coaching a soccer game to explain the type of leadership needed in schools today. The coach of the soccer team has to rely on split-second decisions made by team members rather than trying to direct every action on the field, as a band director does. It is time for principals to intentionally move from serving as the director of school actions to being a coach for teacher leaders.

This new view of leading and learning demands intentional actions by principals to build relationships, distribute power and authority, and align teacher leadership with teacher learning. Only with this commitment can schools develop the capacity necessary to address the complex learning needs of today's students. In the next chapter, we explore teacher leadership, discuss which teachers assume these leadership roles, and determine how teacher leadership benefits the teacher, the school, and the principal.

# 2

# Investigating the Vision, the Roles, and the Reasons

"Be the change that you wish to see in the world."

Mahatma Gandhi

Because teachers played such a key leadership role in the early development of our nation's schools, a certain irony exists in the current interest in developing teacher leaders. This revived interest in fostering some long-overdue attention to classrooms, where the real work of the schools occurs, is also creating conditions for administrators and teachers to reconnect. In this chapter we offer the story of the early steps in the development, encouragement and support of teacher leadership at Markham Middle School (MMS). This story illustrates ways in which the principles described in Chapter 1 were used intentionally by a principal to build a school culture that embraces change. Immediately following this original story is an attempt to describe another phase in the school's development through accounts of Theresa's challenges and opportunities in a formalized teacher leadership role, MMS Dean of Instruction. We believe Theresa's story provides a new dimension to the continuing development of MMS as a community of learners and leaders. Next, we look at the meaning of the term teacher leadership. Our emphasis is on teacher leadership as an organizational quality that emerges as teachers assume a wide range of informal and formal roles. Finally, we explore some reasons why principals would want to lead in this new way.

## Markham Middle School: The Start of the Story

Theresa is completing her master's degree, and her current course is focused on teacher leadership. On the first night of class, she could not imagine why this course was required for her degree. After all, she did not think she was a leader, and what did this have to do with her degree in middle-grades education? At the end of the course, each student must share information about a school in which leadership practices helped promote teacher leadership to improve student achievement. Theresa now knows that she does not have to visit another school because her school is perfect for this report! She realizes how teacher leadership makes a difference in her school, and she is excited to write her report.

Markham Middle School (MMS) is located in a community with changing demographics. Children who are poor and/or speak languages other than English are the majority of the students in this school that once served students primarily from middle-class homes where only English was spoken. Most of the faculty members have either taught for more than 15 years or are in the first few years of their teaching experience. The school operates using a modified middle-school configuration, with four teachers on most teams representing mathematics, language arts, social studies, and science. In addition, there are teachers who teach the elective subjects, physical education, and special education. Similar to schools across the country, MMS is struggling with reduced funding, increased learning expectations for a disadvantaged student population, and high-stakes accountability testing.

Theresa has taught at MMS for nearly 15 years. She would never have been able to do this report 5 or 6 years ago when the working conditions were quite different. But now, Theresa cannot think of anyone on the faculty who does not like working at the school. There is no doubt in Theresa's mind that a major reason MMS is operating as it is today has to do with the principal, Jay Denton. When Jay came to the school 5 years ago, the student achievement at MMS was considered low performing by the state's accountability standards. Given a mandate by the superintendent to improve student achievement, Jay knew this was a school where teachers worked in isolation and had few opportunities to talk about the craft of teaching. The previous principal was popular with many of the teachers because he left the teachers alone; that is, he did not interfere or otherwise raise questions about their teaching.

Jay brought an interesting combination of experiences to MMS. He came from a principalship in an elementary school, but his teaching experience was at the middle-school level. These experiences gave Jay immediate credibility with the staff as a teacher and as an administrator. The important part, however, was that Jay did not leave it at that. Immediately, he gathered information and posed questions to faculty members individually and in groups about their interests, ideas, and dreams for the school. Jay was the first administrator to ask faculty about the school they wanted rather than tell them about the school he or she planned to create. While no one knew it at the time, Jay believed in building a professional learning community that relied heavily on teacher leadership. He never actually said this was his goal; he just took actions that reflected this belief.

Theresa wants to emphasize in her report the important context changes that have occurred over the last 5 years. All of these were changes in the way the school operated. Now everyone remembers only dimly "how things used to be," but Theresa recalls that not all changes were welcomed; in fact, some were resisted by many of the faculty at the time they were introduced. On the other hand, as Theresa reflects on the situation, these early initiatives, such as collaborative decision-making, allowed other changes to occur.

When Jay first came to the school, decision-making about critical issues, such as the use of time and hiring teachers, remained with him. Within the first semester, he worked with the faculty, staff, and members of the community to develop a shared vision for the school. As trust increased between the administrative team and the teachers, Jay formed and became an active member of the Leadership Team, composed of members representing the school community. The Team's first task was to decide what would be solely Jay's decisions, when they would give Jay advice, and when there would be a collective decision. This prevented misunderstandings as the team worked together. Members of the Leadership Team learned facilitation and meeting skills to be effective. Early in the development of the team, teachers participated in external training to gain these skills. Now the outgoing members of the Leadership Team provide this professional development for new members. Today, this is where other teachers bring their ideas so that the team members can help to develop and implement them. In addition to this example of representative leadership, there is an open invitation to all teachers to be involved in decision-making. Faculty meetings, team-level meetings, and other structures allow all teachers to be as involved as they wish.

The interactions between and among the teachers are frequent and varied in length and intensity. These interactions are not just among individuals in a grade level or subject area but throughout the school. For example, Theresa, who works with seventh-grade students in language arts, collaborated with colleagues from both sixth and eighth grades to select materials for the literacy program. While the language arts teachers were the core committee members for this effort, teachers from mathematics, social studies, and science were also involved. The discussions had varied perspectives regarding what materials might provide the best content for the students. Theresa knows she learned a great deal about the connections among these content areas, and it seemed to her that the other teachers did as well.

The committee to select literacy materials was facilitated by Yolanda, the school's literacy coach, a formal teacher leader role. The central office funded this position in schools where there were student demographics similar to those at MMS. Yolanda was a natural choice for this position based on her competency in the classroom. Teachers throughout the school admired Yolanda's ability to work with the most recalcitrant students. Even before Yolanda took the position, teachers would take time during their planning periods to observe her work with students. Yolanda agreed to assume the role on the condition that she would continue to teach two classes a day. Using the same constructivist approach she used with her students, Yolanda invites teachers to find their own voices about their teaching. Rather than working in large groups, Yolanda skillfully invites teachers, either in small groups or individually, to inquire with her about their teaching. In addition, Yolanda is a member of the school system's Curriculum Council, teaches at a local university, and participates in an external network of teacher leaders who are studying literacy.

As in most schools, professional development resources are limited, and the Leadership Team members are conscientious about how these resources are used. The Professional Development Committee members use student data to decide what type of professional development would assist the staff in working more effectively with students. The format of professional development varies depending on the need of the students and the teachers. There are times when an external expert in an instructional strategy is invited to share. At other times, teams of teachers attend conferences, visit other schools, or participate in training that is relevant to the student needs. Finally, the school frequently taps into the expertise of teachers. Regardless of the approach, there is always a plan for follow-up. At times, small groups of teachers arrange student groups in such a way that one teacher is able to have time to co-teach or observe in another teacher's classroom. An important element put in place for the school, as a whole, was the time for faculty to meet together. Theresa knows that most of the faculty members now take that time for granted. As she listens to other people in her graduate courses, she learns that MMS is quite different from many schools in this regard. At MMS, there is common team planning time, and Jay has been able to provide substitute teachers for individuals and groups to work together on curriculum projects. Over the years, Theresa and her colleagues have found that when additional time can be purchased it is appreciated, but if this is not possible, teachers find time to implement new strategies, talk with each other about how they are working, offer feedback, and try again.

The commitment to professional learning is reflected in Jay's participation in most of the activities. This ensures that everyone is familiar with the new approaches, shares a common language, and can both reinforce and support each other. An example of the school's approach to professional learning started in the early stages of reform at the school, when the administrators and teachers were engaged in a literacy training program sponsored by the school system. One of the powerful strategies from this program that helped develop this "make it happen" culture over the years is the sharing of student work. Theresa has been a part of faculty development efforts in which student work was archived from each classroom over a six-to nine-week period. The student work was used to focus the conversations of the teachers on what implementing the new materials or strategies was intended to do. Archiving the work was not just a way of creating a reference point for conversation and change; it was a way to see evidence of student growth and a cause for celebration.

An example of how resources are provided for teacher learning is when Jaime, a seventh-grade team leader, learned about a new critical-thinking strategy. He found a teacher leader from another school who knew how to use the strategy. After his team members met with this teacher, Jay allocated money to bring the teacher back to the school to coach Jaime's team members as they started using the strategy with the students. Having this resource helped the teachers feel more comfortable with what they were doing and gave credibility to the process.

Like Jaime, other teacher leaders spread their influence throughout the school. For example, through Matt's interest in the use of action research, developed during his master's degree program, he learned the value of embedding inquiry into his teaching. At first, Matt used the strategies to investigate how to best serve the students who are English Language Learners (ELLs) in his classroom. Then, in casual conversations, he shared what he was discovering with colleagues on his team. The other teachers decided to join Matt and develop a program that would provide the ELL students instruction within heterogeneous groups across their team. During the next 2 years, the team collected data that showed how valuable the strategy was for their students. At the end of the 2 years, the team members presented their results to the Leadership Team and then to the whole faculty. The faculty agreed to work with Jay to develop a schedule that would provide a similar experience for all ELL students. Now there is no tracking of these students.

Faculty turnover at this school is quite low. The one exception is when teacher leaders move to another school or a central office position when they want a new challenge, usually with Jay's encouragement. For example, Matt is currently the coordinator of the ELL program at the central office. Theresa has found through conversations in her graduate courses that low attrition is not the norm in many schools. Again, in her reflections on why MMS has a low attrition rate, she has identified three ways of operating that might explain the phenomenon.

First, when new teachers come to the school, they join the school, not just a grade-level team or a content-area department, and they are expected to be responsible for the success of students beyond their own classrooms. Even many of the old-timers, like Theresa, have changed grade levels to better meet the needs of the students. At first this was disconcerting to the faculty, but it has turned out to be an essential element in the school's transformation. Also, many have taken lead roles in a variety of instructional and support projects in which faculty from all areas of the school have been involved. Second, teachers serve on the hiring committee that includes representatives from across the school. Over the years, participating in the hiring procedures has generated feelings of ownership for everyone and a willingness to ensure the success of teachers hired.

The third system in place to reduce attrition is an induction program designed for new teachers, even for those who are not new to teaching. Once a teacher is hired, they have support over a 2-year period. Theresa has served mostly as a mentor to veteran teachers new to the school. When the induction/mentoring program was first initiated, Theresa worked with a beginning teacher; she found out quickly that this was not for her. She does much better with teachers who have a background in teaching at other schools. Working with colleagues at this level allows Theresa to share the organizational aspects that an experienced teacher new to the school needs. There are other teachers who prefer to work with the beginning teachers. In fact, Theresa's colleague, Susan, has earned the nickname "Mentor Mom" for her patience with the new teachers who need help in incredibly basic ways. Susan took the lead in organizing the mentoring/induction program about 4 years ago. She pulled the pieces and practices for this program together in a way that allows flexibility for both mentors and the new teachers. Participating in the program is not a requirement for all veteran faculty members, but almost everyone takes part.

There are teachers who work as informal leaders through understated actions that result in remarkable changes within their own and other teachers' classrooms. For example, within the school system, MMS has the highest percentage of teachers who are certified by the National Board for Professional Teaching Standards. This trend began around 6 years ago with Tim, who took the risk of working through the rigorous process. In turn, after receiving his certification, he coached other teachers on the staff on how to develop a portfolio for certification. Now Tim and other certified teachers collaborate annually to coach people who are willing to go through certification.

Theresa knows that many of the students in her graduate course will not believe much of what she will share in her report. Unfortunately, these teachers work under conditions that are not as supportive of teacher leadership. As Theresa completes her report, she now realizes and admits that she is indeed a leader at MMS.

This description of Markham Middle School captured only a snapshot of how this school capitalized on the resources of their teacher leaders. The MMS story represents the new view of school leadership presented in Chapter 1. Few of the instances of teacher leadership in this story would have occurred without *intentional* leadership from Jay, the principal. As the Leadership Team developed, Jay worked with the faculty and staff to develop a shared vision to guide the team members' decisions. We assume that at first Jay frequently had to remind the group that the decisions they made must be focused on the students' learning needs. Once decisions were made, he then provided the resources, structures, and support for teacher leadership. Examples of Jay's support included securing the funding to bring a teacher leader from another school to work with Jaime's team and designing a schedule to build in time for individual teachers and groups of teachers to work on curricular and instructional projects.

*Leadership was built through relationships.* Early on, Jay took time to listen to teachers and determine what social relationship networks existed. Matt's relationships with his team members helped put the program for ELL students in place. Jaime learned about a new teaching strategy and influenced other teachers to learn and use the strategy with their students.

Obviously, Jay believed *leadership requires authentic distribution of power and authority,* as evidenced in the structures developed to support teacher leaders. The Leadership Team functioned as a formal structure to move the school toward the shared vision. Yolanda, a formal teacher leader, had the autonomy and responsibility to work with teachers to improve instruction. Finally, teachers became involved in the hiring and induction of new teachers.

*Leadership for professional learning* permeated the school. There was a school-wide connection with an external literacy initiative, and Jay was a co-learner with the teachers in this project. Individual teachers, like Tim, influenced others to engage in professional learning. A formal structure was established for making decisions regarding the use of resources for professional development and a mentoring program was designed to help all teachers new to the school.

When Jay entered MMS, positive examples of teacher leadership were not the norm, but even so, he found pockets of teaching excellence as well as the problems typical when people work together in any organization. The early efforts in this school give us a glimpse of the variety of roles teachers can take in leading a school as it makes change.

The following figure (Figure 2.1) is intended to present a concise visual description of the individuals and their role changes during the original MMS story.

Figure 2.1. **The MMS Leadership Team Then and Now**

| Role | Name of Leader | Where Are They Now? |
| --- | --- | --- |
| Principal | Jay Denton | Continues as Principal at MMS |
| Literacy Coach | Yolanda | Continues her work at MMS |
| Teacher Leader | Matt | Coordinator for ELL Program at Central Office |
| Teacher Leader | Jaime | Continues his work as 7th-grade Team Leader |
| Teacher Leader (Team Leader) | Theresa | Applying for the new position as Dean of Instruction at MMS |
| Teacher Leader | Susan | Continues her work at MMS as "Mentor Mom" |
| Teacher Leader | Tim | Continues to coach teachers for national certification at MMS |

As MMS professionals remain committed to becoming a professional learning community (PLC), Jay continues to believe teacher leadership is the foundation upon which to build. Jay believes the role of Dean of Instruction at MMS will be critical to the success of the emerging PLC.

---

## The MMS Efforts Continue: What's Next for Theresa?

*Theresa was excited to have completed her master's in middle grades education. She was in her 15th year of teaching at Markham Middle School (MMS). As she thought about her future, she contemplated her next steps. She had numerous options: Would she continue at MMS but in a different role? Or, would she take on a new position in another school? Should she consider applying for the assistant principal position at the nearby school? Should she continue at MMS in her current, and very satisfying, role? So many choices!*

*Her leadership mentor, Principal Jay Denton, had championed teacher leaders at MMS. She wondered if the other schools had similar mentors and advocacy. Would she continue to have the same support and encouragement that Jay provides at MMS? One of the most remarkable things about Jay is his ability to see leadership potential in teachers and develop it. Theresa experienced, firsthand, Jay's commitment to growing leaders at the campus level. She learned that in addition to direction and results, developing leaders who understand change, know how to build relationships and capacity, and encourage distributed leadership is just as critical.*

*Jay had recently received approval from central office to hire a Dean of Instruction. Although Theresa wanted to apply for the position, she was also afraid. Was she really ready? Had her limited leadership roles thus far been enough to prepare her for school-wide leadership? These questions and a hundred others swirled in her head as the deadline for applying neared.*

*After much consideration, in the end, Theresa decided she would not only continue her work at MMS but also apply for the position of Dean of Instruction. With this decision made, the new thoughts swirling in her head focused on her long- and short-term goals and actions, if she was fortunate enough to be selected.*

---

## What Is Teacher Leadership?

Whether seeing MMS through events in the original story or through the lens that Theresa is now using in her career decisions, a discussion of the term *teacher leadership* is needed. Lumpkin, Claxton, and Wilson (2014) reminded us that "teacher leadership is not a new concept." Calls for involving teachers in K–12 improvement efforts have been occurring for over 50 years. Even so, the term *teacher leadership* is often misunderstood. This lack of clarity can lead to confusion resulting in obstacles for teachers who take on leadership roles. Most people outside education, and even many educators, do not completely understand the concept of teacher leadership. The term too often brings to mind the adversarial roles with which teachers and administrators have traditionally struggled.

Fortunately, a body of knowledge about teacher leadership has emerged in the last few decades. In one review of literature, York-Barr and Duke (2004) defined *teacher leadership* as "the process by which teachers, individually or collectively, influence their colleagues, principals, and other members of school communities to improve teaching and learning practices with the aim of increased student learning and achievement" (pp. 287–288). This definition does not identify a person or a set of characteristics; instead, it views leadership as an organization quality influenced by teachers, staff members, and others. Fullan (2005) supported this perspective by stating that "leadership (not 'leaders') is the key to the new revolution" (p. xi) in transforming schools. The principal's role in this "process" is to create a school culture in which teachers' knowledge, interests, talents, and skills are maximized. Ultimately, teachers come forward to take on leadership roles and responsibilities to become powerful change agents who make a difference.

## Who Emerges as Teacher Leaders?

As an organizational phenomenon, teacher leadership is the surfacing of individuals who take on leadership roles in diverse situations. Lumpkin, Claxton, and Wilson (2014) shared that teacher leaders

> are experienced and respected role models, are innovative, organized, collaborative, trustworthy, and confident facilitators of learning. They model integrity, have strong interpersonal and communication skills, display the highest level of professionalism, a commitment to students, and expertise, and demonstrate a passion for student learning, while taking the initiative as influential change agents . . . use data and other evidence in making decisions, recognize opportunities and take the initiative, mobilize people around a common purpose, identify resources and take action, monitor progress and adjust the approach as conditions change, sustain the commitment of others, and contribute to a learning organization.
> (pp. 59–60; Lumpkin *et al.* base these characteristics on their review of works by Bowman, 2004; Danielson, 2006; Katzenmeyer & Moller, 2001; Muijs & Harris, 2003; and York-Barr & Duke, 2004)

The list of descriptors for teacher leaders grows every year. To focus the description of teacher leaders for our purposes, we use the basic dimensions proposed by Katzenmeyer and Moller (2001). According to them, successful teacher leaders exhibit competence, are credible with other teachers, and build relationships so that they are approachable.

## Competent and Credible

Schlechty (1997) defined *teaching* as a leadership act that resides in the primary job responsibilities of the teacher. Similarly, in a more recent work, Collay (2011) stated, "Teaching practice is inherently an act of leadership" (p. 2). We believe that while teacher leader actions may focus on diverse interests, the priority work of teachers is student learning, and teacher leaders want their efforts to contribute to this. Teacher leaders often have expertise in teaching and learning and are able to work with diverse students in motivating them to learn. These teachers are themselves willing learners and want to share learning with others.

## From the Field

Accomplished teachers must become ambassadors for the teaching profession. Our actions and language, within and beyond the classroom, can serve as a catalyst for change.

Jessica Cuthbertson<br>
English/Language Arts 6th–8th-grade<br>
Aurora, CO

---

Teachers usually recognize their competent teacher colleagues as knowledgeable and skilled in their work. Therefore, not only are these professionals competent, they are also credible in the eyes of their colleagues. Teachers look for resources to help them survive in the complex world of teaching, and credible teacher leaders often become one of those resources. Within schools, there may be a known but unspoken acknowledgment these teachers know how best to work with students. Casually glancing into these teacher leaders' classrooms, listening to their comments in meetings, and actually talking to their students are strategies other teachers use to learn about improving their teaching. In an isolated profession, there is rarely time to talk about their practice; additionally, a school culture that inhibits such conversations forces teachers to use these resources. Regardless of how teachers determine the competence and credibility of these teacher leaders, they do it. They intuitively know who is worthy of their confidence regarding instructional issues.

## Approachable

Teacher leaders are *approachable*. They understand the importance of nurturing collaborative and trusting relationships because they are aware of the social and political structures within the teaching culture. To accomplish their work, teacher leaders establish social networks in which they have influence. Teachers who are approachable are physically present so other teachers know how to find them. They are visible in the library, the administrative offices, and in other teachers' classrooms. When a problem arises, a teacher leader's classroom often becomes a haven for helping others and sharing dilemmas.

The ability to influence other teachers to improve their practice, whether by design or by chance, depends on how teachers view each other in terms of their competence, credibility, and approachability. This process is often informal, resulting from teachers learning together in work sessions, in the hallway, or as they eat lunch together. This leadership shows up in a variety of informal and formal roles.

## What Are Teacher Leader Roles?

Silva, Gimbert, and Nolan (2000) described three waves of teacher leadership roles that emerged during the recent school-reform efforts:

1. **Formal leadership roles**, such as department chairperson, master teacher, or a similar position designed to maintain "an efficient and effective educational system" (p. 3).

2. **Primarily outside classroom positions** more closely aligned with teaching and learning, such as curriculum developer or staff developer.

3. **Teachers as leaders within the day-to-day work of teaching** make up the "third wave." These classroom-based teachers did not have special titles, but they were working in collaboration with their colleagues to improve student learning.

We believe that the teacher leadership described in each "wave" serves a purpose, depending on the context of the school.

In the real life of schools and school systems, teacher leadership emerges in a multitude of roles, each of which can provide valuable services. Rarely, though, are all teachers willing to collaborate and formally or informally lead within a professional learning community. Rather than advocating for any specific roles for teacher leaders, we advocate seeking whatever teacher leadership best supports the improvement of teaching and learning; this may vary from school to school. For example, in a school with a history of low student performance, a need for a formal lead teacher to collaborate with classroom teachers to change instructional strategies may be the priority. The creation of the Dean of Instruction position at MMS is another example. Theresa's work in the formal role at MMS is needed for sustaining gains made, supporting increased collaboration and initiating plans for leadership succession. In another school, such formal roles may be less desirable and a better approach would be to build on existing team collaboration informally. Consequently, trying to create a single role description for teacher leaders is futile; there must be flexibility depending on the situation.

Figure 2.2 illustrates some of the different roles teacher leadership took at MMS. A teacher leader may work as an individual in a formal position, such as Yolanda, the literacy coach at Markham Middle School. There are situations when a formal leadership role may be necessary to move a school toward a student-learning goal. In contrast, there are individual informal leaders who are equally powerful in their influence, such as Matt, who used an instructional strategy to help his ELL students and then influenced his team members to try it with their students. Teacher leaders also work in community with others, like Jaime, a formal team leader, who learned with his team members. Then there are informal teacher leaders who work in community as leaders, such as Tim, who took an interest in helping other teachers at MMS gain national certification. Finally, on occasion a new formal position, such as the one Theresa is pursuing, is created to work with issues from a whole-school perspective. Instruction, in particular, needs a perspective that no one in subject-area groups or grade-level assignments can see. Such a position exists in the space that

**Figure 2.2. Different Roles Teacher Leadership Took at MMS**

|  | *Formal Teacher Leadership* | *Informal Teacher Leadership* |
|---|---|---|
| Individual | Serve in the established position of literacy coach (Yolanda) | Use an instructional strategy in own classroom before influencing team members (Matt) |
| In Community | Serve as team leader (Jaime) <br> Serve as Dean of Instruction (Theresa) | Mentor colleagues (Tim) |

is neither classroom teacher nor administrator, yet must function effectively with individuals in both of those roles. These examples demonstrate the need for various leadership roles at different times, and although this leadership may come primarily from the teachers, it may also emerge from the students, the staff, or the parents.

Principals who capitalize on teacher leadership accept both informal and formal teacher leader roles as equal in importance regarding the influence they exert, even though they are quite different in makeup and responsibilities. To better understand teacher leader roles, the next section provides concrete examples.

## Informal Teacher Leader Roles

We start with informal teacher leader roles because they can be the most powerful influences for improved teaching and learning. In fact, when teachers are asked to identify teacher leaders based on who is *competent, credible,* and *approachable,* they frequently name those teachers who do not have formal roles or titles. In Whitaker's (1995) study of effective middle-school administrators, he found these principals were able to identify key teacher leaders and involve them in the school's change process, whereas "less effective principals in the study were unable to recognize their informal teacher leaders" (p. 77).

Informal teacher leaders fulfill such a variety of roles that it is difficult to group them into categories. The driving force behind these committed individuals is their passion for whatever issue they are addressing. Their energies may be focused on a teaching and learning issue, a student activity, or even a facility problem. These informal leaders usually see a problem, identify how to solve it, and rally the needed resources to make it happen. In addition, informal leaders are available for other teachers when they most need help both professionally and personally.

Later, we discuss how to identify informal leaders and build a network to take advantage of their talents. The principal's tasks are first to understand that informal teacher leadership is powerful and then discover how to incorporate this leadership into a productive system.

## Formal Teacher Leader Roles

Teachers assume formal leadership roles in community with other teachers through selection by leaders at either the school site or the central office. In contrast, there are teachers who provide formal teacher leadership as individuals through their ability to reach beyond their schools to find the professional learning or recognition they do not find locally.

## Formal Teacher Leaders in Community

There are myriad ways teachers emerge as formal leaders when schools and school systems reach out to talented teachers to help reduce the gaps in student learning. Individuals in formal teacher leadership roles work collaboratively with other teachers as school reform leaders, district or school-site resource teachers, and the more traditional managerial/leadership roles.

## Teachers Selected to Be School Reform Leaders

Many national, state, and local school-reform programs select outstanding teachers to participate in intensive, long-term professional learning experiences with the expectation they will use the new knowledge and skills to help other teachers at the school site or within the school system learn. For example, with the infusion of funds for science and mathematics education, there are several national and state programs where teacher leaders study with scientists or mathematicians so they gain deep knowledge in their content area. Some literacy programs help teachers develop in-depth knowledge of writing or reading so they can provide quality teaching in these areas. As teachers apply their new content-area knowledge and skills, the program directors identify leaders who can learn how to teach and coach other teachers. In time, a critical mass of teacher leaders forms a cadre from which schools or districts can draw expertise. These teacher leaders may also participate in leadership development activities in order to prepare them to work with other teachers.

## District or School-Site Resource Teachers

Based on student needs data, a school or district may determine that teacher leaders are needed to work with other teachers in formal instructional leadership roles. These teachers may work at one or several schools to provide support in various ways, such as facilitating professional learning activities, modeling effective teaching strategies, and coaching other teachers. Titles assigned to these teachers vary—lead teacher, staff developer, literacy facilitator, coach, or technology specialist, to name a few. The advantage of a school-site position is the teacher works within the context of the school and can adapt to its culture, whereas district resource teachers may be spread among so many schools they are unable to provide this level of service.

## Managerial/Leadership Roles

Teacher leaders serve in traditional roles such as department chairperson, team leader, athletic director, or school improvement team chairperson. These roles can be crucial to the effective operation of the school. In many cases, these teacher leaders provide leadership in instruction as well as the day-to-day operational functions. Principals can also enlist these leaders to work in vertical teams to help address school-wide issues.

## Individual Formal Teacher Leaders

There are teachers who want to learn continuously but work in a school culture that does not support their growth and development, so they seek out their own professional learning experiences. There are obvious advantages for the school in capitalizing on these teachers' talents. Principals are in a position to identify opportunities to engage such individuals in collaboration with their peers. Even when teachers succeed in their efforts to learn, schools and districts do not always tap into their leadership potential for a variety of reasons. Principals may be so busy they do not realize some teachers have taken on this additional responsibility for their own learning, or they may not understand the level of accomplishment the teachers achieve and therefore cannot link others to this learning resource. School leaders may also hesitate to invite these teachers to contribute because they may be unduly concerned about the negative responses from other teachers. Sadly, in many cases, being exceptional in one or more subjects or skills creates animosity rather than admiration between and among peers.

## Teachers Who Seek Professional Learning

Teacher leaders sometimes find it difficult to discover like-minded teachers in their schools. This may be a lack of opportunities to work with other teachers or because there may not be teachers in their areas as passionate about their work. As a response to these situations, national and state organizations have developed teacher leader networks where teacher leaders can find colleagues who want to pursue conversations or study in their field of interest. These networks form around content areas, school-reform issues, and even teacher leadership itself. Check some of the sites listed in the Resources at the end of the chapter; those listed are only a small percentage of what is available.

## Teacher Awards/Certification

There are numerous teaching awards for which teachers can self-nominate or be nominated by others, such as teacher of the year. Also, the National Board of Professional Teaching Standards supports a rigorous national certification process. When teachers are involved in applying for awards or certification, they engage in professional learning.

Today we have more highly qualified teachers than at any other time in our profession, and most are not being fully utilized as resources for solving the significant problems in our schools. The Institute for Educational Leadership Task Force on Teacher Leadership (2001) stated the issue succinctly: "It is not too late for education's policymakers to exploit a potentially splendid resource for leadership and reform that is now being squandered: the experience, ideas, and capacity to lead of the nation's schoolteachers" (p. 2). Likewise, Berry, Byrd, and Wieder (2013) reported that Roland Barth suggested, in a panel discussion at Harvard, that our public schools need to "unlock the tremendous overabundance of underutilized talent that gets left in the parking lot every day" (p. 142).

There are thousands of teachers who are nationally certified and others who are involved in leadership roles within school-reform efforts, often external to the school. Schools and school systems invest significant resources in placing teachers in these roles. Teacher leaders are participating in national networks such as the National Writing Project, where teacher leaders learn from each other. Even with all these formal efforts to build professionalism into teaching, the engagement of teachers as leaders remains absent in most schools.

# Teacher Leadership from Multiple Perspectives

In some instances teachers take on overlapping informal and formal leadership roles. Teachers can lead based on their level of knowledge, skills, interests, and specific needs at the campus. Harrison and Killion (2007) identified roles through which teachers can contribute to the success of their school. Among those identified are: resource provider, instructional specialist, curriculum specialist, classroom supporter, learning facilitator, mentor, school leader, data coach, catalyst for change, and learner.

# What Makes Teacher Leadership Essential?

One of the most important elements affecting the acceptance of a new way of leading is a perceived need for the change. Principals have to believe that staying where they are in their practice is more painful than adopting something new. In truth, most of us do not change unless we can see the benefits or "what's in it for me." Most of us pursue only those things we perceive as benefiting us by bringing us recognition, helping us to succeed, or aiding us in keeping our jobs or getting a better one.

We identified benefits for putting effort into developing teacher leadership. These benefits are divided into three categories. First, there are reasons specifically connected to individual teachers and teaching. Second, there are advantages for the school as a whole. Finally, principals will reap benefits related to their role.

## Individual Teachers and Their Teaching

### Increase Student Learning

The private act of teaching, a norm in most schools, allows inequity in instruction to be a veiled secret. The student assessment results from one teacher can be dramatically different from another teacher's students, as illustrated in Figure 2.3. Although there are variables, such as student placement, that affect these results, these data suggest that some students are learning more when they are taught by certain teachers. Boles and Troen (2003) have suggested that "egalitarianism is the pervasive myth that every teacher is as good as every other teacher" (p. 2). If the school as an organization is to provide quality education for all students, improvement will depend on quality instruction being consistently implemented across all classrooms as a school-wide professional community (Sanders, 1998; Louis & Wahlstrom, 2011; Leithwood & Seashore Louis, 2012). Teacher leaders can work in collaboration with other teachers and influence them to make their practice public so that these inequities are evident and can be addressed.

Figure 2.3. **Illustration of Differing Student Assessment Outcomes with Different Teachers**

| Course | Teacher | Percentage of Students Who Meet the Assessment Criteria |
|---|---|---|
| American Government | 1 | 44% |
| American Government | 2 | 100% |
| American Government | 3 | 58% |
| American Government | 4 | 57% |
| English I | 1 | 90% |
| English I | 2 | 59% |
| English I | 3 | 100% |
| English I | 4 | 81% |
| English I | 5 | 81% |
| English I | 6 | 11% |

### Improve Teacher Quality

Teacher leadership can help move teaching toward a higher level of professionalism. Leading and learning are closely aligned; so, as teachers take on leadership roles, they learn, and as they learn, they lead. This is why considering how all teachers can assume leadership roles is important. Given the right circumstances, even teachers who are not as skilled as others may not only provide leadership but also improve their own instructional skills. The adage of "we learn what we teach" holds true for everyone. Blasé and Blasé (2006) discovered that administrator support of informal teacher leadership led to an increase in teacher efficacy and professional learning and capacity to meet diverse student needs. They also shared that the implementation of professional learning communities encouraged teachers to collaborate.

## *Reduce Attrition of Teachers*

Because it is becoming more difficult to find quality teachers, no school can afford the attrition of talented faculty. Sadly, although record numbers of teachers are being produced in the United States through both traditional and alternative certification programs (Glazerman *et al.*, 2008), too many educators leave within a few years of entering the profession (Roberts & Pankake, 2012). Ingersoll and Smith (2003, 2004) estimated in their study of teacher turnover that 40 to 50 percent of beginning teachers leave education within 5 years. Over 78 percent of these teachers cite four areas of inadequate working conditions as their reasons for leaving: student discipline problems, lack of support from school administration, poor student motivation, and lack of teacher influence over school-wide and classroom decision-making. Each of these working conditions reflects the absence of a collaborative school culture. Teachers stay in schools where they feel a sense of belonging and are offered opportunities to be contributing members in the organization. There is a positive relationship between teacher leadership and teacher commitment and retention (Pounder *et al.*, 1995, cited in York-Barr & Duke, 2004). A higher level of teacher commitment results when teachers are involved in authentic professional participation. Creating a collaborative culture will be discussed more thoroughly in later chapters.

## From the Field

We can't say we want high-quality teachers in every classroom if we're not going to allow them to do high-quality teaching. Otherwise, a free quality public education for every American child remains only a partially filled dream and an empty promise.

Renee Moore
Mississippi Delta Community College
Cleveland, MS

## *Benefit from Diverse Leadership Styles*

Principals who deal with teachers unwilling to change often say, "If only that teacher would retire." Many of these teachers are not incompetent, but they have only average or mediocre skills. Principals should put energy into encouraging them to become good teachers rather than simply wait around for them to retire. Here is where diverse leadership styles and social networks can make a difference. Just as students respond to different types of teaching styles, teachers are influenced by different leadership styles. In many cases, a teacher leader may influence another teacher whom the principal is unable to reach for whatever reason. In fact, one of the most powerful sources for initiating changes in schools and classrooms is one teacher to another. Providing a variety of leadership styles will increase the likelihood of teachers improving their practice.

# The School

## *Reduce the Power Struggles*

When the goals of the principal and the teachers are not aligned, these "differences of opinion" can result in power struggles. Symptoms of these conflicts may include withdrawal from interactions, rumors and coalitions building among subgroups within the school, one-sided conversations, or strong disagreements in public spaces. These relationships are not healthy for the school climate, and they can certainly make the principal feel uncomfortable.

Building teacher leadership will reduce power struggles in three ways. First, teachers will have more information on which to base decisions and understand why decisions are made. Second, teacher leaders are usually those teachers who can communicate collective decisions effectively to others both within and outside the school. Finally, teachers who take on leadership roles and are more informed move away from their dependence on the principal and assume responsibility for collective decisions rather than blaming unpopular ideas on the principal, central office, or other external policymakers.

## *Keep the Focus on the Improvement of Teaching and Learning*

Teachers' work lives are busy and focused on their students' learning; thus, the most logical areas in which teachers might be willing to lead are related to instruction. This helps address the principal's dilemma of balancing both managerial and instructional leadership responsibilities. With the current emphasis on improving learning for all students, principals cannot ignore instructional leadership tasks; however, they need not be alone in leading all the work related to improved student learning when teachers can keep the focus on this goal. Teacher leaders can be significant sources of advocacy and support for instructional practices intended to improve student learning. Without teacher advocacy, the work of convincing already overloaded teachers to invest time and energy in developing new classroom practices will be more difficult, if not impossible.

## *Use Limited Resources Effectively*

Most of us would agree there is more work to do in a school than there are people to do it. With reduced resources and few discretionary funds, the principal must create novel ways to increase services to students. The most overlooked and underused resource in most schools is the professional staff. Creating a context in which teachers increase their capacity as leaders will result in a commensurate increase in resources, such as more effective use of materials and equipment and careful selection of programs that align with organizational goals.

## *Accomplish the Accountability Agenda*

The *accountability agenda* is often translated into "increased student test scores." Although the quality of current measures of this success—standardized tests—is debatable, few of us would argue against the need for accountability. In spite of the focus on testing, most accountability systems at the state level, and even more so at the local level, involve more than test scores. Accountability measures and other assessments can provide data for decision-making about what instructional practices, organizational patterns, curricular emphases, and/or instructional materials best improve performance. A principal can facilitate this process of using data but teacher leaders will contribute significantly in attaching meaning to the data and turning that meaning into classroom actions.

## *Sustain Continuous Improvement*

Many school systems fail to recognize the importance of leadership stability and leadership succession. This is unfortunate since leadership succession "can dramatically affect organizational stability" (Schechter & Tischler, 2007, p. 2). Repeatedly, studies have demonstrated that a strong instructional leader can influence schools to increase their effectiveness (Cotton, 2003), but longitudinal studies have also demonstrated that when these strong instructional leaders exit the school, the improvement agenda is slowed or halted, and in some cases even reversed (Hargreaves & Fink, 2004). Obviously, leadership succession is a serious issue with consequences for individuals and the organization as a whole. According to Hargreaves (2005),

> distributing leadership makes succession less dependent on the talents or frailties of particular individuals. When a good leader leaves an organization, it should wobble a bit and there should and will be a sense of loss. But temporary unsteadiness should not turn into widespread feelings of despair or institutional states of collapse. Schools need to cushion the departure of key leaders and develop leadership capacities to provide a pool of growing talent from which future successors may be selected.
>
> (p. 172)

When efforts are made to develop teacher leaders, the school's improvement program has a much greater chance of surviving changes in formal leadership. From their first day on the job, principals should spend time considering how leadership development will proceed. Even this less formal leadership training and development will help with succession issues (Schechter & Tischler, 2007). As teacher leadership grows within a school, the organization can become more self-monitoring and self-improving. In fact, teacher leaders often induct and inform new principals about the work of their organization so that the support of improved teaching and learning continues (Goodbread, 2000; Lambert, 2005).

## The Principal's Role

### *Help Address the Principal's Ever-Expanding Job*

Principals who succeed know they did not accomplish that success singlehandedly, because schools are too complex for one or even a few people to lead. Anyone who has been a principal knows each year brings more responsibilities. It is highly unlikely that help will come in the form of additional administrative positions; rather, it is more probable that the principal will be asked to make better use of the existing, limited human resources. The "super principal myth" (Copland, 2001b, p. 528) must give way to engaging all teachers in varying levels of leadership so that principals can survive. If principals are to meet these ever-expanding demands, they need help. Teachers who assume various leadership roles are significant players in helping the principal succeed—or not. Whether teacher leadership is focused on individual classroom instructional responsibilities or school-wide issues, the success of the whole system, including the principal, is helped. Our advocacy is for leadership to be viewed as a characteristic of the organization, not inherent in any specific position. "Individuals with this perspective believe that leadership can and should be found in thought and active practice throughout the organization—in every classroom, office, bus, cafeteria, foyer, playground, and so on" (Pankake & Abrego, 2012, p. 4).

### *Distinguish Principals as Leaders of Leaders*

When teachers expand their leadership influence as they engage in school-system projects, external networks within large-scale programs, and professional organizations, they become emissaries for the school. In turn, principals are viewed by the external leaders of these initiatives as innovative because they work to improve schools with the help of excellent teacher leaders. In time, these teachers may be chosen to take on larger leadership roles in another school or at the school-system level. As difficult as it is to lose talented teacher leaders, principals have more to gain by encouraging teachers to move into these more challenging roles than to discourage them, even if it means losing their skills and abilities. These circumstances cause principals to be perceived as leaders of leaders.

## Summary

Teacher leadership is ubiquitous and can be overlooked by principals and other formal leaders within both school and district. In spite of this, the proliferation of teacher leader roles demonstrates how teachers are increasingly being recognized as an untapped resource for improved teaching and learning. In the vignette about Markham Middle School, we saw how both informal and formal teacher leadership emerges with support. Investing energy, time, and resources in this new way of leading and learning can result in numerous benefits for individual teachers, the school as a whole, and the principal. The continuing story of Theresa's growth as a leader in her new role and her efforts to encourage growth in others through a more coordinated and collaborative school culture evidence the idea of leadership as an organizational characteristic, worthy of pursuit.

This is not easy work. It demands a commitment from the principal to make it happen. Knowing what the roadblocks to building a culture of change are will help make the journey easier. In the next chapter, we invite principals to consider predictable phases of change, individual reactions to change, and how to prepare relevant others.

## Resources

2.1 Harrison, C., & Killion, J. (2007). Ten roles for teacher leaders. *Educational Leadership, 65*(1), 74–77.

2.2 Center for Teaching Quality (CTQ)—CTQ is a national nonprofit that has been around since 1999 (previously Teacher Leaders Network). CTQ's vision is "a high-quality education system for all students, driven by the bold ideas and expert practices of teachers"; and their mission is "to connect, ready, and mobilize teacher leaders to transform our schools." CTQ provides access to a variety of teacher leadership resources, including a virtual community for teacher leaders. Retrieved from www.teachingquality.org

2.3 Tapped In—This website is now closed; however, numerous items (newsletters, publications, members' perspectives, and transcripts) are archived at the site. It is still a site worth visiting—exploring for any school leaders and teacher leaders looking for a variety of online professional learning tools, and resources. Retrieved from http://tappedin.org

2.4 Teacher Leadership Project—The Teacher Leadership Project is no longer operating. However, the evaluation report on the project has some helpful information that could assist schools with technology integration. The Teacher Leadership Project (TLP) was designed to assist teachers in their efforts to integrate technology into the school curriculum. The Evaluation Report can be found at https://docs.gatesfoundation.org/documents/tlp2003report.pdf

2.5 Teachers Network—This website has a variety of dimensions focused on teacher leadership in classrooms and in larger contexts. The site lists the core purpose of Teachers Network as: "To empower, recognize, and connect teachers to improve student learning, and to advocate for teacher leadership, all for the public good" and the vision as: "Our leadership would empower all teachers to transform public schools into creative learning communities so every student would succeed and contribute to the public good." Resources include teacher developed lesson plans, curriculum units, links to other sites, videos and video reviews, and more. The site also has a specific section devoted to a Teacher Leadership Institute. Retrieved from www.teachersnetwork.org

2.6 Center for Teacher Leadership: Organizations—Provides access information for key teacher leadership organizations. Retrieved from www.ctl.vcu.edu/

2.7 Teacher Leader Model Standards—A website devoted to presenting recent development of Model Standards for Teacher Leaders. Content includes information regarding the development process and the individuals and organizations involved. Statements of the vision and mission of the developers and a downloadable PDF document of the complete set of standards can also be found here. Retrieved from www.teacherleaderstandards.org

2.8 About ED: Educational Association and Organizations—The U.S. Department of Education provides contact information about grants and programs; laws & guidance; and data and research. Retrieved from www.ed.gov/

# 3  Developing a Culture of Continuous Improvement

"Most people want to be part of their organization; they want to know the organization's purpose; they want to make a difference."

Lewin & Regine in *The Soul at Work*

> Theresa waited patiently as the committee prepared to begin the interview. She was interviewing for the newly created position of Dean of Instruction at Markham Middle School (MMS). Theresa recently completed her school leadership certificate at a local university and wanted to continue her work as a teacher leader at Markham Middle School.
>
> Teachers, administrators and community representatives made up the interview panel. During the interview, one of the teachers said, "We've never had a Dean of Instruction at MMS. Why do we need a Dean of Instruction?" And, "What do you think that role will be in this school?"
>
> As Theresa looked across the interview table, she realized most of the committee members were colleagues and not strangers to her or to MMS. She found that both comforting and disconcerting. She responded, "One of the things I think the role of Dean of Instruction can bring is a realistic and holistic instructional perspective to the teachers in the school. In other words, instead of interacting with teachers as individual units, the Dean of Instruction, in my view, is going to encourage even more teamwork and collegiality amongst teachers. That's been part of our vision and mission at MMS from the beginning! I believe it's important to continue down that path. Furthermore, I see the Dean of Instruction role as one that encourages and supports teacher leaders in various ways throughout the school. Teacher leadership continues to strengthen our practice individually and as a team of learners, so that together we help meet the learning needs of our students."
>
> Theresa took some time following the interview to reflect. She was happy she applied for the position and appreciative of all she had learned during her nearly 15 years at MMS. One thing she had observed and liked about MMS was the "whatever it takes" attitude that permeates the climate at the school. She had come to appreciate Jay's efforts as principal in creating a professional learning community. Whether she was selected or not, Theresa was confident that she had matured professionally to a point that she could give back to the organization in ways she was never able to

> *before. She had been supported in her development as a teacher leader and was anxious to do the same for others. Her feelings about the interview were mixed: she really hoped they would select her, but at the same time she was afraid they would select her! Now all she could do was wait to hear.*

Schools cannot maintain the status quo for many reasons. Demands from the larger system and from changing student needs require continuous improvement and ongoing changes. Principals sometimes feel overwhelmed trying to lead uncontrollable changes. Additionally, school staff members determine programmatic or operational changes that are controllable but equally challenging to put into place. Promoting teacher leadership introduces a deliberate, local change in the power structure of the school. It engages teachers as partners in collective decisions addressing difficult problems facing the organization. Instructing student populations whose demographics are rapidly changing, bringing special needs students into the learning mainstream, and ensuring all students have a quality teacher generate issues on a day-to-day basis. Undoubtedly, the most appropriate individuals to design and implement solutions to these problems are the professional staff members who live with them every day. We advocate building a system through which collective efforts continue and change is sustained, even following leadership change.

Preparing for this type of leadership includes understanding the complexity of building a culture of change. In this chapter, we examine the phases individuals move through when they confront a new way of working. Next, we look at how individuals' differences can influence their passages through the phases of change and, in turn, influence how the organization moves through change. Then we address other entities principals need to get ready for this change, such as the school administrative team and central office leaders. Finally, we offer advice to principals about sustaining the long-term commitment necessary to fully realize this new view of leadership.

We believe principals can take intentional actions to build teacher leadership; however, predictable risks exist in moving from being the person responsible for all the answers to facilitating many problem solvers—teacher leaders. Disrupting the current way of working makes people anxious. Asking teachers to take ownership of problems upsets their traditional expectations of what a principal is supposed to do. Reactions to these changes are somewhat predictable. There will most likely be teacher actions to undermine or resist a change in leadership methods. If principals are aware of these possible reactions, they can be prepared rather than blindsided.

Making changes to improve student learning must be continuous and based on the diverse needs of students and teachers. Principals are likely endorsing new perspectives and practices regarding professional learning, as well as introducing a new way of leading. As teachers' learning and leading increase, they will feel discomfort from being asked to examine their beliefs, attitudes, knowledge, and skills in order to improve student learning. Effective principals balance an understanding of teachers' disequilibrium with a gentle but continuous press for change. Norton (2004) suggested "this balancing act—this ability to set high expectations while building a professional relationship with teachers—is the hallmark of today's successful principal" (p. 2). These are complex changes, and it is not easy work.

We believe principals must be skillful in leading planned change. A good first step is to study the schools' history of planned change and how this influences teachers' willingness to be involved in yet another project. Next, we provide an overview of information about how individual teachers generally react to change, depending on factors such as their adult development, career situation, philosophy of teaching and learning, and personal issues. Everyone resists change at some point, but people respond differently to change initiatives depending on their personal circumstances. We provide several interventions principals may use depending on the context and teachers' individual needs.

## A History of Change

A major factor contributing to whether or not a change will be successful in a school is the school's history of change efforts (Fullan, 2003, 2016). Not surprisingly, where there is a history of success, new proposals have a greater chance of succeeding. If previous change initiatives have fared poorly, new proposals are likely to suffer the same fate. Teachers' lack of enthusiasm may be influenced by previous experiences, so they find ways to protect themselves to prevent being disappointed again.

Even the most eager teachers hesitate if there is a history of multiple innovations that subsequently lacked the support to be fully implemented. A history of failed changes does not mean initiating change will be impossible, but the challenges may be greater in number and intensity. Principals should be cautious regarding the pace and what assistance should be in place when these conditions exist. If a school has multiple change initiatives underway, each should be clearly identified to reveal where efforts may be fragmented and if consolidating or discarding particular initiatives is needed. Teacher leadership and learning form the foundation for how program initiatives are introduced, supported, and continued. There must be an integration of this new way of leading and learning with existing initiatives.

## Themes Common to the Change Process

We identify four common themes synthesized from three widely referenced models of change: Bridges' (1991) recommendations for managing transitions, rather than managing change; Fullan's (2003, 2016) advice for initiating, implementing, and continuing an initiative; and the work of Hall and Hord (2001, 2015) in supporting teachers as they move through "Stages of Concern." Even with their unique perspectives, they all support the following themes related to change and can guide principals in their work with teachers.

### From the Field

Some people are very hard to change. They don't want it to be different. They want everything the same. Why should I have to change? But, sometimes change is really good. You have to do it . . .

Deborah Davila<br>
Elementary Teacher<br>
Harlingen, TX

- *Change is a personal phenomenon.* Most principals know they cannot announce changes and then expect everyone to fully adopt them. Instead "change is a process through which people and organizations move as they gradually come to understand and become skilled and competent in the use of the new ways" (Hall & Hord, 2001, p. 5). Individual teachers change, not the school. Thus, principals must strategically plan for individual needs in order to achieve organizational change. Trying to bring about change in schools, while ignoring the individual, results in resistance and wasted resources.

- *There are discernable stages.* Change does not happen immediately; instead, there are distinct phases. For example, Bridges (1991) pointed out, letting go of beliefs and behaviors is necessary before new ways of working can occur. Even principals seeking to successfully implement a new view of leadership must let go of old ways of working and move toward new behaviors in order to facilitate this process for others.

- *Time is a factor.* Fullan (2016) found that "even moderately complex changes take from 2 to 4 years, and larger scale efforts can take 5 to 10 years, with sustaining improvements still problematic" (p. 58). The time needed for change increases from elementary school to middle school and high school levels. This reality is too often ignored, resulting in leaders abandoning initiatives when they do not see immediate results. Fullan (2016) used the term *infrastructure* in describing failed change within the context of time: "The main reason that change fails to occur in the first place on any scale, and is not sustained when it does, is that the infrastructure is weak, unhelpful, or working at cross-purposes" (p. 16). Thus, to encourage teachers to believe that the change will be supported and sustained over time there must be trust in the infrastructure.

- *Intentional actions can move the process in the desired direction.* The leader's actions or interventions keep the change process going; more specifically, particular actions will influence and guide the speed, direction, and acceptance of the changes. This reinforces the notion that teacher leading and learning are successful when principals exercise intentional leadership.

## Three Predictable Stages of Change

These themes should encourage principals to help teachers move through three stages of change: getting started, trying it out, and accepting a new way of doing business. Following are selected actions that principals can use in promoting, building, and sustaining teacher leading and learning.

### Stage 1: Getting Started

- *Start with the problem, rather than the change.* People rarely change unless they see a need. Teachers will respond to problems they see as important to them rather than accepting a change or solution that has no apparent link to their work. Looking at relevant problems or needs can result in conversations about how the school faculty and staff might work together differently to address them.

- *Determine which individuals have something to lose.* Identifying who has a vested interest in the current system will help principals be aware of sources of resistance regarding the change. Vested interests take a variety of forms including emotional, social, financial, as well as more tangible dimensions.

- *Recognize that everyone will lose something.* People will feel loss. Even the changes we want require us to let go of or leave behind current ways. Bridges' work can be particularly helpful in understanding this phenomenon.

- *Be prepared for anger, anxiety, and other emotions.* Too often, principals approach teachers with logical explanations about why a change is needed or try to talk teachers out of their feelings. People experiencing loss do not hear the logic; rather, they feel the emotion. Principals must address this need for emotional support. In this instance, listening is a more powerful tool than explaining.

- *Provide differentiated support.* If change depends on individuals, then the support must be geared to those teachers who have the highest levels of concern. Providing reassurance is crucial for these teachers.

- *Be an advocate for the change.* Be consistent: Put the best perspective on everything. Realize teachers will have concerns along the way. Your support during the implementation of change will reassure faculty that you are an advocate for the change initiative. Negative comments or uncertainty about the change should be addressed as a team as early as possible—if not, momentum in implementing the change can be lost.

- *Honor the past, but show a future connected to students.* Acknowledging that the past was not bad, just unresponsive to the needs of current students, helps teachers understand their work is really never complete but ongoing. As the principal encourages a new way of leading and learning, some teachers may feel left behind or confused. Finding ways to celebrate and let go of the past moves teachers toward a new way of working.

### Stage 2: Trying It Out

- *Provide tangible examples.* Invite teachers into conversations about how teacher leading and learning will look. Send a team of teachers to visit similar schools where the principals and teachers work collectively. These concrete examples can spark conversations when teachers return.

- *Build supportive structures.* Schools are busy places, and unless structures are in place to support teacher leadership, such as routine and dependable committees, teams, and task groups, change will not happen. No one can change another person, but principals can facilitate the building of relationships through structures that bring teachers together.

- *Communicate again and again.* Teachers know the principal is serious about change when there is consistency in communication. For example, when speaking with teachers, parents, students, and others, the principal continuously reminds everyone how teacher leadership is an underused resource and will no longer be ignored.

- *Exert both pressure and support.* During this stage, many teachers will want to abandon this new way of working because of conflicts, time constraints, and uncertainty. The concept of "implementation dip" comes into play here; what seemed to be such a good idea and was initiated enthusiastically becomes more difficult as the realities of making it happen get underway. The principal's gentle pressure and strong support are both needed to keep things moving forward.

- *Try to limit additional changes.* Sometimes asking teachers to take on more change because of external demands cannot be avoided. Still, there should be an effort to limit the number of changes teachers experience as they start to lead and learn together. If externally initiated changes intrude, it may be necessary to put local initiatives on hold or at a maintenance level temporarily.

- *Learn leadership skills together.* As co-learners, principals and teachers can acquire the requisite leadership skills needed to work together. With the current emphasis on collaborative work in schools, principals have access to numerous resources for needed leadership development.

- *Celebrate successes and analyze mistakes.* Most people like to celebrate successes, but growth in leadership depends on learning from mistakes as well. To show disappointment when a teacher makes a wrong decision sends a message that taking a risk as a leader is dangerous. Instead, principals can show how these mistakes are valuable lessons in building leadership.

### Stage 3: Accepting a New Way of Doing Business

- *Offer frequent reminders of the purpose for a new way of leading and learning.* Teacher leadership will expand in this stage. The communication necessary within the previous stage is just as critical, because new people will be engaged and veterans will be at new levels of engagement.

- *Compare Stage 1 with Stage 3.* If teachers can see how they have increased in their leading and learning, they can better appreciate their efforts and be more inclined to "stay the course." This reassures teachers the new way of working will not go away.

- *Provide recognition.* Teacher leaders often report the lack of recognition in their schools. Principals must find ways to recognize teachers' leading and learning either publicly or privately, depending on the teachers and the school culture.

- *Continue support.* Principals relinquish part of the responsibility for promoting and building teacher leadership as teachers take on more of this responsibility. However, ongoing support from the formal leader, including making adjustments to structures and the use of resources will still be needed.

- *Plan to sustain the change.* Helping teacher leaders plan for transitions can make a difference for the school and the school system. Involving teachers in conversations on how to sustain progress, even with a change in formal leadership, is an important means for continuing support. Teacher leaders, regardless of their competence and years of experience, are hesitant in their leadership when a new principal arrives.

Intentional leadership actions in each of these stages helps achieve valued outcomes. Remember, outcomes valued by some are not necessarily those valued by everyone—consequently, different reactions to change are inevitable. Some teachers will quickly embrace this new view of leadership, others will be more cautious, and a few may reject the idea altogether. Finding ways to work with all of these reactions is incumbent on the principal.

## Individual Reactions to Change

When any change is introduced, some teachers may be so enthused they volunteer to lead study groups or visit other schools, while other teachers go to great lengths to avoid any professional conversations about the initiative. As previously discussed, most everyone will move through stages of change, but not everyone will move at the same pace. It may be difficult to match specific support for each individual teacher's needs, but examining reasons for these differences can help principals understand and accept, or at least tolerate, the diversity of perspectives. This knowledge helps principals plan for appropriate levels of support for the majority of teachers.

We recommend principals consider why teachers may or may not be motivated to lead. We review four areas in which teachers' differences can influence their willingness to lead and learn. The first area is the teachers' adult growth and development through systems that explain their "ways of knowing" (Drago-Severson, 2004, p. 24; Drago-Severson, Blum-DeStefano, & Asghar, 2013, p. 27) and influence how they will react to change. We suggest strategies to support teachers within each system during a change process. Next we consider where the teachers are in their career cycles (Steffy, Wolfe, Pasch, & Enz, 1999; Eros, 2011). Then, we identify some of the personal issues competing for teachers' attention. Finally, we recommend principals acknowledge and accept that teachers do not always share the same philosophy of teaching and learning.

## Adult Growth and Development

Drago-Severson (2004) studied 25 principals who supported teacher professional learning and used Kegan's (1994) constructive-developmental theory to understand how the principals' work supported teacher growth and development. Using this model, principals can better understand how teachers "construct—or *actively make sense* of—the reality in which they live (with respect to cognitive, interpersonal, and intrapersonal development)" (p. 24).

These categories are not rigid, but do offer descriptions of behaviors that may help principals recognize how teachers differ in constructing their realities. This knowledge allows principals to take advantage of the strengths teachers bring to the process. Thus in their most recent book entitled *Learning for Leadership: Developmental Strategies for Building Capacity in Our Schools*, Drago-Severson, Blum-DeStefano, and Asghar (2013) shared findings from a 15-week graduate Leadership for Transformational Learning (LTL) course about learning leadership for adult development:

> As with all kinds of learning, we remember best what we use most often . . . and for these leaders, developmental mindfulness and intentionality have proven effective and key parts of their leadership lives and work in support of adult development.
>
> (p. 88)

Previously, we referred to "time" as one of the themes of change. In addition to examining teachers' adult growth and development, consideration of how much time it may take for them to adopt change is important. Several authors have developed descriptions of different types of people and the amount of time it takes them to move through a change process; we believe that the "labels" (Figure 3.1) help us visualize and identify likely behaviors.

## Instrumental Way of Knowing (Drago-Severson, 2004)

These adults are primarily oriented toward their own self-interests, purposes, and wants. They are less likely to see the perspectives of other people unless those perspectives interfere with what they want. They will adopt change only if they see it as in their best interests. Teachers who view the world through this lens are likely to fall toward the far right on the time-it-takes-to-change continuum. These teachers do not easily give up what they are doing for something new. Principals will notice these teachers are cynical and cautious, and use their energy to resist the changes rather than adopt them. Their skepticism can also be viewed as strength, especially when their critical questions require principals and other advocates to provide a rationale for change. Strategies principals can use with these teachers include:

- At first, limit the time and energy spent with resistant teachers while always extending to them the invitation to be a part of the effort.

- Invite peers who have adopted the change and are valued by these teachers to work with them.

- Provide as much information as the teachers need to help them believe that the change is safe to adopt. (Adapted from Schlechty, 1993, pp. 49–50)

## Socializing Way of Knowing (Drago-Severson, 2004)

This system may represent the majority of teachers in most schools. These teachers depend on external authority and seek approval from the principal or peers who influence them. Additionally, these teachers are sensitive to feelings—their own and others'. They derive satisfaction from involvement with other teachers, but are not going to be out in front when change is taking place. Though they will fall toward the right on the time continuum in Figure 3.1, they are less resistant and more

Figure 3.1. Labels on the Moving-Through-the-Change-Process Spectrum

| Source | A Little Time | | Early majority | Late majority | A Lot of Time |
|---|---|---|---|---|---|
| Rogers (2003) | Innovators | Early adopters | Early majority | Late majority | Laggards |
| Quaglia (1991) | Yahoos | | Yes/Buts | | Come-ons |
| Schlechty (1993) | Trailblazers | Pioneers | Settlers | Stay-at-homes | Saboteurs |
| Whitaker (2002) | Superstars | | Backbones | | Mediocres |
| Joyce, Mueller, Hrycauk, & Hrycauk (2005) | Gourmet omnivores | Active consumers | Passive consumers | | Reticent consumers |

persuadable than those at the far right. Their strength is their ability to ask for realistic examples of the change. Strategies principals might consider in working with these teachers include:

- Help these teachers know what the expectations are for them.
- Develop support systems to prevent them from quitting when the work becomes frustrating.
- Design recognition strategies to use in celebrating achieved benchmarks in the change. (Adapted from Schlechty, 1993, p. 49)

## Self-Authoring Way of Knowing (Drago-Severson, 2004)

These teachers evaluate and criticize themselves based on internally generated values and standards. Rather than seeking the approval of others, they are concerned with their own competence and performance, and see conflict as potentially useful in clarifying issues. These teachers may separate into two groups of change agents. The first group includes those who are "trailblazers" (Schlechty, 1993) or "innovators" (Rogers, 2003). These are the teachers who love risk and are motivated by new ideas. They do not need to know what is expected of them; in fact, they take off without a plan. However, they still need a connection to the formal leadership, especially the principal. These teachers may isolate themselves from colleagues and be viewed as preoccupied with their own agendas. Strategies principals can use to support these individuals include:

- Find unique ways to provide support, such as connecting them with external networks of like-minded teachers.
- Encourage them to see their work in the context of the mission of the school, rather than as isolated from other teachers.
- Capture what these teachers are doing in order to help other teachers when they adopt the change. (Adapted from Schlechty, 1993, pp. 47–48)

The second group of teachers in this system might be called "pioneers" (Schlechty, 1993) or "early adopters" (Rogers, 2003). These teachers are often motivated by their trailblazer/innovator colleagues, and are willing to take risks but are a little more cautious. This group includes the teacher leaders who are respected by their peers and can influence others to move in the direction of the change. When they adopt a change, it is likely others who have not yet done so will join or seriously consider it. Strategies principals can use to support these teachers include:

- Provide encouragement for believing that adopting the change will make a difference in student learning.
- Invite them to observe demonstration lessons.
- Offer resources so they can build collaborative groups. (Adapted from Schlechty, 1993, pp. 48–49)

Both these groups of teachers are to the far left on the time to change continuum.

## The Strongest Resistors

The final group of teachers exhibits the strongest resistance toward change. It is difficult to link their behaviors to a system or "way of knowing" because they take on these roles for a variety of reasons sometimes not related to where they are in their adult growth and development. The best term we found in the literature for these teachers is "saboteurs" (Schlechty, 1993, p. 50) or "reticent consumers" (Joyce, Mueller, Hrycauk, & Hrycauk, 2005). They undermine and attempt to destroy change efforts they believe should not take place. Often they have been repeatedly disappointed with so many change initiatives that they refuse to be involved in another and try to influence other teachers to resist involvement as well. Practical strategies for principals to consider when dealing with this type of resistor include:

- Listen to find out the cause of their resistance.
- Do not ignore them; attempt to bring them into the conversations about the change even if they are disagreeable.
- Do not reward them by not asking them to take on responsibilities expected of other teachers. To do so would be to reinforce the undesired rather than the desired behavior. (Adapted from Schlechty, 1993, p. 5)

Using what is known about adult development and its impact on teachers' acceptance or resistance of change can help principals feel less frustrated when faced with individuals' unwillingness to change. It does not make it easier, but it does make it more understandable. This knowledge alerts principals to teachers' needs regarding pressure, resources, and encouragement. The good news is "people (and their constructions of reality) can *change or develop* over time with developmentally appropriate supports and challenges" (Drago-Severson, 2004, p. 24). To develop strategies to nurture and confront teachers' reluctance to continuously improve, principals and teacher leaders must be knowledgeable about adult growth and development. Figure 3.2 was developed to describe how this balancing of support and challenge must be purposeful. Too much of either support or challenge can be counterproductive. When asking teachers to meet the various challenges of change, commensurate support must be provided to avoid unnecessary or overly stressful risk situations. In Figure 3.2, we offer a visual of how to think about these two dimensions.

At point A in the figure, the risk of the situation is low and therefore requires a lower level of support to avoid stress for the individuals involved. Point B in the figure demonstrates the higher level of support needed to minimize stress for those involved in this situation of higher risk. Both points A and B are examples of support and risk levels being commensurate. As the risk increases, so should the intensity and types of support. Point C, on the other hand, indicates a mismatch between the level of support and the level of risk. Point C indicates that while the level of risk involved is high, the support level is low; this sort of mismatch is ripe for creating stress, even to the point of fear, for participants. Too many incidents where the level of support does not match the level of risk involved will reduce the likelihood that teachers will want to risk getting involved when they are unsure that the necessary level of support will be provided.

## Developing a Culture of Improvement ♦ 47

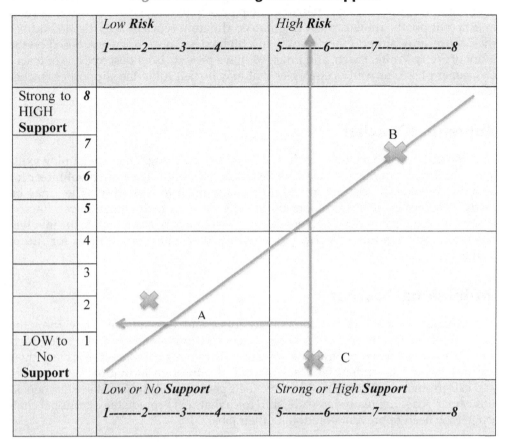

Figure 3.2. **Matching Risk and Support**

Where teachers are in their adult growth and development is only one piece of the puzzle in understanding teacher differences. There are other aspects of teachers' lives that influence their willingness to lead and learn. Next we examine where teachers are in their careers and how this may influence them.

## Teaching Career

Principals should not make assumptions about who may be willing to lead. Many beginning teachers are mature adults who decide to move to teaching from a previous profession. Consequently, there may be teachers who are "self-authoring" in their adult growth and development but entering the classroom for the first time. One might predict teachers who are just beginning would be reluctant to take on new roles beyond their survival in the classroom. Yet there are first-year teachers who reach out for leadership roles to help end their isolation and feel a part of a collaborative community. Some teachers nearing retirement may lack interest in starting something new, while others may take on responsibilities because they want to leave a professional legacy. In between these two extremes in a teacher's career are different phases in the cycle. Teacher leaders can emerge from every phase of the career cycle.

As expected, teachers do not move through all career phases. Recognizing the needs of teachers at different phases can help principals understand why individuals at different points in their career might need different types of activities to address their concerns or support their growth to a higher level of competence. Based on the work of Steffy, Wolfe, Pasch, and Enz (1999), we provide brief descriptions of teachers' career phases as well as strategies that may be helpful in the support of teacher leaders.

## Apprentice Teacher

Apprentice teachers are in their first 3 years of teaching. They are gaining skills and confidence, but they still experience much self-doubt. They often volunteer for activities outside the classroom and are usually open to new ideas. They may be ready to accept leadership responsibilities this early in their career, depending on their adult growth and development. Mentor assignments may facilitate the involvement of these beginning teachers in activities that will prepare them for future leadership.

## Professional Teacher

Professional teachers are competent, solid, and dependable. They form the majority of the faculty in most schools; teachers at this stage generally enjoy their work and rarely have aspirations for administrative positions. They view their greatest reward as student feedback, specifically through individual notes, visits, and calls from former students. They see their peers as colleagues. Many teachers in this career phase are ready for leadership roles that will provide the additional challenge they need to prevent boredom in their jobs.

## Expert Teacher

Expert teachers move beyond competence to a level of instinctively knowing what to do with students from all backgrounds who have a variety of needs. Many of these teachers seek and achieve national certification; all of them demonstrate the knowledge and skills for this certification. They look for new ideas to improve teaching and learning, and often become involved in the profession at the local, state, and national levels. Principals will not have to encourage these teachers to be leaders because, through their own initiative, they are leaders. Expert teachers need resources that allow them to expand their leadership. Many teachers in this career phase are concerned about leaving a legacy and are anxious to mentor less experienced teachers.

## Distinguished Teacher

Distinguished teachers influence policy and legislation at the local, state, and national levels. Decision makers often consult these individuals. They are often award winners in teaching. Teachers in this phase have moved beyond the school level in their leadership, and should be encouraged to continue this work. Action research is an avenue through which distinguished teachers can influence practice and satisfy their interest in moving beyond the traditional forms of professional development.

## From the Field

As an accomplished classroom teacher, I work at the membrane through which policy becomes practice. That gives me day-to-day experience with the impact that policy has on teaching and learning. Therefore, I will use my unique, inherent credibility to speak on issues in education and advocate for changes in institutional policy and practice that I believe will most benefit student well-being and the teaching profession.

August "Sandy" Merz III, NBCT
8th-grade Mathematics
Safford K8 1B Candidate School
Tucson, AZ

At any phase, teachers may move into stages of withdrawal. Being able to diagnose the level of withdrawal can help principals select appropriate interventions to prevent withdrawal or at least decrease its intensity. Steffy et al. (1999) identified three levels of withdrawal: initial, persistent, and deep.

- **Initial**—Teaching is adequate, but the teacher begins to experience feelings of inadequacy and decreased competence. The teacher becomes quieter and more isolated even during group gatherings. Individuals may not be aware of what is happening to them.
- **Persistent**—At this stage, the withdrawal moves to active criticism and even obstructionist behaviors. These teachers often demonstrate strong resistance to change and sometimes serve as gatekeepers, keeping out any changes to which they wish to be unresponsive or resistant.
- **Deep**—In deep withdrawal, teachers spiral downward in their attitudes and skills. Professional growth is no longer a part of their development and they often become "defensive and difficult." (Adapted from Steffy et al., 1999, pp. 15–17)

Principals' understanding of these phases of withdrawal offers two important points. First, these phases provide an explanation for behaviors that may have previously caused principals exasperation and anger. Second, understanding these phases can form the foundation for developing strategies to assist teachers in moving out of the withdrawal and/or prevent any deeper withdrawal. When a principal identifies a teacher in initial withdrawal, steps should be taken to bring the teacher back to his or her level of competence. Busy principals can easily overlook these early symptoms and rely on teachers to "fix themselves." In many cases, however, relatively simple actions by the principal can reengage the teacher. These actions may include:

- Invite the teacher to participate in an off-site professional learning event.
- Engage the teacher in a task force focused on an issue of particular concern to the teacher.
- Stop by the teacher's classroom frequently to talk about issues unrelated to their teaching.

- Place interesting articles related to an interest in the teacher's mailbox (e-mail or snail-mail).
- Orchestrate interactions for the teacher with positive, engaged colleagues in committee work, room assignments, and professional development activities, etc.

Other influences on a teacher's willingness to lead come from outside the school. An individual at different points in their personal life may experience stresses and conditions that cause them to react differently.

## Personal Issues

Teachers may want to commit to leading, but other parts of their lives can cause them to be reluctant, perhaps resist or even withdraw. These pressures come from external sources and from intrapersonal stress the teacher is experiencing. Regardless of the source, balancing personal and professional lives is tough, especially for leaders.

### External Demands

Teachers' lives extend beyond the school and are influenced by demands in their personal lives. Pressures come from family, community, and other commitments. Presently, the teaching population is heavily distributed at the beginning and at the end of the teaching career. Both ends of the continuum have personal concerns that distract from work. Younger teachers may have childcare issues that rule out early morning or late afternoon meetings, whereas older teachers may be responsible for elder care.

These family demands must take priority, making teachers reluctant to let added school responsibilities take precedence over such issues. Some teachers may face situations in which they are discouraged by family members from taking on additional leadership roles or even working outside the home (Zinn, 1997). Sometimes volunteering in community organizations provides greater satisfaction for teachers than taking on additional responsibilities at work. The pressures and challenges faced by families today differ from the past few decades. The work and effort to support the "changing face of the family" structure requires a better understanding of the different configurations that make up the modern family (Lieberman & Miller, 2004). Those structural changes impact the level of involvement and commitment at the school. Finally, there are issues with personal health or the health of family members that drain teachers' emotional and physical strength causing them to be unable to offer their leadership.

### Intrapersonal Demands

Not every teacher believes they can be a leader. In school cultures, teachers are, in most cases, not encouraged to lead and sometimes actually discouraged from taking the lead, especially by their peers. To lead may be viewed as being the "boss," or cause the individual to be viewed as "apart" from the group rather than being "a part" of the group. This would not help these teachers maintain relationships with their colleagues.

## Philosophy of Teaching and Learning

Many conflicts within schools can be traced to differences in teachers' beliefs about how students learn and what teaching strategies should be used. For example, when an instructional strategy is introduced that requires teachers to follow a script, and the majority of teachers believe students should learn through problem solving, resistance occurs. Although most teachers study different philosophical traditions in their undergraduate programs, they seldom connect these to their disagreements with team members regarding how to address student needs. Until principals and teacher leaders bring these differences to the table for discussion, there may be passive or even aggressive resistance to changes in instruction with teachers having little to no understanding of why.

## Preparing Others

A change in the way of leading and learning should not be a surprise to other formal school leaders such as assistant principals, guidance directors, and others. Although primarily a school-based initiative, a number of external entities and groups will be affected by this change also. Individual schools are part of larger systems, and a change in one part of the system affects the entire system. With a move toward distributed power and authority, others outside the school will need to be prepared for implementation of this new view of leadership. Proactively providing information and building relationships along the way are smart strategies for most any change initiative, large or small.

Principals must take the steps necessary to create a state of readiness on the part of these entities. If done well, hardly anyone will notice; if done poorly, incompletely, or in a neglectful way, the negative results may never be overcome. We identify one internal group (the administrative team) and three external groups (the central office, parents and the community, and teachers' organizations) principals need to include as the school moves forward in developing its shared vision for greater distribution of leadership.

### Administrative Teams

Administrative teams vary in definition from school to school. In some schools, the administrative team includes only the principal and assistant principals. In other schools, the team may include lead teachers, guidance counselors, and other formal leaders. Providing clarity early on regarding the definition of teacher leaders including who they are, what their responsibilities and authority entail, and how their work aligns with and is not in conflict with the administrative team is essential. Internal strife assures failure, even if external entities are supportive.

Principals, especially in larger schools, delegate formal leadership responsibilities to others, such as assistant principals. These individuals often have the most frequent contact with classroom teachers. When principals are off site, the assistant principals step in to support teacher leaders. Even when principals sincerely believe in teacher leadership, if other formal leaders are not in agreement, problems will occur. If they are to work to promote teacher leadership, everyone on the administrative team should be involved in substantive decision-making.

If a principal is new to a school, an administrative team may already be in place; alternately, principals may have input into the selection of all or some formal leaders.

Regardless of the situation, the principal must build relationships with the team to establish a unified support system for teacher leaders.

## The Central Office

Keeping immediate supervisors informed regarding initiatives at the school site is always a wise idea. Watching the supervisors' reactions gives clues about the pace at which the principal should initiate change. While the new view of leadership is still at the "thinking stage," a meeting with the principal's immediate supervisor to get input and advice should be scheduled. Even if the conversation does not seem to produce much interest or enthusiasm from the supervisor, the principal has performed an important service in terms of building relationships with those within the central office and preparing them for the changes ahead. As the distribution of power and authority increases, teacher leaders will become primary contacts for various central office administrators. Making these officials aware of the change from one leader to many leaders will better prepare everyone.

Central office leaders are responsible for keeping the system in equilibrium. When a principal introduces change that upsets this balance, central office leaders may be unwilling to support the principal. Most central office leaders will support innovation if they are kept informed and the change does not negatively affect the larger system.

## Parents and the Community

Parents and community leaders get involved in schools when they believe it to be in their best interests. Distributing power and authority should be seen by external entities as a positive endeavor. Parents need to know if a teacher leader will be taking major responsibility for a project or program involving their children. This information can be provided through letters, the school's website, telephone calls, electronic mail, social media, newspaper articles, and face-to-face meetings. Teacher leaders should be introduced to parents and community members as the primary contact for the specific school initiatives they are leading. They should be the representatives when presentations regarding the projects are requested. Knowing who the leaders are and how to contact them helps prepare parents and community members to understand this new view of leadership.

## Teachers' Organizations

Teachers' organizations are important entities to involve regarding the distribution of power and authority. Making sure everyone understands no additional layers of administration are being created, that teachers are not being overloaded with additional responsibilities, and that the work does not infringe on contracted workloads is important. These issues need to be shared, understood, and evaluated frequently. This will go a long way in building and maintaining positive relationships with the leaders of teachers' organizations. Conversations regarding how this new view of leadership impacts items in the negotiated agreement need to begin early and involve representatives from the teachers' organization, the central office, and the school. Involving teacher leaders from the school will facilitate these conversations. Teachers should not be put in a position of having to divide their loyalties between their work at the building site and their membership in their professional association.

## Making the Long-Term Commitment: Advice for Staying on Target

As we bring this chapter to a close, we want to reemphasize that the work to be undertaken must be intentionally led, but the way principals do this will depend on their tenure with the school and the school system. Principals are in a variety of situations as they begin this effort, and there is no one set of experiences or circumstances ideal for the journey. We have provided "Good News/Challenging News" in Figure 3.3 to describe some of these various circumstances. Each situation can be positive and in support of the work; simultaneously each situation presents some rather unique challenges. We invite principals to find their own situation on the chart and factor in this information as they make decisions about their work with teacher leaders.

The three framework principles provide structure for the next chapters. None of the three result from hopes, wishes, and waiting to see. If positive relationships

Figure 3.3. Principal's Situation: Good News/Challenging News

| Principal's Situation | Good News | Challenging News |
|---|---|---|
| New principal in this school, but worked as a principal in another school in the same school system | Do not have to unlearn ways of leading; "style" is open to develop without restraint from the past experience in this school. | Need to devote a good percentage of time and energy getting to know the school and local surrounding attendance zone. |
| Current principal in the school | Can focus on the change itself because much of the job is routine. | May make too many assumptions about a situation. In doing this, may overlook important opportunities. |
| Worked as a principal before, but new to the school system and school | Everyone is expecting new ideas of operating within the school system and the school. | There is much about the individuals and the organization both in the school and the school system (and local community/values) that is not known. Well-intended but naïve actions could generate resistance. |
| New to the school with no previous experience as a principal | What an opportunity to redefine the leadership roles in the school! There is no "history." An excellent context for change. | There is much to learn and the year will be very busy focused on just surviving. There may be little time and energy for nurturing others. It may be challenging to focus on your personal well-being and professional learning. |

are to be developed, power and authority to be distributed, and teacher leadership to be aligned with professional learning, then planned change must be undertaken. Some teachers may push too hard to make these planned outcomes realities; others will work diligently to keep them from ever being realized. Then there will be the "mass in the middle"—open to, but cautious about, the planned changes. They will be expecting strong leadership to get started, and require supportive conditions, as things get under way.

Here is advice for principals as they commit to the implementation of the needed changes to usher in this new view of leadership:

- *Raise the difficult questions.* There will be times when information from external and internal sources will have to be shared though it will not be welcomed, even by the principal. Principals can develop the "capacity to deliver disturbing news and raise difficult questions in a way that people can absorb, prodding them to take up the message rather than ignore it or kill the messenger" (Heifetz & Linsky, 2002, p. 12).

- *Be persistent.* The changes involved in successfully implementing this new view of leadership are complex and will take time, perhaps years. Not everyone will be excited about everything and not all things will go well. Others will be looking to the principal to see if this change is really important or just something that gets time and attention when nothing else is happening. Principals need to demonstrate their continued advocacy for this new view by purposefully supporting the change process day after day, month after month and, likely, year after year.

- *Be flexible in leadership style.* Principals need to exercise a variety of leadership styles to successfully implement planned changes. Depending on what is happening and who is involved, principals should be prepared to function both as a directive leader and a facilitative leader, as well as sometimes using an artful mixture of both.

- *Stay focused.* With the "busyness" of schools, it will be easy to be distracted and unable to keep conversations and work focused on the school's shared vision of leadership. But if the principal stays focused, teachers will stay focused. Principals can take actions to minimize distractions and keep these planned changes at the top of the daily agenda.

- *Align decisions about resources.* Once the school members develop a shared vision for student learning, the principal must make sure resources are aligned with this ideal. Comparing the current situation with this ideal inevitably reveals discrepancies. The principal must secure resources and facilitate collective decision-making that aligns them in ways to reduce the gap between existing and ideal student learning outcomes. Resources can be many things, including but not limited to tangible items and money. The following Figure 3.4 offers some excellent examples of intangible, but powerful resources in the form of actions principals can exercise in aligning leadership resources to assist in achievement of the school's vision for student learning and a new view of leadership.

Figure 3.4. **Do Less, Do More**

| Do Less, Do More | |
|---|---|
| **Do LESS** | **Do MORE** |
| Less rush to change | More assessment of organizational readiness |
| Less top down decision-making | More teacher empowerment |
| Less isolation of faculty and staff | More intentional collaboration between faculty and staff |
| Less competition of faculty and staff | More intentional collaboration between faculty and staff |
| Less competition over resources and withholding of professional practices | More intentional sharing of successful instructional practices and resources |
| Less Me | More We (Team approach) |
| Less distrust of teacher's ideas and viewpoints | More confidence in teacher |
| Less adding of competitive initiatives | More focus on teacher learning through PLCs |
| Less individual learning | More collective learning |

Rubin, R., Abrego, M.H., & Sutterby, J.A. (2014). *Less Is More in Elementary School: Strategies for Thriving in a High-Stakes Environment.* New York, NY: Routledge. Used with permission.

# Summary

To continuously improve, the faculty and staff must be involved in change. One approach to promote continuous improvement is to involve teachers in leadership responsibilities. If principals are moving from traditional leadership to the new view of leadership advocated here, there will be change. Seeing the need for a change and successfully making that change happen do not necessarily travel together. With knowledge about the phases of change and how teachers individually experience change, principals are better prepared to promote intentional teacher leading and learning.

Principals may acknowledge that individuals react differently to change, but this should not prevent moving forward with what is best for students. The principal's job is to have courage to face negative reactions, to stay focused and not waver from the goal regardless of the displeasure, complaints, and even anger that may emerge.

# Resources

3.1 Education Topics: School Culture/Climate—ASCD provides an overview of school culture and climate and includes videos of authors Todd Whitaker and Paul DeWitt addressing specific aspects of these topics. Retrieved from www.ascd.org/research-a-topic/school-culture-and-climate-resources.aspx

3.2 Whitaker, T.W. (2014). *Dealing with difficult teachers* (3rd ed.). New York, NY: Routledge—Addresses something that all principals face in their schools to one degree or another: difficult teachers. Includes strategies for motivating, creating discomfort in, communicating with, and reducing the influence of difficult teachers.

3.3 Conner, M.L. (2005). *How adults learn: Ageless learner, 1997–2004*—Conner introduces the most significant concepts and terms in adult learning. Included in the work are an overview of adult learning theory, books on adult learning, and links to other websites. Retrieved from http://agelesslearner.com/intros/adultlearning.html

3.4 Zinn, L.M. (2001). A resource for teacher leadership: Philosophy of education inventory (PEI). In M. Katzenmeyer & G. Moller, *Awakening the sleeping giant: Helping teachers develop as leaders* (2nd ed.), 139–166. Thousand Oaks, CA: Corwin Press—Zinn's PEI provides teachers with an instrument that measures how they believe students learn and their preference for teaching methods. The instrument can be purchased directly from the author at Lifelong Learning Options, phone: (303) 499–0864. Instrument and instructions can be found at https://ctl810.wikispaces.com/file/view/paei.tex.pdf

3.5 Ferrero, D.J. (2005). Pathways to reform: Start with values. *Educational Leadership, 62*(5), 8–15—This article is a good companion when teachers are examining their educational philosophies.

3.6 Goleman, D., Boyatzis, R., & McKee, A. (2013). *Primal leadership: Realizing the power of emotional intelligence.* Boston: Harvard Business School Press—The authors explain how a leader's emotional intelligence can impact the organization. Of particular relevance is the focus on leadership styles. This updated edition adds to an already interesting and informative book.

# Part 2: Putting the Principles into Action

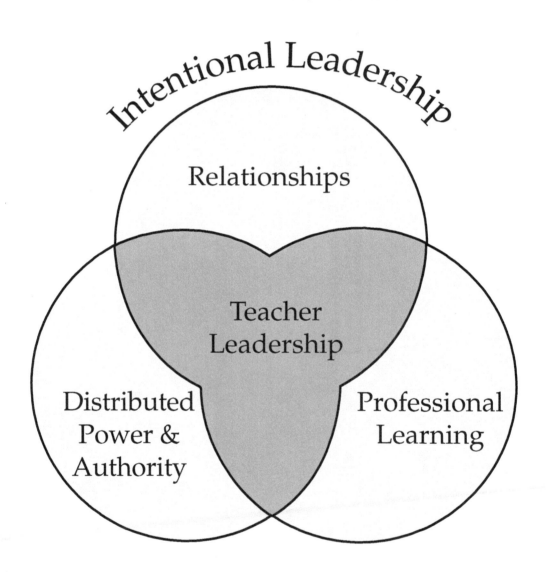

# Part 2: Putting the Principles into Action

In Part 2, the principles in the Framework for Intentional Leadership—building positive relationships, distributing power and authority, and aligning teacher leadership with professional learning—are addressed. Each chapter includes an introduction, self-study activities, and actions principals can take. We recommend reading these chapters in the sequence presented. We believe principals first pay attention to relationships before establishing structures for distributing power and authority. Successful distribution of power and authority is dependent on the relationships between and among principals, administrative team members and teachers. The offering of and the willing acceptance of distributed power and authority require mutual respect and trust throughout the school. Once this foundation of relationships and distributed power and authority is formed then the alignment of teacher leadership with professional learning follows.

Chapter 4, "Building Positive Relationships," begins by asking principals to seek out existing human and social resources that can be used to increase teacher leading and learning. Attention is then given to how relationships can be built among teachers and between principals and teachers. Finally, there are suggestions on dealing with the inevitable conflicts that emerge as people collaborate. In Chapter 5, "Distributing Power and Authority," we ask principals to examine their beliefs and values about "letting go" of control. If principals acknowledge a desire for and some level of readiness to distribute power and authority, we offer strategies for working with teachers to develop a shared vision for student learning, collectively make decisions, and effectively delegate. We also recommend structures principals can establish to facilitate the distribution of power and authority. Chapter 6, "Aligning Teacher Leadership with Professional Learning," invites principals to think differently about professional learning. Specific recommendations are provided for engaging teachers in leading and learning. We discuss both the more traditional definitions and processes of professional learning and those that have emerged with recent technological advances. At the end of this chapter, we address identifying and working with reluctant teacher learners.

# 4  Building Positive Relationships

"The most valuable resource that all teachers have is each other. Without collaboration our growth is limited to our own perspectives."
Robert John Meehan in *Treasury of Quotes for Teachers*

## Scenario: Theresa's New Job Begins

Theresa's interview went well and the feedback from everyone involved was pretty positive. Jay was pleased to extend an offer to her to be the first ever Dean of Instruction at MMS. From Jay's perspective, he wasn't losing Theresa, and he was strengthening the MMS network of leaders. What a great beginning to a new academic year!

After getting herself organized for the new school year and her new responsibilities as Dean of Instruction, Theresa met with Jay to discuss her beginning steps and the long-term perspective for the year ahead. Without hesitation, Jay advised Theresa to spend some time working with individual faculty members and some small groups to learn what they were thinking about this new position and to share some of her own thoughts. Jay reminded Theresa that only those individuals on the hiring committee had really heard her thinking about this new position and the influence it should had. Spending time listening to and talking with all faculty members, in one forum or another, would be time well spent in these first days and weeks of the new year. Jay also suggested that most of these conversations be informal. There would be plenty of whole-group meetings in the days before the students arrived.

He suggested they talk again after the first few days with the students in attendance and review what she learned. He also shared that he would announce the formation of a project team to collaboratively work on putting together a personnel committee with the goal of developing interview questions to help select qualified applicants to fill school vacancies. Jay added that in his announcement, he would designate her as the leader on this project.

Among the important lessons she'd learned from Jay and her colleagues at MMS was that building and maintaining positive relationships based on trust would be essential for long-term success. The informal conversations were going to help Theresa and MMS faculty in getting acquainted in deeper ways both personally and professionally. The more formal interactions through the personnel project committee would be Theresa's first opportunity to work with faculty in her role as Dean of Instruction. This project would provide an opportunity to work collaboratively and pursue an end result that would benefit the entire school. What could be more related to instruction than hiring quality teaching staff!?

Through her various conversations with faculty, Theresa confirmed her colleagues, like herself, were both excited and a bit nervous about this new position at

> MMS. Though she had worked with many of these people for years, things were different now—she knew it and sensed that they did as well. However, everyone agreed that while strong relationships at MMS exist, they could and should be stronger and much more collaborative. So, in order to maintain and sustain the strong relationships that exist at MMS, but also help move them to the next level, it's important to work collaboratively in the design and use of interview questions that deliberately identify potential candidates who believe in the benefits of building and sustaining positive relationships. What a great beginning to this new formal teacher leadership role.

Personal, professional, and social relationships support a web of school leadership. This web must be built on trust, or it is certain to fail. Most of us know positive relationships enhance our work, whereas negative relationships strongly influence our desire to leave a school, sometimes even the profession. The quality of relationships built over years determines the success of the principal and the school itself. Bryk and Schneider (2002) stated that "when an individual sustains a relationship with some person or organization, these long-term social connections can take on value unto themselves. . . . Individuals come to define themselves as connected to that person or organization" (p. 15). These "long-term social connections" are resilient, and promoting positive and more deeply professional relationships among these connections is a major leadership challenge principals face.

In this chapter, we discuss the concepts of human and social capital and how they are essential to understanding why building positive relationships can be beneficial for the school, the school's mission, and the principal. Then, we offer principals practical strategies to use in gathering information about the existing human and social resources in the school and how best to use and build on those resources. Next we provide suggested activities principals can use in building relationships—teachers with teachers and principals with teachers. We close the chapter by addressing the inevitable conflicts that occur regardless of the efforts put into building positive relationships.

## Investing in Teacher Leadership to Build Human and Social Capital

Principals can lead, but others must agree to follow; this is the essence of leadership. Teachers decide whether to follow their principals based on how they act. Teachers' perceptions are influenced by the leader's "capital." Like the business community, where capital is related to money available to generate more money, there are four types of capital that leaders use to influence followers:

- human capital—skills, knowledge, and expertise;
- cultural capital—ways of being;
- social capital—networks, relations of trust; and
- economic capital—material resources. (Spillane, Hallett, & Diamond, 2003, pp. 3–4)

Principals utilize these forms of capital in their daily interactions with teachers, whether they realize it or not. To build teacher leadership, it is necessary to tap into the existing resources, or capital, teachers already possess. We addressed cultural capital in Chapter 3 when we discussed teachers' adult growth and development. Because teachers have minimal access to economic capital, we will look at human and social capital.

Potential for gaining adult human capital through increased social capital in a school resides with the teachers individually and collectively. Coleman (1988) defined *human capital* as "changes in persons that bring about skills and capabilities that make them able to act in new ways" (p. 100), and said that *social capital* "exists in the relations among persons" (pp. 100–101). Three forms of social capital make it an effective means of social action: 1) obligations, expectations, and trustworthiness; 2) information channels and norms; and 3) effective standards of reciprocity (Coleman, 1988; Woolcock, 1998). These elements are requisites for social capital to serve as a benefit to people. However, like other forms of capital, maximization will depend on how it is managed. Teachers' competence in their classrooms and their chosen social contacts are valuable resources. Left alone, these human and social resources remain virtually unavailable to the school.

Bryk and Schneider (2002) found that in effective schools "the arrangement of social exchanges is an important consideration in the overall productivity of any organization, [but] these concerns take on a heightened salience for schools. The social relations of schooling are not just a mechanism of production but they are a valued outcome in their own right" (p. 19). A principal can purposely structure connections to increase value by being aware of teachers' knowledge, interests, talents, and skills, as well as the social networks in which teachers influence others. Relationships can be encouraged among teachers as well as between teachers and principals to add value to the entire organization. Although many principals use this process intuitively, it is often unsystematic, resulting in overlooked teacher leadership potential.

## Self-Study: Potential for Increasing Human and Social Capital

A self-study of human and social capital includes three steps. First is to gather information about the knowledge, interests, talents, and skills of individual teachers, as well as information about the social connections of these teachers. Next is an analysis of the existing relationships to determine if they add value to the school and then identify opportunities that could be created to increase value to the campus. Third, based on this information, principals can build structures in which positive social networks may develop and thrive, thus increasing social capital. This exercise helps principals see where there are dysfunctional relationships that decrease social capital and take steps to minimize their effects. The size of a school and level of responsibility will govern the amount of time a principal can devote to the activities suggested here. In some cases, a principal may deal with only a section of the teacher population. Whatever the approach, this is a different way of looking at personnel, and we encourage principals to accept the challenge of using these tools. Sometimes, this proactive strategy will save time dealing with relationship issues in the future.

## Gathering Information

Looking for information that reflects the strengths of the teachers rather than focusing on weaknesses is important. People build on their strengths more readily than they respond to instructions to correct their weaknesses. In fact, sometimes others may view what a principal considers a teacher's weakness as a strength. To make good use of human and social capital, principals must determine what information is needed and then collect, organize, and analyze the data in ways that make them useful.

### *What Information Is Needed?*

The purpose of collecting this information is not to select teacher leaders, but to recognize existing and potential teacher leadership. Principals should avoid making assumptions about what human and social capital exists. This is essential, especially for veteran principals who believe teacher leadership is a desired goal. When principals have been in place for an extended period of time, they sometimes think they know all there is to know about the school. Suspending those assumptions as much as possible and beginning with a fresh, and as yet, unformed perspective is important. This information will provide new perspectives, perhaps dispel inaccurate assumptions, and even spark new respect for the accomplishments and interests of individual teachers. Some examples of information principals might seek include:

*Human Capital*
- Evidence of exemplary student learning
- Committee and project lists for the last few years, noting who chaired these committees
- Staff development records looking for who participated and who used the new knowledge and skills
- Honors and awards for teaching, scholarship, and service that reflect leadership or specific knowledge

*Social Capital*
- Teachers who socialize, learn, or volunteer to work with certain other teachers
- Civic and professional association service where leadership is exhibited outside the school
- Teacher of the year, especially if selected by other teachers and the selection criteria are also developed by teachers
- Collegial connections at the district level and in other schools

### *Where Is the Information?*

Reviewing documents, conducting individual interviews, and observing interactions are critical means for addressing the following questions: What knowledge, interests, talents, and skills are present? What relationships already exist?

## Search Documents

Principals should access existing information before trying to generate new information. Personnel files often have important information regarding teachers' previous work and educational experiences, including experiences and interests they had prior to working at the school. We often overlook the level of decision-making many teachers take on in roles they assume in their families and in their communities, such as taking care of ailing parents, maintaining more than one job, or organizing community events.

Searching through records of school communications, such as faculty meeting minutes and committee assignments, can reveal which teachers are involved in school initiatives as well as which teachers voluntarily attended staff development opportunities. Looking for names that appear repeatedly, principals can discover faculty members who are involved, are looked to for leadership, seem to be interested in their professional learning, and show interest in particular subjects or tasks. All of these are indicators of prime candidates for involvement in the leadership efforts at a school. These individuals are already leaders; they are the everyday behind the scenes teacher leaders that make things happen without having to be in the limelight. Other teachers at the school have probably already identified these particular colleagues as leaders. Therefore, principals need to carefully encourage and support their transition from behind the scenes to a wider audience of teachers who might benefit from their innate leadership skills.

## Interview Teachers

According to John Maxwell (2014), "Good questions inform; great questions transform!" (p. 25). Individual interviews conducted either throughout the school year or during the summer are additional sources of information. Effective use of questions and listening techniques are the most important skills in this data gathering. Using open-ended and structured questions, such as those in Figure 4.1, generates information helpful in identifying the full scope of the resources teachers bring including their knowledge of other human and social capital. Open-ended questions are best used with teachers who speak freely; structured questions are more helpful when a teacher is more reticent.

Figure 4.1. **Open-Ended Versus Structured Questions Illustration**

| *Open-Ended Questions/Requests* | *Structured Questions* |
|---|---|
| Tell me about your major responsibilities at the school. | Do you feel your strengths are being well utilized? *Probe:* Why do you say that? |
| Describe leadership in this school. | Who are the leaders in this school? *Probe:* What criteria did you use to determine that these individuals are leaders? *Probe:* How do they lead? |

Figure 4.1. **Continued**

| Open-Ended Questions/Requests | Structured Questions |
|---|---|
| Is there anything about the school you would change if you could? | What one thing would you change about the school if money were not an issue?<br>*Probe:* How is this different from the way things are now? |
| What activities, such as sports or volunteer work, are you involved in when you are not at school? | Are you involved in any activities, such as sports or volunteer work, outside the school?<br>*Probe:* Could you give me an example of one of these? |
| Tell me about work you have done with your colleagues at the school. | Which two or three colleagues would you select to help you with a project?<br>*Probe:* Why did you pick these individuals? |
| Tell me about your professional learning. | Are you involved in any type of formal professional learning?<br>*Probe:* What would you like to learn? |

## *Observe and Listen*

Information can be discovered by listening to teacher interactions at committee meetings, faculty functions, and in the hallways or office area. Staying alert to comments faculty members make regarding such things as colleagues they admire (or not), individuals from whom they have received assistance (or not), or those teachers with whom they have worked on committees or projects can provide important insights about the existing and potential human and social capital. Visiting with teachers formally and informally about students can also be enlightening. More direct information comes from observing faculty members' teaching. Most school systems require observations to meet the formal evaluation obligations, but a reliable source of information is the informal "walk-through" that takes place for short periods, occurs unannounced, and happens frequently throughout the school year. Principals who spend time in classrooms are often able to quickly identify which teachers are leaders or have the potential for leadership.

Using documents, interviews, and observations can help principals begin developing a picture of teacher leadership potential in the school. Depending on the size of the school and the time available, adjustments in what information to gather and how to gather it should be made. Additionally, principals must be aware of temporary lapses in a teacher's leadership focus, possibly due to outside commitments such as family obligations or a return to graduate school. Perhaps a teacher needs time to "heal" from an earlier leadership experience that was frustrating. Principals need to question their assumptions, ask questions, listen, and analyze the data.

## Analysis of the Information Gathered

Data are merely information until meaning is attached. Where is the human capital that adds value? Do existing relationships add value to the school? Are there relationships that need to be addressed? Are there relationships that need to be built in order to maximize the potential for change initiatives to succeed? Are there relationship opportunities that could be created to increase value to the organization?

### *What Relationships Exist?*

Principals now have the baseline data for building teachers' leading and learning, just as student achievement and attendance data are for school improvement planning. To facilitate analysis, the principal can develop a sociogram to show who is connected to whom inside and, if possible, outside the school. Plotting this information in a web, such as the one in Figure 4.2a, provides a picture of the human capital and the potential for using social networks to build human capital for improved instruction. Figure 4.2a illustrates the social relationships that existed when Jay arrived as principal of Markham Middle School (described in Chapter 2). For example, Theresa, at that time, was the 7th-grade language arts teacher, had

Figure 4.2a. **Example of a Sociogram for MMS (at the Time of Jay's Arrival)**

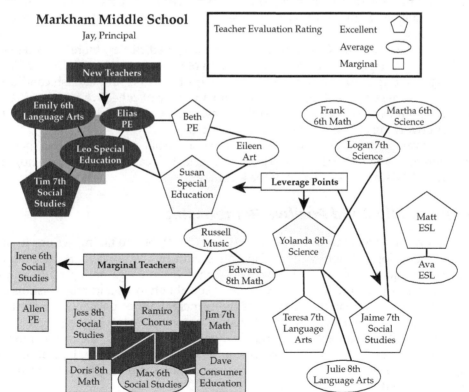

Adapted from Copland, 2001a.

social connections with Yolanda, who later became the lead teacher, and with Julie, another language arts teacher. Similarly, Susan was connected to two of the new teachers. Notice how Jaime was linked with Yolanda and Logan, who were socially connected to other teachers. Importantly, the marginal teachers formed networks with other more successful teachers.

The sociogram here is formal and fairly detailed. Again, depending on the size of the school and the time available, principals may need to be more informal. However, even hand drawn circles and lines that cause the principal to think about existing relationships and what they mean in terms of influencing the school provide important information for future actions.

## *What Existing or Potential Relationships Can Add Value?*

Once the sociogram is complete and other information about individual teachers is collected, principals can study the data to determine where value-added relationships exist, where opportunities for value-added relationships could be created, and where relationships exist that are harmful to the school's mission. Connecting the talents of competent teacher leaders who have relationships with teachers who need to improve their skills provides principals with leverage to influence other teachers. For example, in Figure 4.2a, Yolanda, Susan, and Jaime, all excellent teachers, are parts of social networks that stretch across the school. Jay discovered this during his analysis and saw these individuals as leverage points for influencing others. He used this information to build interaction opportunities for teachers. Conversely, understanding the detrimental social networks gives principals the information to design strategies to disrupt that influence while building other social networks to help the school.

Other than classroom responsibilities and assigned duties, there are relatively few tasks a principal can mandate, so, teacher volunteerism is crucial. Developing a sociogram and gathering other information helps the principal establish conditions in which teachers may volunteer to deal with a variety of collective concerns. These data are unique to a school, and can shift as new structures provide opportunities for social networking and as personnel changes occur.

For example, at this time, several shifts in social networking and personnel changes have occurred at MMS over the last decade. A current sociogram (Figure 4.2b) demonstrates some of these differences.

## *Intentionally Build Positive Relationships*

According to Rubin, Abrego, and Sutterby (2014), before taking actions to nurture and develop a school-wide collaborative culture, it's important to reexamine the existing quality of relationships. Thus, once the data gathering and analysis are complete, opportunities for new positive social networks and relationships can be created. These intentional actions of the principal are of particular importance because: a) it is "interactions and relationships among people, not the people themselves that make the difference in organizational success; and b) the factor common to every successful change initiated is that relationships improve. If relationships improve, things get better. If relationships remain the same or get worse, ground is lost" (Fullan with Ballew, 2004, p. 80).

There are no guarantees that interactions between and among individuals will be positive; however, there are steps that can reduce the risks of negative results.

Building Positive Relationships ♦ 69

Figure 4.2b. **Example of a Sociogram for MMS (Current)**

**Markham Middle School**

Jay, Principal and Theresa, Dean of Instruction (teacher leader)—gray scale covers entire faculty.

The culture at MMS currently displays the following:

♦ Teacher leaders influence other teachers whether new or seasoned. All share in developing and supporting teacher leadership.
♦ Dept. heads/mentors interact with and support new and veteran teachers.
♦ All teachers deserve to be supported.
♦ Two-way communication is typical (⇠┈┈⇢) behavior at MMS.
♦ Communication is the expectation; but as in any organizations, not all members communicate effectively (denoted by straight line); MMS is aware that professional learning helps to better prepare faculty to have smart conversations. At MMS, the school community stresses that "smart organizations have smart conversations" (Perkins, 2003).

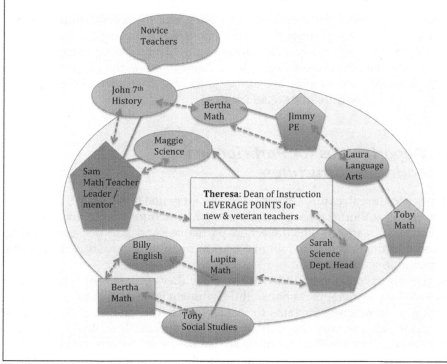

Major factors in reducing the risk of negative relationships developing are careful actions along with the principal's use of their tacit knowledge of the school and knowledge they now have based on their data collection and analysis. Providing opportunities for interaction is intended to generate "relational trust." ELEducation defines *relational trust* as referring "to the interpersonal social exchanges that take place in a group setting" (http://eleducation.org). They go on to say, "Trust is essential if a school is to succeed—both in beliefs and action." And so, whether principal leadership or teacher leadership, "the most effective leadership situations are those in which each member of the team trusts the others" (Kouzes & Posner, 2012, p. 220).

## Building Teacher-with-Teacher Relationships

### From the Field

Site-based decision teams, vertical teams, grade level teams—you have to establish those because if you don't establish those then you make all the decisions yourself; there's not gonna be any buy in, but when it come from them . . .

Juan Manuel Garcia
Principal
Harlingen, TX

---

Teacher-with-teacher relationships are the essence of the school culture. Principals can take actions to build these positive relationships. By using the human- and social-capital information they gathered and purposely embedding what they now know about personal and professional issues, they can guide the process of building strong relationships. Following are six examples of actions principals can take to build positive teacher-with-teacher relationships.

### *Provide Opportunities for Participation Within Leadership Structures*

Within schools are structures that exist or can be created to facilitate the distribution of power and authority throughout the school. Structures may include committees, task forces, or teams in which teachers participate and lead decision-making. Inviting and selecting teachers to join in one or more of these structures can enable social exchanges that build trust.

Most schools have a core of individuals who either volunteer or others expect will be selected for leadership responsibilities. Principals can use data collected in the self-study of school relationships to include more teachers. Based on the data collected, principals can identify individuals with specific knowledge, interests, skills, and talents. Once identified, principals can determine which social networks would be affected or perhaps created with the inclusion of these people. Additionally, the sociogram information may reveal a combination of individuals that should be avoided.

Early on, principals may need to model building positive relationships. This, according to Piercey (2010), may be a challenge. He writes in response to the question "Why don't teachers collaborate?" Among the many issues he identifies is the principal's own lack of knowledge and skill in collaboration. He offers this ending as a response to the original question, "Perhaps, then, the simplest answer to the question, 'Why don't teachers collaborate?' is that their leaders won't collaborate or can't demonstrate and model the necessary attributes" (p. 56). Piercey's admonishment is worth the principal's personal reflection. An honest assessment of personal knowledge and skills regarding collaboration will go a long way in fostering trust in working together in this new leadership culture.

As the new networks and relationships mature, and teacher leaders emerge, more invitational strategies can be employed. Teachers can assume the responsibilities for building schedules and structures that nurture and sustain these positive teacher-with-teacher relationships. There is an intensity of time needed to accomplish these purposeful decisions; however, if principals keep their eyes on the long-term goal of developing relational trust, they will see that the amount of time needed will decrease as healthy social networks are established.

## Build or Use Existing Structures Where Teachers Lead and Learn Together

When we use the term *structure*, our reference is not to buildings or spaces. Rather, we are talking about opportunities, processes, and procedures created to bring teachers together for their learning. Possibilities include:

- *Study groups.* These groups can focus on an instructional strategy, analysis of student work, or perhaps a recent book on a topic of importance to student learning needs.

- *Teaching teams.* Teachers who share the same students or teach the same subjects can form collaborative groups for sharing their personal practice in order to improve student learning. Common planning time supports opportunities for team teachers to work with each other.

- *Curriculum development.* Working on curriculum provides a structure where teachers across grade levels and subjects can learn together, as can teachers within grade levels and subjects.

- *Electronic discussions.* Teachers who may not share common planning time can be part of a group that meets, questions, shares, plans, and discusses electronically through discussion boards, as well as Skype; Zoom; Facetime; Facebook pages/live feeds; local, state, national, and international virtual communities; Twitter; and other social media. Thus, teacher leaders can pose questions, moderate the discussions, provide resources, and encourage others to share ideas through online media.

## Invite Teachers to Travel Together to Meetings and Conferences

Anyone who has traveled with professional colleagues understands how this can be a strategy for building relationships. Topics covered during the hours spent in a car, on a plane, or waiting for the meeting to start often are quite different in kind and depth than the brief encounters within a typical school day. Sharing the experiences of solving problems such as locating the hotel or meeting room, deciding where to go for dinner, and making sure the appropriate materials are packed creates bonds that remain long after the event itself has ended. The trip home provides another opportunity to discuss what was learned, how this might be useful in achieving the school vision, and what actions are required to get started.

## Develop Teacher Schedules

Most principals can remember being teachers and how the colleagues they knew best were those with whom they came in contact most frequently, such as teachers in the same grade level, team or department, subject area, or same area of the school. In addition, teachers who shared common duty schedules, lunch periods, or planning periods often became colleagues. Proximity is a powerful tool for building relationships. Giving careful consideration to who is working with whom in a particular schedule can make good use of existing human capital and generate new social capital. Scheduling teaching teams with teachers who are at similar or diverse career phases may create new friendships or impromptu mentor–mentee relationships. Making duty assignments based on information regarding personal obligations will reduce stress for the teachers and increase focus on work during the school day. Taking notice of teachers exhibiting early stages of withdrawal and then scheduling them with individuals still fully engaged in their careers may give those fully engaged a chance to nurture the others and serve as catalysts for their reengagement.

## Plan Social Events

Every school has social events, such as holiday gatherings and beginning- and end-of-the-year socials and ceremonies. These are rich opportunities for building relationships. Principals can organize committees that result in faculty members coming together to work on these events. Providing support by offering space, funds, and communication mechanisms to keep everyone informed reinforces these developing groups. Occasions for celebration may bring together teachers who might otherwise not know they share the same birthday month, were hired in the same year, or have children graduating from high school at the same time. These social functions offer new possibilities for the social exchanges necessary in building relational trust.

## Restructure Faculty Meetings

Much like schedules, faculty meetings are part of every school year. Because they already exist, making use of them as mechanisms for intentionally building relationships seems obvious. Principals may need part of the agenda to address school-wide issues, but other agenda items can be teacher-planned and teacher-led. Social interaction at the meetings can be purposely designed also. People generally sit with individuals they already know; this can limit opportunities to get to know individuals outside their usual circle. Principals might consider asking teacher leaders to generate schemes for mixing up traditional seating, for example:

- Sitting together by birthday month
- Sitting together according to favorite type of vacation
- Sitting together by family member sequence (all of the only children together, oldest children, youngest children, etc.)

Once in new groups, conversation starters can provide informal exchanges at the beginning of the meeting; teachers can then remain in the new groups or return to their usual seats before the meeting proceeds. Another strategy that focuses on school issues invites teachers within an existing group to divide and visit with other groups, then return to their home groups and report on the thinking of other colleagues.

## Building Principal-with-Teacher Relationships

Teachers and principals are dependent on their mutual relationships. Principals depend on teachers to do what is best for students and the school; teachers rely on principals and other formal leaders to be fair. Principal-with-teacher relationships are crucial in building teacher leading and learning. In this section, we offer strategies for building these relationships.

### Increase Knowledge About Teaching and Learning

### From the Field

So then we made lesson plans and I put an assistant principal in each one of their [English teachers'] classrooms full time. The only time (the) assistant principals had off were the 90 minutes that the teachers had off. . . . The teachers in the beginning were like, "You are going to be in my classroom?" I said to them, "Yes, but you know what, we are good people. We want to be in there when our test scores go up and we want to be a part of that."

It only took a couple of times for us to be in there that they realized, yeah, they are not here to criticize; they are here to help. We had no discipline problems, and we scored 90 percent and above in every part of the writing. Those kids worked hard.

Aurora Hurtado<br>
Former Principal<br>
Galena Park Middle School<br>
Galena Park, Texas

---

Principals who are knowledgeable about teaching and learning build closer relationships with teachers, because they know the work of the schools. Rather than a "hands-off" approach to curriculum and instruction, these principals assume responsibility for knowing what instruction is taking place and for bringing the right people together to solve instructional problems.

Honesty about their knowledge of curriculum and instruction is an important self-assessment for principals, because teachers can easily determine if principals are only pretending to know. Regardless of their teaching backgrounds, principals should know or be willing to learn about effective teaching. The best people to learn from and with are accomplished teachers. Generally, people are forgiving if the principal does not have all the knowledge and skills, as long as he or she is willing to learn.

## Visit Meetings and Planning Sessions of Various Groups and Project Teams

Just as there are "walk-throughs" for classroom observations, we advocate "stop-bys" as a strategy for building relationships. Principals are unable to attend every scheduled meeting. However, they can, with a little planning, "stop by" to check in on how things are going with most meetings. Finding time to stop by accomplishes at least three things. First, the principal's presence signals that the work being done is important, and teachers perceive this as an acknowledgment that their efforts are being recognized and appreciated. Second, it allows principals to be in tune with what's going on and who is involved. As brief as "stop-bys" might be, they still provide an opportunity to gather information about the focus of the meeting and the participants. Finally, something learned during a visit could later generate a question from the principal to a teacher in the project, such as, "Were you able to get that draft completed at your meeting yesterday?" or "Is there anything I can do to help you with scheduling that activity?" These actions of support help build principal-with-teacher relationships. There may also be an opportunity to build new networks of positive relationships between groups based on information gathered.

## Use Questioning and Listening Skills

Principals often believe an efficient strategy is to give solutions to problems. However, this practice can contribute to a dependency relationship between the principal and teachers. Principals can use questioning and listening skills to help teachers solve their own problems. Probing questions get to the real issues involved, and the principal can use specific types of questions depending on the situation:

- Getting specific information: Can you clarify that?
- Tuning in to others: What do you think about that?
- Getting feedback from others: Did I understand you correctly when you said?
- Giving feedback to others: What type of feedback would be most helpful to you?
- Closing: Are we in agreement?
- Consequences: What might the long-term results be? (Leeds, 2000, pp. 273–280)

Listening is an essential skill for leadership, but it is rarely taught. Too many of us believe we listen better than we actually do (Schein, 2013). This is the skill most frequently identified by teachers when describing effective principals (Moller et al., 2000). These principals are intense listeners and know how to ask the right questions to get at the problems a teacher is experiencing. A principal who is using effective listening skills:

- Does not appear to be in a hurry
- Talks about a specific aspect of the teacher's work
- Makes eye contact rather than being distracted

- Allows the teacher to finish speaking and pauses to ensure the teacher is finished before speaking
- Makes brief comments and stays focused on the issue rather than trying to handle several issues at the same time
- Sits or stands so that there are minimal distractions
- Avoids sharing a similar experience the principal had and how it was solved

Listen, ask questions, listen, and ask more questions—this represents the ideal rhythm of interactions when a principal is working with teachers to solve problems.

## *Provide Human and Fiscal Resources*

Resources are not limited to dollars, but include personnel, time, space, talent, ideas, and more. While resources may be expended individually, it is the collective allocation and use of these resources that fuel the operation of the organization. The matching of resources with teachers' needs is one of the principal's primary responsibilities and can be helpful in building relationships. Decisions about resources must be driven by the school's vision for student learning; however, the vision is accomplished through individual teachers' efforts. Effective principals use all available resources and are constantly seeking additional sources of support for teachers. Principals must learn to balance fiscal responsibility with sensitivity to teachers' needs and wants.

## *Give Extra Attention to New Teachers*

The culture of the school is built through relationships. New teachers are acculturated through their relationships with other teachers and with the principal. To sustain a culture that supports teacher leading and learning, principals cannot ignore building relationships with new teachers.

The time a principal spends with new teachers reaps benefits in four ways. Principals can:

- learn more about the individual human and social resources the teacher brings to the school;
- provide additional materials, equipment, and other support that new teachers do not know how to access;
- assess the new teacher's potential for teacher leadership; and
- prevent attrition of talented teachers, as well as identifying teachers who are not able to meet the school's expectations.

Teachers stay in schools where they are supported by the administration. A principal's investment in building relationships is a powerful contributor to this support.

## *Be Accessible*

Teachers often judge whether a principal is accessible by the way the principal's time is allocated. Finding time to meet the paperwork requirements of the job as well as interact with others is a challenging time-management issue principals face. There are no easy solutions, but principals can begin by sharing this concern with faculty and staff, and try to find ways to delegate some administrative paperwork. In understaffed schools, this may be difficult; however, principals may be surprised by who is willing to take gathering data for reports previously considered the responsibility of the principal. Helping office staff understand how important their contributions are in addressing paperwork can be invaluable as well.

## Match Individual Interests with School-Site Opportunities

### From the Field

Some years we have like "super Saturday" where on a Saturday in the fall . . . we have an all-day in-service where you go to sessions and you go into things that relate to whatever you're teaching. Like I went to one that was about writing or I went to one about science . . .

Monica Alvarado<br>
Elementary Teacher<br>
Harlingen, TX

---

Ever-watchful principals can determine individual teachers' interests and attempt to match these with opportunities. What appeals to one teacher may not appeal to another, so principals are wise to consider individual differences as they seek ways to encourage teachers' growth and development. If teachers are provided a variety of options, much like food choices on a buffet, there will be some teachers who step up to certain invitations and others who find different options attractive. Lovely (2005) stresses the importance of building on teachers' interests and strengths by stating, "Teacher leaders need to be cultivated in accordance with their talents and interests. Finding tasks that suit each individual best allows every member of a faculty to experience a sense of accomplishment" (p. 18).

Once those interests and strengths are identified, it is important to note that teachers will have different needs and interests throughout the span of their careers. Thus, "school systems should implement flexible roles and staffing structures that adjust teaching roles to meet teachers' interests and responsibilities" (Teach+Plus, 2015, p. 13).

For additional discussion about the challenges principals face when recruiting teacher leaders, as well as possible strategies to encourage shared leadership, we offer Tool 4.5 (see the eResources).

## Encourage Teachers' Involvement in School-System, Regional, and State Projects

Principals are often asked to nominate, recommend, or appoint representatives to projects initiated by the school system. Regional agencies, such as educational service centers, school study councils, leadership consortia, and other networks may also have need for teacher participation. Similarly, though not as frequently, state organizations such as state departments, professional associations, state-level commissions, and task forces will request principals suggest teachers to be invited for service. When asked, principals should have in mind the school's available human and social resources in order to provide opportunities to individuals that may be an especially good fit for the activity. Participation in these experiences gives teachers a chance to lead by serving as a liaison between school and external systems. Principals need to be proactive in promoting teachers for these opportunities.

## *Avoid Possessive Language*

Often principals use possessive language such as "my teachers" or "my school." The use of this language sends a subtle message that the principal is in control and teachers are merely players in the principal's master plan. While most principals do not actually feel this way, their language contradicts efforts to build collaboration. Instead principals should use inclusive language, such as "we," "our," and "us."

## *Attend Professional Learning Activities with Teachers*

One of the most important roles principals play in supporting and nurturing professional learning is participating as active co-learners. Principals cannot participate in every professional learning experience, but they should be active learners in the school's primary initiatives. When principals do not attend, it sends a clear message to teachers that the learning is only important for them, not the administrator. There is a growing trend in school systems to require principals to actively participate alongside their teachers to encourage professional learning across the campus.

## *Attend Teacher-Planned Social Events*

The social events discussed earlier can also be sources for building principal-with-teacher relationships. Principals may discover these events provide opportunities for them to observe who interacts with whom, who is leading and managing the activities, and how problems are solved when they occur. These events provide windows for observing teacher leadership. Also, attending teacher-planned social events allows the principal to be viewed in a different role. While never completely eliminated, the power and authority of the position are minimized during these events, allowing conversations between teachers and the principal that might never occur in more formal work settings.

There will be events in teachers' personal lives when it would be appropriate for principals to support them. For example, a personal illness, the marriage of a child, or loss of a family member can be stressful and pull a teacher's attention from his or her professional work. The principal's actions could include offering classroom support at the school, attending events, or simply writing a note to the teacher acknowledging the stressful situation.

## *Share Information About Personal Interests*

Principals and other administrators often try to separate their professional and personal interests, especially when interacting with the people they supervise. The causes for partitioning one's life are numerous, but a commonly cited reason is a concern about stepping beyond the typical boss–subordinate relationship. Administrators are socialized into the culture of their work, just as teachers are taught how to act within the teaching culture. Fishbein and Osterman (2001) found that administrative interns were taught by their mentors to protect themselves, while teachers also tended to protect themselves from administrators. Furthermore, some teachers, especially new teachers, resist confiding their concerns in administrators due to fear that they may be perceived as weak; however, they do share their concerns and questions with other mentors and colleagues (Howard, 2016).

Principals who want to improve relationships with teachers share—including personal information. If teachers see the principal as a person who balances professional and personal commitments, they are more likely to believe the principal will understand their unpredictable personal situations. Additionally, as principals, teachers, and other staff members share about themselves, revealing common areas of interest can promote relationships. The boundaries of professional relationships can be maintained even when principals let others know them as individuals.

### *Follow Through Consistently*

The act of following through on commitments seems obvious to most people, but with the busy lives of principals there is tendency to put off, forget, or ignore some of these. For teachers, a principal's follow through is an indicator of how well the principal listens to them; consistent follow through builds trust by demonstrating responsibility for agreed upon actions.

Principals may sometimes feel overwhelmed, but teachers are watching to see if there is follow-up on commitments, especially if the action relates to them personally. A principal who makes promises but does not follow through on them damages relationships. To avoid forgetting a promise made, principals should find ways to keep track of these. Many principals have developed their own strategies for avoiding this problem with everything from a pen and notepad to the use of one or more electronic devices to make notes, send messages to self and others, set alarms or alerts for meetings or specific classroom visits, and more.

### *Provide Authentic Recognition*

Sadly, it is not unusual to hear about the absence of recognition even when teacher leaders accomplish extraordinary tasks. Most teachers do not seek elaborate forms of recognition, especially in front of their peers, but they do crave at least some small indications that they are doing a good job. A simple note from the principal placed in a teacher leader's mailbox or sent electronically may be saved for months or even years. Teachers, like students, do not respond to general praise as well as they do when the principal cites a specific behavior. As teacher leadership grows, teachers may become more willing to accept public praise from the principal and peers. The principal can move away from providing all the recognition by encouraging teachers to give recognition to each other.

## From the Field

The common thread that unites these ideas is our belief that authentic teacher appreciation begins with us. If we seek understanding and appreciation from the communities we serve, accomplished teachers must become ambassadors for the teaching profession. Our actions and language, within and beyond the classroom, can serve as a catalyst for change.

Jessica Cuthbertson
6th–8th-grade English/Language Arts
Aurora, CO

## Conflict Is Inevitable

Nurturing a professional learning community is difficult work for a number of reasons, but perhaps the most challenging is dealing with conflicts. The predictable changes in faculty due to ongoing attrition of teachers and the principals' often limited authority to select replacement teachers can result in a mix of viewpoints. Diverse perspectives are seldom explored because there are few opportunities for teachers to learn about each other except in pockets of friendships that develop among like-minded teachers. Most of us like to work in harmony with others; however, in a genuine professional learning community where the conversations go beyond congeniality to discuss what is valued most by teachers—their teaching and students—there will be conflict. Principals have an obligation to help people embrace these differences in productive ways. This obligation brings us back to the primary purpose for building teacher leadership within a learning community, which is to build a democratic workplace where the shared values allow for the expression of different perspectives from individuals and groups.

### *Dealing with Conflict*

The principal's day is filled with conflict involving students, parents, teachers, custodians, bus drivers, secretaries, cafeteria workers, central office personnel, and others. There are many days principals go home only to realize they accomplished little of what they had planned because they were embroiled in dealing with conflicts of one sort or another. Teachers, however, are often inducted into a culture that expects little or no expression of disagreement and at least an appearance that collegiality pervades all interactions. Most teachers are in situations where there are options for not working together, avoiding conflict, and therefore not moving beyond the issue. To move beyond this escape route, principals and teachers need to work in safe structures, or "holding environments to contain and adjust the heat that is being generated by addressing difficult issues or wide value differences" (Heifetz & Linsky, 2002, p. 102).

A strategy to prepare faculty and staff in their dealings with conflict is to engage them in building a common language around the issue of conflict. When people use the same words for emotionally laden experiences, it helps defuse the situation. Providing safety for public discussions of differences and skillfully managing conflict is essential; if conflict is handled poorly, it will affect the school culture and stall improvement efforts. There are three ways to deal with conflict:

- *Avoid dealing with conflict.* This strategy is too often selected because people do not want to be upset or do not have the skills to confront or collaborate to manage conflict. On the other hand, there are times when it is wise to avoid conflict because confronting it may only make the situation worse, or the time might not be right for dealing with the issue.

- *Confront conflict.* There are situations in which a person must stand up for what they believe and defend a position, but teachers are not often willing to do this; they know that silence is safer in the teaching community. Principals may need to bring conflict to the surface without trying to solve the problem. This may require encouraging people with unusual ideas or those who have an opposing view to speak out. If used with skill, confrontation can result in compromise and increased understanding.

- *Collaborate to manage conflict.* A compromise resulting from confronting conflict may result in unequal satisfaction among the people involved. Collaboration, though, works to find mutual agreement acceptable to everyone. This strategy takes more time and requires the people involved to explore each other's interests, needs, and perspectives. At first, principals can facilitate collaborative management of conflict, but in time, teachers must learn the skills and work together to find creative solutions themselves.

Principals and teachers can be proactive in learning skills to handle conflict in their work with each other. Programs for helping children learn skills in resolving conflicts are common in schools; surely, if these skills are important for children, they are for adults as well. Ignoring this important interpersonal skill development can result in unplanned chaos throughout the school that may spill out into the community.

## Summary

Leadership is all about relationships. Yet when aspiring principals go through many graduate programs, there is often relatively little emphasis on the importance of the skills needed to build relationships. Although they study human resource management, aspiring principals rarely learn how to build a professional learning community. Through personal experiences, usually on the job, principals learn the hard way how neglecting the building of relationships makes a difference in the ways schools respond to diverse students, accountability demands, and community pressure. Collective action to address student learning cannot happen without intentional actions on the part of the principal to build positive relationships with teachers and between and among teachers.

Teacher leadership can increase human and social capital focused on student learning. After completing a self-study of the existing human and social resources, we recommend that principals intentionally build social networks. As relationships change and become more fluid, conflict will emerge, which both principals and teacher leaders must acknowledge, honor, and work to manage. The conflicts are predictable, but when principals understand this and have the skills to be constructive in their handling of interpersonal issues, there is hope for teacher leadership to emerge and grow.

Principals can use the Intentional Leadership Rubric for Positive Relationships (Figure 4.3) to determine their current skills.

If principals intentionally build trust through positive relationships, they can turn their attention to establishing structures for distributing power and authority. Before starting, though, it is important for principals to be clear about their own beliefs and values regarding distributing power and authority. Unless principals are firm in their commitment for this move to a new way of leading and learning, any actions will be perceived as contrived and will violate trust with the teachers. Once the decision is made, there are specific leadership actions that can ensure the effort will be worthwhile.

Figure 4.3. **Intentional Leadership Rubric for Positive Relationships**

| Quality Teacher Leadership Requires Essential Positive Relationships | |
|---|---|
| Level | Outcome |
| Unsure and Unskilled | Teachers are known to the principal and to each other; some self-selected groups are intact. Everyone is cordial, but limited in their interactions with each other. |
| Moving Along | Teachers' talents, skills, and interests as well as their social networks are known to the principal; the number of purposefully established groups has increased and most teachers are participating in one or more school structures. |
| Leading Teacher Leaders | Teachers' talents, skills, and interests as well as their social networks are known to the principal and to other teachers; groups are established voluntarily, by invitation, and by assignment; the principal, teacher leaders, and teachers themselves take the initiative to link individuals together in realizing the school vision. |

## Resources

4.1 Tschannen-Moran, M., & Gareis, C.R. (2015). Principals, trust, and cultivating vibrant schools. *Societies, 5*(2), 256–276; doi:10.3390/soc5020256—This is an academic paper that explores evidence of the role that faculty trust in the principal plays in student learning. Information on how principals can develop this trust is also included. Retrieved from www.mdpi.com/2075-4698/5/2/256/htm

4.2 Brewster, C., & Railsback, J. (2003). *Building trusting relationships for school improvement: Implications for principals and teachers.* Portland, OR: Northwest Regional Educational Laboratory—The authors describe the importance of trust and how to build relationships between teachers and between the principal and teachers. Retrieved from www.nwrel.org/request/2003sept/teachers.html

4.3 Schroth, G., Beaty, D., & Dunbar, R. (2003). *School scheduling strategies: New ways of finding time for students and staff.* Lancaster, PA: ProActive Publishers—This book is a principal's guide to time-effective, learning-focused scheduling. Each step in the scheduling process is detailed and illustrated with practical examples for elementary, middle, and high schools.

4.4 Faculty Meetings on Pinterest—Check it out! Go to Pinterest.com and type the words Faculty Meetings in the search area. The result will be an array of ideas and recommendations for conducting faculty meetings, energizing meetings, creative awards and more.

4.5 Webne-Behrman, H. (n.d.). Conflict Resolution, Office of Talent Management website—Provides information about conflict, common problems in dealing with conflict, and eight steps to resolve conflict. Retrieved on September 09, 2016, from www.ohrd.wisc.edu/home/HideATab/FullyPreparedtoManage/ConflictResolution/tabid/297/Default.aspx

4.6 Piercey, D. (2010). Why don't teachers collaborate? A leadership conundrum. *The Phi Delta Kappan, 92*(1), 54–56—This article has some excellent information, especially as regards the ways in which principals may, themselves, be among the greatest barriers to teacher collaboration. The contents, once read, should lead to serious personal reflection.

4.7 Scott, S. (2004). *Fierce conversations: Achieving success at work and life, one conversation at a time.* New York, NY: A Berkley Book—This book addresses organizational communications in plain language. Scott's seven principles of fierce conversations offer a means for exploring how to engage in and facilitate the conversations needed to move an organization forward.

# 5  Distributing Power and Authority

"Leaders make it possible for others to do good work. They know that those who are expected to produce the results must feel a sense of personal power and ownership.... Leaders enable others to act not by hoarding the power they have but by giving it away."

Kouzes & Posner in *The Leadership Challenge*

> ### Scenario: Theresa Encourages Shared Leadership
>
> *The teacher personnel committee was excited to be part of the hiring process. The group realized that helping new teachers not just survive but thrive in their first years would need the involvement of the entire campus. The teacher personnel committee viewed this task regarding new teachers as a good place to begin. While Theresa agreed, she also asked the group to think beyond this first task. She spent some time with these leaders drafting a mission for the group and then listing some additional tasks related to that mission. As the group started with the new-teachers projects, others on their list included developing an interviewing/hiring process guide and a mentoring program for teachers new to the school, but not to teaching. During her tenure at MMS, Theresa learned that teachers, regardless of whether they are new or veteran teachers, have great ideas and want to contribute to the improvement of the school.*

An often-heard comment by leaders is, "It would be easier if I just did it myself." In many cases this is true, but distributing power and authority is not just about making the principal's work more manageable. It is also about building teachers' leadership capacity so that, over time, the school's initiatives can be self-sustaining and not dependent on a single leader or a small group of leaders.

This chapter offers four reasons principals might want to distribute power and authority. Then, through a self-study and self-reflection, we suggest actions to help principals examine their beliefs about relinquishing power and authority. Next, we recommend ways to intentionally build and sustain a system that supports teachers as they take on leadership roles. Finally, we look at structures that foster collaborative leadership.

## From the Field

School administrators have a choice in how they see and treat teachers—and that choice profoundly affects how schools operate. If we see teachers as 'those that can't do,' then administrators will remain overwhelmed with responsibilities and teachers will continue to feel underutilized and underappreciated. But if we see teachers as highly intelligent, caring committed professionals, our responsibilities can shift to inspiring, empowering, and assisting teachers as they 'do' the critical work of helping to lead their schools.

Adam Tidlove, Head of School<br>
Jewish Community Day School of Rhode Island<br>
Andrea Katzman, Principal<br>
Providence, RI

## Reasons to Distribute Power and Authority

The first reason to distribute power and authority is to break the bonds of dependence between principals and teachers. There is a tendency in schools for those without authority to expect to have their needs satisfied by those with authority. Conversely, principals may choose to satisfy their own needs by being caretakers rather than helping teachers become self-initiating and self-managing problem solvers.

As the dependency relationship decreases, the workload becomes more manageable for the principal because leadership moves beyond one person. Principals must acknowledge the possible existence of these emotional needs and build structures and experiences to move self and others toward collaborative leadership. If teachers always seek approval and permission from the principal, it is impossible to have a democratic workplace. The driver of decisions and actions must be an articulated, shared vision rather than permission from any one person.

A second reason for distributing power and authority is to build leadership throughout the school. This helps ensure improvements are not totally dependent on the person who sits in the principal's chair. The "hero leader" is a liability that denies teachers responsibility for learning, leading, and sustaining continuous improvement long beyond the tenure of any one principal. An increase in teacher leadership buffers the predictable turnover of principals with a critical mass of teacher leaders who can ensure improvement efforts continue. Distributing power and authority relieves principals of the unrealistic expectation that they are the sole instructional leader and requires them to take responsibility for building communities of leaders and learners.

The third reason for distributing power and authority is to increase leadership resources. Many principals begin their tenure believing they must fulfill every leadership demand placed on them. If not, others will view them as incompetent. Fortunately, it doesn't take long for principals to realize they cannot be "all things to all people" and they must make choices about how to cope with the myriad responsibilities. Rather than feeling guilty about not meeting every expectation, we encourage principals to consider viewing power and authority as tools for expanding leadership. Principals who hold this view believe that power is infinite rather than finite. They find ways to involve as many leaders as possible, resulting in levels of service to students that one person could never accomplish.

Finally, the hero myth is detrimental not only to the school but also to the principal. Heifetz and Linsky (2002) went so far as to say, "The lone warrior myth of leadership is a sure route to heroic suicide" (p. 100). Trying to move a vision forward alone can result in "marginalization" (Heifetz & Linsky, 2002, p. 32) that puts the principal on the fringe of the professional school community and makes them a target for conflict (Weiner, 2016).

Even when principals want to distribute power and authority, they have concerns about teachers' willingness to accept the challenge of leadership. Not all teachers welcome invitations to be leaders; their reluctance may be nested in behaviors and attitudes a long time in the making or based on their relationships with previous principals who needed to be in control of everything. Creating an organization in which distributed leadership is the norm requires reciprocity between administrators and teachers. Granted, teachers cannot be empowered without accepting the power; nevertheless, principals must begin to develop a school culture where teachers are authentically engaged in leadership. Eventually, principals can selectively give up control, trust others to be responsible for their leadership, and, in time, watch teachers as they become self-organizing in their leadership.

Acting on the belief that power can lead to more power is risky and requires courage from the principal, but it can result in unlimited opportunities for the school. However, the first and most necessary decision principals must make is whether they are willing to share power and authority. This decision must be based on the principal's personal belief about collaboratively working with teachers. The next section offers ways principals can explore their beliefs and their willingness to move in this direction.

# Self-Study: Beliefs About Distributed Power and Authority

If the hesitation to distribute power and authority by the principal and, in turn, the reluctance of the teachers to accept it is to be resolved, both teachers and principals must begin to view power and authority as a shared commodity. While it would be ideal if everyone could come to this recognition simultaneously, it is the principal who must take the first steps.

When principals view power as fixed in the principalship, then distributing power and authority is anathema to them. On the other hand, if principals view power and authority as resources to be shared, distributing them becomes a way to increase power both organizationally and individually. Principals need to spend time visualizing where they might place themselves on a continuum anchored with "a strong belief in sharing" at one end and "too risky for me" at the other. Principals should start by being honest with themselves concerning their personal beliefs about the distribution of power and authority. Teachers are quick to discern what the principal sincerely believes. So, asking them to support an endeavor in which the principal has little or no confidence is at best a façade and perhaps more realistically a ruse—not a good context in which to develop trust and teacher leadership.

## Examining Beliefs About Distributing Power and Authority

Spillane (2006) states that distributed leadership is "about leadership practice, not simply roles and positions. And leadership practice is about interactions, not just the actions of heroes (p. 4)." Consequently, principals must begin by examining their leadership beliefs and their personal leadership experiences, acknowledging the risks involved, and examining what is known about collaborative leadership. Only then can they make a decision about their willingness to commit to distributing power and authority. If they do commit to this, then we recommend they write a personal vision statement to help in guiding their actions.

## Reflect on Personal Experiences as a Teacher Leader

One strategy principals can use to assess the strength of their belief in teacher leadership is to reflect on their experiences as teachers. Individuals in formal leadership positions have generally exhibited leadership, both formal and informal, throughout their lives. In reaching their goals and surviving in the context of the school, most principals developed leadership skills through personal initiative and the support of others. Although past experiences as a teacher leader help principals recognize the concept, their involvement as teacher leaders may have been haphazard and have taken place in a variety of contexts.

Principals usually start their careers in education as classroom teachers. To be considered for a principalship, individuals have exhibited leadership to someone who made the decision to recommend them for that position. Although a graduate degree in educational leadership is a prerequisite in many states, the determining factor for selection is often behavior demonstrated through past leadership roles.

To link the concept of teacher leadership to principals' personalized contexts as teacher leaders may be challenging, depending on the number of years they have been in an administrative role. However, most principals can remember their classroom teaching experiences as well as how and when they, as teachers, either formally or informally provided leadership. (Refer to our teacher leadership stories in the opening of the book as examples of such recollections.)

## Acknowledge Risks in Distributing Power and Authority

In most cases, principals' understanding of schools is more complex and comprehensive than that of other staff, so principals can foresee problems more easily at the macro level. Their experiences with conflict and other interpersonal predicaments often make them legitimately hesitant to distribute power, because they know ultimately their supervisors will look to them as being responsible for any decisions made. Therefore, principals may have valid concerns about the wisdom and risk levels involved in distributing power and authority. Below are questions principals often pose about teacher leadership. Responses to each question will vary, so principals should consider each one within the context of their own situations.

- Can negative teachers ever become positive teachers?
- Will scheduling collaboration time be viewed positively by the community?
- Can teacher leaders be rewarded without others viewing this as favoritism?
- Will traditional department or team chairs be willing to share power?
- Can the administrative and the teacher leaders' agendas be aligned?
- How can younger, less experienced principals work successfully with veteran teacher leaders?

- What happens if teachers make poor decisions?
- Will I be seen as not doing the job I am being paid for if I share power?
- Will other principals see me as someone to emulate or someone to isolate?

## Examine Your Knowledge Base About Distributing Power and Authority

Busy principals often find it difficult to take time for their own learning. A colleague of ours often makes this point with educators by saying, "You can't teach what you don't know any more than you can come back from where you've never been" (Dr. James Boyer, personal communication, October 22, 1992). Principals come from their personal experiences as teacher leaders, but they must also be grounded in current knowledge about distributing power and authority.

These suggestions are offered for helping principals learn the basics about distributed power and authority:

- *Read books, journal articles, and websites explaining this concept.* Literature to learn about distributing power and authority is plentiful. Reading in the area will reveal a variety of terms used to describe this concept (see Figure 5.1).

Figure 5.1. **Distributed Power and Authority: Terms and Sources**

| Terms | Sources |
|---|---|
| Parallel leadership | Crowther, Kaagan, Ferguson, & Hann, 2002 |
| Building leadership capacity | Lambert, 2003; Drago-Severson, Blum-DeStefano, & Asghar, 2013 |
| Providing opportunities for leadership | Drago-Severson, 2004 |
| Shared and supportive leadership | Hord, 2004; Hord & Sommers, 2008; DuFour & Marzano, 2011 |
| Shared leadership | Hughes & Pickeral, 2013 |
| Distributed leadership | Spillane, Halverson, & Diamond, 2001, 2004; Spillane, 2006; Hall, Gunter, & Bragg, 2013 |
| Multipliers | Wiseman, 2010 |
| Teacher-led schools | Berry, Byrd, & Wieder, 2013 |

- *Visit schools where teacher leadership is the norm.* Principals can contact state-level administrators or teacher professional associations (association websites often give details) to identify schools with positive reputations regarding teacher leadership. Phone conversations, site visits, and reviews of documents from schools where teacher leadership is common practice can provide important information on the process used and the results attained. Consider taking one or two classroom representatives to visit and encourage them to talk with their peers in these schools.

- *Attend professional learning experiences.* Although many central office leaders strive to establish community among principals, in many systems a subtle competition inhibits these conversations. Principals can seek like-minded peers at summer institutes or other renewal activities designed to help practicing principals learn from each other about a variety of issues, especially about working with teachers to build a community of learners.

- *Check online.* The Internet is rich with resources on most every topic imaginable. Access to speeches, electronic presentations, websites, blogs, and more by both the famous and the unknown can be located with a simple search. Two sources with which to begin would be *YouTube* and *TED*. Specific to teacher leadership topics is the *Center for Quality Teaching* website. Once at these sites, search for topics of interest. Additional items and sites are added almost daily, so, check frequently.

Only by knowing what the distribution of power and authority entails can principals understand what the concept means for the school. When the image has been formed, principals can knowledgeably compare their personal beliefs with what will most likely happen in practice. Initially, principals may not fully embrace teacher leadership—although that would be desirable—but they may, at least, see distributing power and authority with teacher leaders as a possible goal to pursue.

## Commit Time and Energy

After reflecting on personal experiences as a teacher leader, acknowledging the possible consequences of distributing power and authority, and examining the knowledge base about the idea, it is time to act. Principals can make the choice to either commit time and energy to pursuing the next stages of increasing teacher leadership or to put distributing power and authority aside and look for another model of leadership that better aligns with their personal beliefs. Without a strong level of commitment, moving to strategies for building teacher leadership is ill-advised and most likely doomed to failure.

## Write a Personal Vision Statement

If principals make the commitment to continue, the next step is to write a personal vision statement describing how they want distributed power and authority to play out. A vision statement draws many ideas together into a few sentences (sometimes even a single sentence) that provide a focus on the desired way adults will lead and learn together. This personal vision statement will be a stimulus for the principal's actions that in turn will link to the school's shared vision for working together to improve student learning.

When principals are clear in their own minds about how schools can function with distributed power and authority, teachers are more likely to be leaders in countless ways. This written personal vision statement should be revised as the process unfolds; principals can use it as a touchstone throughout this journey, as the complexity of the endeavor is revealed, or when the losses seem to outnumber the gains.

# Acting to Distribute Power and Authority

This section presents several actions that principals and teachers can take to move forward in distributing power and authority. First is the development of a shared vision to drive decision-making and leadership. Next are ways to support collective decision-making and delegating.

## Develop Shared Vision for Student Learning

The school must have a compelling vision that pulls everyone to take actions that move toward its realization. The vision must be embedded in the school culture, and in turn, the culture must support the achievement of the vision. Earlier we recommended principals write a personal vision statement as part of their self-study for examining their own beliefs about distributed power and authority. At this point, principals need to move beyond themselves and facilitate the collective development of a school vision to guide the decisions and actions of everyone. A vision helps formulate an image of the desired future regarding school operations for improved student learning. A school vision involves everyone—if not in the development, certainly in the ratification, implementation, and achievement of the vision. The ultimate purpose of all schools—the continuous improvement of learning for all students—must both energize and direct every element of the vision development. Here are three actions to help in developing a shared vision.

## From the Field

I was on the committee two times and we would go through and really write down what we thought should be the mission statement and the goals and it was a long, arduous task. We would really sit down and . . . pros and cons on wording and how to make it global and all this other stuff, so that's how that was done.

William D. Gooch
Middle-School Teacher
Harlingen, TX

### *Step 1: Imagine the Ideal School*

Ask all participants to imagine the ideal school and record their input describing the desired future. There could be any number of these statements, depending on the various dimensions needed to describe the ideal. The goal is to get a rich description of every dimension of desired student learning from as many different perspectives as possible.

### *Step 2: Synthesize the Information*

Synthesizing the recorded input should first be done by category and then into an articulate whole to allow the creation of a statement describing the ideal school envisioned by the group. For example the category of literacy might have descriptors such as "all students are literate." The category of professional learning might use words such as "continuous follow-up." Next, the task becomes how best to include literacy and professional learning in a statement that most accurately describes the desired future state of the school, such as: "The ideal school will engage in quality professional learning resulting in strategies to ensure all students learn."

### Step 3: Share and Use the Vision

Once developed, the vision statement needs to be disseminated to all primary stakeholders, both inside and outside the school. It must also be used at every level of the organization to guide decisions and actions. Principals can model this by specifically referencing the vision at various points in discussions and always asking how a particular decision or proposed initiative moves the school toward achieving the vision. For example, if a suggestion is made to adopt a particular program, principals can ask questions such as, "Does this action fit with what we have stated as our vision for this school?" When the principal routinely uses the school vision as a guide for decisions, the professional staff will soon adopt the same strategy when considering decisions on teaching teams, on committees, or in individual classrooms.

## Collaborate in Decision-Making

### From the Field

What is unique about my school and other "teacher-powered" schools is the level of collaboration and collective decision-making that occurs among all stakeholders.
Josef Donnelly
9th- and 10th-grade Social Studies
International Community High School
South Bronx, NY

---

Relying on others to make decisions or to help with decisions is a reality of today's complex school organizations. Collaborative decision-making is easy to say but not necessarily easy to do. Ironically, mandates for shared decision-making are common, but the reality of sharing this power is in the hands of the principal. Piercey (2010) identified the major impediment for collaborative decision-making as becoming accustomed to the notion of more than one "chief"; this requires giving up some power so others may be empowered. Principals who are willing to act democratically reflect their beliefs in supportive and shared leadership (Huffman & Hipp, 2003; Abrego & Pankake, 2011).

The process of decision-making is the core of school administration (Ward & Wilcox, 1999; Ubben, Hughes, & Norris, 2016). Decision-making is also an important skill for teachers. Teachers must be good decision makers; every day in their classrooms, they make hundreds of decisions about time, materials, strategies, discipline, and other classroom-related issues. Yet they are rarely invited to participate in making substantive school-wide decisions.

Before collaborating on decisions, determining who should participate in what parts of the decision-making process is essential. The parameters should identify which decisions are the principal's alone, in what circumstances the group would provide advice to the principal, and when the group would be solely responsible. Too often these discussions take place after the principal and teachers are engaged in the process, resulting in frustration for the teachers and anxiety for the principal. Lack of clarity on the decision-making parameters may be a source of more frustrations, disappointment, and distrust than any other issue. Too often individuals commit time and energy to share in decisions, make recommendations, and generate solutions only to have their work rejected, modified severely, or, sometimes, not even acknowledged. Participants need to know at the start whether they are giving the principal advice or actually making decisions. If teachers know they are advisory, they can understand when their advice is not taken. But if teachers believe their decisions are to be final and these decisions are ignored, then conflict and disappointment are inevitable.

Four elements should be considered when determining who should be involved in what decisions:

- *Test of relevance (Bridges, 1967).* Most of us do not want to waste our time being involved in decisions about issues that we perceive as irrelevant. So the first "test" is whether the teachers have high levels of interest in the decision because they hold a personal stake in it. If they do, then they will have more interest in and want more involvement in decisions in these areas. For example, teachers would most likely consider the adoption of a school reform model as relevant to their work. On the other hand, there may be areas of decision-making regarding facility renovation that are not relevant, depending on how they affect the teachers.

- *Test of expertise (Bridges, 1967).* It is possible that teachers may perceive a decision as having relevance to them but have no expertise that would allow them to assist competently in the decision-making process. If there is high interest in the area in which the decision is to be made, then competence must be developed in order to make an effective contribution. For instance, school finance is often a mystery to teachers, but if they perceive it as relevant to their involvement in decision-making, then the principal can provide training in this area.

- *Test of jurisdiction (Owens, 2001).* Principals are vested with the power and authority to make decisions that by law cannot be delegated to the teachers, even if they have a high interest and expertise in an area such as reappointment of teachers. For those problems that have legal or policy restrictions, individuals can consult the appropriate resources.

- *Test of intensity (Pankake, 1998).* Interest in a particular decision can change depending on the stage of a project. At the beginning of a project, teachers may only want information, but this may change to a desire for direct participation as the project matures. Similarly, projects can require different levels and areas of expertise as they develop.

Keeping this developmental perspective in mind helps principals and teacher leaders maintain flexibility regarding the intensity of the involvement.

Once parameters are clarified regarding the procedures for decision-making, they should be reflected in teacher and student handbooks. If a school does not already have handbooks in place, a committee or team to develop them should be created. When these standard operating procedures are developed and disseminated, leadership for solving these issues is distributed throughout the school; with the guides in place, others can make recurring decisions appropriately, and school administrators can reallocate their time to more strategic decisions.

## Delegate Effectively

As teachers take on responsibilities based on collaborative decision-making, the principal relinquishes control and delegates to others. If principals are to create an inclusive model of leadership, effective delegation is a must. Here are seven actions principals can take to increase the effectiveness of their delegating.

- *Ensure the appropriate people are involved, and communicate their responsibilities to others.* Identifying who should be involved at what level and when is part of the planning process. Others need information about to whom authority is being delegated. Failure to do this will create confusion among the staff and undermine the work of the teacher leaders. For instance, the principal needs to refer questions and conversations about projects to the teacher leader to whom the work has been delegated. Updates on various initiatives can be provided during faculty meetings or through written reports by those who are "heading things up." Everyone should know who is responsible for a particular initiative.

- *Communicate the principal's role.* Principals should consult with teacher leaders working on projects to get their views and clearly communicate what roles principals see themselves playing in the projects. This might include agreements such as attendance at meetings or voting privileges. The principal should be able to live with the role agreed upon and follow through with letting go of control. At times, principals' roles will vary depending on the experience of the teacher leaders or the scope of the work. To declare one role and then try to fill another will generate distrust and resentment, leading to a reduced pool of willing volunteers for sharing in the work.

- *Clarify the tasks to be done.* Completing the work will be much easier if there is a clear understanding of what is to be accomplished. Putting the plan in writing is the best way to do this. Deciding together what will exist when this work is successfully completed is important at the beginning and becomes even more critical as things get under way. This helps everyone understand the task.

- *Define process issues to which teacher leaders must conform.* If principals have process preferences, they should share them immediately.

Obscuring preferences with words like, "One way I have found that works well is . . ." implies that what principals are describing is optional. If the approach is not optional due to policies, central office directives, professional preferences or previously agreed upon procedures, the principal should make comments like, "I want you to . . ." or "A part of what you are to do is . . ." In turn, when reviewing the project, the conversation should focus on outcomes, not on the processes used, unless there is a lack of progress. Offering someone the opportunity "to run with it" but then criticizing and redirecting their methods even though they are accomplishing the identified outcome will create distrust and perhaps even cause the teacher leader to opt out. If it is not illegal, immoral, unethical, or socially unacceptable teacher leaders should be encouraged to do it their way, as long as there is progress toward the defined outcome.

- *Create completion timelines and "big picture maps" for viewing multiple projects simultaneously.* A multitude of activities occur simultaneously in schools. While there may be a sequence for each, the actual operations of the school are not linear. "Big picture" maps with timelines that clearly identify both routine and special events will help minimize redundancies and overlaps and keep everyone informed. Everyone is busy enough without trying to do jobs that someone else is already doing. Helping teachers identify how their work coordinates with others is essential.

- *Provide resources for accomplishing the tasks.* Once the task to be accomplished and the processes to be used are agreed upon, conversations turn to what resources are needed. No one can be expected to work without resources such as money, support staff services, time, and/or physical space. Additionally, teacher leaders should know how to request resources and principals should inform support staff regarding who is empowered to request services. If there are budget limits, teacher leaders need to know them before their work begins. It is better to cancel or modify the project than to create disappointment and distrust through inadequate resource availability after work is underway.

   A resource often overlooked is information. Teacher leaders need access to information relevant to the tasks in which they are involved. Information is gathered in schools for a variety of purposes, particularly reports for the school system, state, and federal entities. Also, principals have access to information that can help teacher leaders when it is connected to their work.

   Finally, time for people to work together is an essential resource for getting things accomplished. Ways to connect can include face-to-face opportunities, conference calls, and electronic exchanges. A few meetings before and after school are understandable; however, locating time during the workday is essential to demonstrate to teacher leaders the priority their efforts take.

- *Create continuous feedback loops for evaluation and planning.* Principals take on the roles of mentor *and* evaluator. Principals can delegate work, but they cannot abdicate responsibility for the work. They can, however, keep themselves apprised of a project's progress through a monitoring system established to provide teacher leaders the opportunity to share how things are going, get feedback on their work, and have a skilled coach to help them improve. Monitoring can be defined as "focusing on [paying attention to] a project, process, or program by gathering information that (a) indicates whether or not expectations are being achieved, and (b) if not, provides relevant data for designing needed adjustments or corrective actions, which will result in the achievement of expectations" (Pankake, 1998, p. 108).

## From the Field

Delegation will not only save your sanity—it is important for the growth of your staff.

Annette Christiansen
Co-Chair, 11th- and 12th-grade English/Language Arts
Stevenson High School
Utica Community Schools
Sterling Heights, MI

## Structures to Facilitate the Distribution of Power and Authority

Accomplishing a shared vision for student learning requires structures to support the work of teachers. "If the structure is overlooked, an organization often misdirects energy and resources" (Bolman & Deal, 2003, p. 67). These structures are focused on decision-making and professional learning.

The structures will vary depending on the school context, but there is one aspect that is nonnegotiable—collaboration. Structures should be designed to ensure all teachers' voices are heard. Of course, there will be teachers who, even with these structures in place, will remain silent, but if principals design and communicate the purpose of these options, other teachers can gently pressure the reticent to bring their concerns forward. For too long, relying on teacher volunteerism to collaborate has resulted in pockets of excellence rather than improvement for all students. Collaboration must be an expectation embedded in the culture rather than an invitation or a suggestion (DuFour, 2003; DuFour, Eaker, & DuFour, 2005; DuFour, DuFour, Eaker, & Many, 2010). Principals and teacher leaders can establish structures with guidelines for participation and intentionally support teachers to ensure that they work together to focus on student learning.

All schools have existing structures, but as principals look to promote teacher leadership, a few structures may need to be created, while others may need to be redesigned, or perhaps even eliminated. There are structures that are ongoing and focus on governance issues, and others that are specialized and may be continuous or formed on an as-needed or *ad hoc* basis. In either case, the important point is that once the teams are formed and their task(s) made clear, they are empowered to move forward with autonomy and authority to accomplish the task. Listed below are a few examples of structures that could be intentionally designed to build and support teacher leadership:

- *Leadership teams.* Leadership teams include members representing different groups of the school community. The members make collective decisions regarding strategic school-wide decisions. Many states mandate this decision-making structure; policies may dictate what groups must be represented (for example, parents, teachers, or students). Sometimes called shared decision-making or school improvement teams, leadership teams can be critical structures in authentically facilitating the distribution of power and authority. Initially, the principal may be directive in organizing the team, but in time, procedures to ensure that the team has a composition that allows for multiple perspectives and a rotating membership that brings in new people on a regular basis should be in place. Clarity regarding the role (or roles) the administrators play on these teams is essential if authentic collaboration in decisions is to be realized.

- *Professional development committee.* This group is responsible for making decisions in collaboration with the leadership team regarding the use of limited resources for professional learning. These two groups must work together closely. In too many schools, the professional development committee allocates resources based on teacher seniority or other criteria that are unrelated to the school's vision for student learning. When this committee is effective, members of the group track down internal and external resources to support professional learning. This includes writing grants, visiting other schools, attending external professional development to evaluate its value, identifying and securing technological options, and performing other tasks that help them make wise decisions about professional learning.

- *Communication structures.* Information is power. If teachers lack information, their power to lead is diminished. Often principals and other leaders have information that they want to share with teachers, but the busy demands of the school day prevent this information from being distributed. While this is usually unintentional, the results are the same as if the principal chose to keep the information secret. To avoid this, structures must be built to ensure that critical information is shared with everyone appropriately and in a timely manner. These structures might include electronic communications, weekly staff newsletters (paper copy and/or electronic), or even the low-tech large message board near the school office or other centralized gathering place.

    Communication "trees" can be established through which the principal shares information with one person and that person then shares with designated others. Additionally, minutes from meetings should be physically or electronically posted and filed so everyone has access to a record of these discussions and any resulting decisions.

## From the Field

Collaboration takes many forms, and I've found that the most engaging encounters are the casual "hallway chats" with colleagues or informal discussions at lunch time.

Robert Gardner
10th- and 12th-grade Social Studies
McNally High School
Edmonton, Alberta, Canada

---

- *Teaching teams.* Teaching teams—whether grade level, subject centered, or multidisciplinary—support the core of collaboration; it is within these groups that teachers who share common students work together to focus on student learning. Teacher leaders are the key to the success of these teams. Teacher leaders can help ensure scheduled time is used for authentic discussions and make shared decisions about teaching and learning, rather than individual projects or operational tasks.

- *Faculty study groups.* Study groups provide an opportunity to transform even traditional faculty meetings from tedious obligations to anticipated opportunities, if the principal is willing to use them for activities other than information dissemination. Depending on the size of the faculty and the focus of the school change, the structure of these groups will vary, but they should allow for all faculty members to have input into how the change will emerge. Most often, teachers can lead these meetings, either jointly with the principal or with the principal as a participant only.

- *Curriculum teams.* Curriculum teams frequently are developed to design and implement the strategic plan that focuses on the vision for student learning. These teams make decisions regarding teaching and learning, such as selecting materials, analyzing students' learning data, determining the curriculum scope and sequence, and evaluating the curriculum. Teachers with specialized knowledge of subject matter or curriculum development are needed for this work.

- *Management teams.* Management teams are organized to handle the day-to-day issues facing every school. Too often, leadership teams get bogged down in the minutiae of issues such as student extracurricular activities, teacher duty schedules, or access to supplies. Separating discussions on these topics to another team helps keep the leadership team focused on student learning.

    For example, schedule development is an activity that affects students, teachers, parents, cafeteria workers, custodians, office staff, and administrators. Schedules also play a significant role in the instructional process. There are a variety of factors in schedules, such as classes (required and elective), recesses and study halls, labs/special purpose rooms, lunch periods, assemblies, special instructional programs, and others as the situation demands. Schedule development could be an administrative task or it could be a task for a management team; in either case, input from the various stakeholders should be solicited and considered.

- *Procedures for hiring new staff.* Selecting and hiring teachers are among the most crucial decisions in any school. The selection of faculty new to the school should take into consideration how they will add value to this new way of leading and learning. Establishing small groups or teams of teachers to participate in the selection process is an empowering activity. Recall that among Theresa's initial tasks as MMS Dean of Instruction is to work with MMS teacher leaders to establish a hiring process.

  Principals need to work with teacher leaders to determine whether the group will play an advisory role or make the final decisions. Additionally, these teacher leaders will need professional development on interviewing techniques, legal and illegal questions, note taking, and ways to judge interviewees' responses.

- *Induction program for new teachers and teachers new to the school.* The induction of teachers new to the profession cannot be left to chance; new teachers have the potential to contribute to the school's human and social capital. These teachers must understand the culture in which they will be working and the expectations for them to lead and learn. Rather than a hit-or-miss approach, there must be a structure in place to work with teachers new to the school. The induction may supply anything from basic information to intensive support for classroom activities. Some teachers may want to work with beginning teachers, while other teachers will prefer to mentor veteran teachers who are new to this particular school; there will also be teachers who may want to help but do not want to be continually involved. This is an area where one teacher leader can assume the power and authority to organize and manage the overall process while keeping the principal informed.

- *Social and ceremonial events and activities.* In most schools, there are planned social and ceremonial events and activities. The purposes of the events vary, but timely planning and careful organization are necessary if the intended purposes are to be achieved. A committee or task force for scheduling and organizing these events and activities is another structure for distributing power and authority. While everyone generally enjoys participating in these events, not everyone likes the planning and organizing. However, in most schools there are those individuals who could probably have second careers as events managers on cruise ships. Building on the interests and skills of these individuals is a way to address important rituals in the organization.

These are only a few examples of structures that can be designed to involve teachers and support their leadership. Structures should be revisited periodically to see if they are fulfilling a need or simply existing because they always have. The members of the organizational structures should have clarity about their roles and responsibilities, including:

- Developing procedures for appropriately selecting and rotating membership so the entire school community is represented

- Establishing clear parameters for making decisions

- Setting up communication and dissemination mechanisms so appropriate and timely information is available to everyone
- Organizing meeting schedules to prevent conflict for teachers who participate in more than one structure

## Summary

Agreeing to distribute power and authority is one of the most difficult decisions a principal will make, because although the school may reap benefits, there will be obstacles both personal and professional. Yet with demands for increased accountability for student learning, principals who want to succeed cannot continue to "go it alone." Instead, they must reach out to teachers for expanded leadership throughout the school. Once the decision is made to distribute power and authority, the principal's work has just begun. Specific actions must occur to build a shared vision, collaborate in decision-making, and delegate effectively. These actions take place within purposeful structures designed to promote, build, and sustain teacher leading and learning.

Principals can use the Distributing Power and Authority Rubric (Figure 5.2) to self-assess beliefs about distributing power and authority. The primary goal for building relationships and distributing power and authority is to promote continuous teacher and student learning. Teacher leadership emerges from teachers who are learners. The principal's responsibility is to ensure that quality professional learning is continuously accessible to teachers.

Figure 5.2. **Distributing Power and Authority Rubric**

| Quality Teacher Leadership Requires Authentic Distribution of Power and Authority ||
|---|---|
| Level | Outcome |
| Unsure and Unskilled | Principal does not trust teachers to lead and be accountable. May have one or two individuals with whom issues are discussed and some projects delegated, but only with close supervision. |
| Moving Along | Principal is beginning to trust a select group of teacher leaders to lead and be accountable. The teacher leaders are generally those individuals in formal leadership roles in the school. |
| Leading Teacher Leaders | Principal has confidence that most teachers will lead and be accountable and is willing to establish structures to support their efforts. |

## Resources

5.1 Lambert, L. (2003). *Leadership capacity for lasting school improvement.* Alexandria, VA: Association for Supervision and Curriculum Development—Lambert provides 11 specific strategies principals can use to "break dependency relationships" (pp. 48–49).

5.2 Spillane, J.P. (2006). *Distributed leadership.* San Francisco, CA: Jossey-Bass.
5.3 MindTools—This website discusses numerous topics important to individual and team development. It is noted here because of an excellent presentation on effective delegation. Much of it reinforces what has been shared in this chapter. Retrieved from www.mindtools.com/pages/article/newLDR_98.htm
5.4 The Muse—A website with all sorts of career improvement advice. Of particular importance to this chapter are the items on delegating. Retrieved from www.themuse.com/tags/delegating

# 6 Aligning Teacher Leadership with Professional Learning

"By Japanese law, first-year teachers receive at least 20 days of inservice training and 60 days of professional development. Master teachers are released from their classrooms to advise and counsel them. In both Japan and China, new teachers watch other teachers at length, discuss problems of practice, present and critique demonstration lessons, and, with group colleagues, imagine and act out how students might respond to certain presentations of material."

Linda Darling-Hammond in Teaching for Intelligence, Second Edition

---

*As Dean of Instruction, Theresa works closely with different groups of teachers at MMS on a variety of instructional issues. As MMS continues to develop as a professional learning community, the focus on learning for teachers and staff is a priority. The importance of building the human and social capacity of all staff is one of the most valuable lessons Theresa learned from Jay. With that in mind, Theresa has spent the past several weeks observing classrooms and attending various teacher-group meetings as a way of getting to know the teachers and learning their specific needs and interests.*

*In an effort to share professional development opportunities across the campus, Theresa is actively recruiting teachers to participate in a community of practice (COP) that will focus on identifying campus-specific needs and interests. Ultimately, Theresa wants to ensure professional learning is teacher-led and focused on the academic needs of MMS students. After sharing her activities of the past few weeks with Jay, Theresa is affirmed in her goal of organizing a COP at the school. Now, she knows the idea is a good one, so it is time to get started on making it happen. Theresa's mind is busier than ever with thinking about the who, what, when, where, and how of this professional learning and leading effort at MMS will emerge.*

---

Quality teacher leadership aligns with professional learning to help achieve a school's shared vision for student learning. For example, the Institute of Education Sciences (2007) reports, "Teachers who receive substantial professional development—an average of 49 hours in the nine studies—can boost their students' achievement by about 21 percentile points" (p. iii). The relationship between the two is mutually beneficial since growth in teacher learning supports growth in teacher leadership, and in time, growth in teacher leadership influences teacher learning. Most importantly, growth in both teacher learning and leading positively impact student learning. National, state, and local school-system reforms rely on this connection between leading and learning, because only with internal leadership can these programs be developed and sustained.

## From the Field

Another important connection between deeper learning for students and teacher leaders is that teachers themselves need to be engaging in collaborative deeper learning.

Tricia Ebner
6th–8th-grade English/Language Arts
Lake Middle School
Wadsworth, OH

Teachers are flooded with both mandated and voluntary professional learning opportunities, some of which are worthwhile. Unfortunately, teachers consider most as a waste of time. Sparks (2005), one time executive director of the National Staff Development Council (now Learning Forward), shared, "My work in the field of staff development for the past 25 years has revealed to me deep feelings of discontent among countless teachers, administrators, and policymakers regarding the quality of professional learning in schools" (pp. 8–9). Yet most teachers know how they learn new teaching behaviors that affect student learning, as evidenced by the results of a national sample of more than 1,000 teachers. Here is what these teachers wanted in their professional learning:

- Sustained and intensive professional learning over time
- Active learning
- Professional learning that is coherent, connected to what I am doing with my students
- Content focused on what I teach (Garet, Porter, Desimone, Birman, & Yoon, 2001)

In this chapter, we first invite principals to think differently about professional learning for teachers than the traditional paradigm has dictated. Then, we encourage principals to conduct a self-study of their own professional learning experiences. Next, we describe some group structures and professional learning designs and offer an example of a comprehensive model that illustrates the teacher leading and learning process. Following this, we recommend strategies for principals to consider in confronting reluctant teacher learners.

## Thinking Differently About Professional Learning

Engaging students who do not respond to traditional teaching approaches, ensuring full inclusion for students with special needs, and monitoring student interactions for bullying incidents are examples of the complex issues today's educators face. This complexity emphasizes that no longer can professional learning be considered simply instruction in models of delivery, such as workshops, study groups, or action research. Instead, the entire school staff must build on their capacity, that is, professional learning, to develop "the collective ability—dispositions, skills, knowledge, motivation, and resources—to act together to bring about positive change" (Fullan, 2005, p. 4). Achieving this "collective ability" requires principals to nurture teachers in the construction of meaning in their work. Professional learning models are tools to be used, but the real learning happens in the cycle of conversations, actions, evaluation, and new actions. This cycle must be supported through the principal's intentional leadership that simultaneously gently pressures and nurtures teachers. This process must be organizationally embedded rather than externally imposed to build teachers' knowledge and skills—in other words, increase human capital—within the school's social networks.

Examining the influence of teachers' adult development on their professional learning helps us understand the level of changes needed in order to teach differently. For adults to move to another level of development, they must see a gap between what they believe to be ideal and what they are currently experiencing. Closing this gap involves transformational learning; this form of learning demands the adult be engaged in honest appraisal, reflection, and actions. This transformational learning happens when what we are actually doing is changing our long-held beliefs based on new experiences. Similarly, teachers do not change their teaching behaviors because they attend a workshop, read a book, or participate in a study group. They must be involved in a variety of professional learning experiences that invite them to examine the discrepancies between how they are teaching and how they need to teach in order to reach their goals for students.

The complexity of this level of professional learning exceeds the traditional model still used in many schools and districts. For example, if there is a problem with the writing skills of students, a school system may mandate that all teachers attend workshops on the writing process. Another example occurs when a new leader comes to a school or system enamored with a particular program; that new leader then mandates that all teachers learn this program. These deficit models ignore that teacher beliefs and their behaviors based on those beliefs are not that malleable. Some teachers will comply for fear of punishment or lack of approval from formal leaders. The majority of teachers, however, will listen, or pretend to listen, and then return to their classrooms and teach based on their own beliefs about how students learn, even if those beliefs are not producing the desired results. "Habits, values, and attitudes, even dysfunctional ones, are part of one's identity. To change the way people see and do things is to challenge how they define themselves" (Heifetz & Linsky, 2002, p. 27). Regardless of the number of supervisors in a school, use of mandated programs cannot be guaranteed. The structure of schools and the culture of teaching generally do not permit this level of prescription and inspection.

If mandated deficit approaches do not work, how do teachers change their teaching strategies to better meet students' needs? Teachers must personally see a gap between their classroom actions and their desired goals for students before they will use new instructional strategies. This proposed professional learning demands more intentional leadership than asking the professional learning committee to allocate funds for teachers to go to workshops or conferences. The outcome, however, is worthy of the effort; not only will teachers learn, they will become leaders. Transformational learning based on teachers' professional needs can create the changes in beliefs and result in actions of classroom teachers to redefine their professional selves. Ultimately these changes cause the structure of the school and the culture of teaching to change commensurately.

## From the Field

And it depends on which ones, what they are, and who's presenting them, because I've been to . . . of course I have to go to a lot of them because of my position and I've been to a lot of them that are totally worthless, but I've been to some that I thought were pretty good.

Mark Conway
High School Teacher
Harlingen, TX

## Self-Study: Experiences with Professional Learning

Principals can realize the importance of aligning teacher leadership with professional learning by reflecting on their own professional learning experiences. Most everyone (including principals) has experienced a wide range of professional learning opportunities, the quality of which ranges from dreadful to fantastic and everything in between. Principals may find it easier to understand the importance of key variables in the quality of professional learning experiences by reflecting on their previous learning opportunities; doing this can help principals more effectively use the information presented in this chapter.

### Step 1: Recall and Respond—Dreadful Experience

First, principals should recall their most dreadful professional learning experiences. They should try making the memory as vivid as possible, including remembering when it occurred, who was there, and the intended learning; then, they should respond to the following statements based on their recollections (see Table 6.1):

Table 6.1. **Recall and Respond: Dreadful Experience**

| The most dreadful professional learning opportunity I ever experienced . . . | | |
|---|---|---|
| Took place in a large group. | Yes | No |
| Involved activities and interactions with other learners. | Yes | No |
| Was directly connected to my work. | Yes | No |
| Was sustained and intensive over time. | Yes | No |
| Took place away from the job site. | Yes | No |
| Gave me an opportunity to apply or practice what was being learned. | Yes | No |

*(Continued)*

Table 6.1. **Continued**

| The most dreadful professional learning opportunity I ever experienced . . . | | |
|---|---|---|
| Was largely content-focused. | Yes | No |
| Dealt mostly with processing. | Yes | No |
| Was held outside the school workday. | Yes | No |
| Resulted in improved student learning. | Yes | No |

## Step 2: Recall and Respond—Fantastic Experience

Now, principals should think back to their most fantastic professional learning experiences. Again, they should try to bring to mind as many details as possible and then respond to the same set of statements (see Table 6.2):

Table 6.2. **Recall and Respond: Fantastic Experience**

| The most fantastic professional learning opportunity I ever experienced . . . | | |
|---|---|---|
| Took place in a large group. | Yes | No |
| Involved activities and interactions with other learners. | Yes | No |
| Was directly connected to my work. | Yes | No |
| Was sustained and intensive over time. | Yes | No |
| Took place away from the job site. | Yes | No |
| Gave me an opportunity to apply or practice what was being learned. | Yes | No |
| Was largely content-focused. | Yes | No |
| Dealt mostly with processing. | Yes | No |
| Was held outside the school workday. | Yes | No |
| Resulted in improved student learning. | Yes | No |

## Step 3: Compare

A comparison of the two experiences usually reveals some components are always present in the fantastic experiences and always absent in the dreadful ones. For example, the size of the group and where the learning opportunity occurred likely make less difference than the relevance to the principal's work, the opportunity to apply the learning immediately, interaction with others, and follow-up.

We suggest that principals use this same activity with the entire faculty and then follow with these steps:

- Invite faculty members to compare their individual results within small groups.
- Chart the results. Taking time to list the questions and tally the number of "yes" and "no" responses for the fantastic experiences and the dreadful experiences will provide a powerful graphic representation

of what is really important in planning and providing quality professional learning opportunities.

- Use the charted information to formulate a set of guidelines for planning and evaluating professional learning opportunities for all school groups.

Once the guidelines are established, the principal and teachers should examine the existing professional learning opportunities and level of support. Any discrepancies between the principal's and the teachers' perceptions should be explored.

## Structures for Professional Learning

Professional learning occurs through a variety of structures designed for individuals, small groups or teams, or the whole school. Developing and maintaining support for these structures can be daunting, and sometimes a principal needs a "map" to keep track, but as teacher leaders become a part of this design, the system can eventually become self-managing.

### Individual Professional Learning

Many teachers take the initiative to learn without direction from anyone. They search for quality professional learning both inside and outside the school and district. The proliferation of websites for teachers indicates the myriad learning opportunities available to meet their wants and needs in spite of any formal system in place for their professional learning. The certification process through the National Board for Professional Teaching Standards is an example of how teachers work individually to document and reflect on their teaching. Although this process was designed to document accomplished teaching practices rather than as a professional development activity, teachers learn reflection skills that continue beyond the certification process (see Hamilton, 2015).

External networks attract teachers who enjoy learning from other teacher leaders in diverse settings. Teachers often seek learning in content-area professional associations and then go on to provide leadership in these organizations. Graduate schools offer teachers a higher level of licensure, usually with the district incentive of a pay increase; during their study, teachers can often find quality learning missing in their workplace. These are only a few examples of how teachers can and do take responsibility for their own learning.

The principal's role in nurturing individual professional learning is one of "matchmaker" between the information they have about professional learning opportunities and teachers' interests and passions—all to improve student learning. When a teacher is invited to attend a professional learning experience related to their learning interests, there is potential for adding to the human and social capital of the school. Additionally, the positive relationship between the principal and teacher is likely enhanced. As follow-up, principals should spend time visiting with teachers about their application of the learning, to identify any additional resources needed, and to provide recognition for these professionals. This attention to individual needs results in benefits that far outweigh the initial investments.

## Small-Group/Team/Partner Professional Learning

Within small groups or teams, social networks contribute to increasing human capital, such as teachers' knowledge and skills. These groupings may be voluntary, selected, or based on roles and responsibilities. As classroom composition becomes more complex, teachers need increased peer support. Here are the examples of different types of groupings for professional learning used in *Lead with Me* (2006): single subject area, focus groups, grade level or department teams, study groups, groups with representatives from each grade, subject, or specialty, and pairs of teachers in mentor–mentee relationships. All of these remain relevant; however, a more recent list of types of learning groups offered by Sullivan and Glanz (2013) provided some alternative approaches to learning of groups: instructional rounds, book study groups, lesson study groups, peer coaching, critical friends groups (CFG), portfolio assessment, and action research.

The initial sharing may be limited, but it can be an incentive to move to deeper levels of collaborative learning. For example, a sequence of activities for building collaborative groups from less risk to more risk may include the following:

> *Low Risk*
> 1. Forming study groups around a common topic
> 2. Offering professional development workshops delivered by teacher leaders
> 3. Looking at student work and discussing it
> 4. Inquiring about teaching through action research, portfolios, or video cases
> 5. Providing time for peer observations of the "expert" teacher with no feedback
> 6. Conducting joint planning with peer observations and feedback
>
> *High Risk*

As groups work on their professional learning, the principal's role becomes one of attending to the process. Realistically, the principal cannot take part in every learning experience, yet it is important for principals to keep their fingers on the pulse of the activities. They can do this by visiting groups on a regular schedule, talking to key members of the groups, or requesting a debriefing meeting to update them on the status of the learning and its implementation. Principals have the responsibility of setting expectations for learning groups to meet on a regular basis and use the time wisely; they must also make sure these expectations are met.

## Whole-Faculty Focus

At first, principals take responsibility for a whole-school focus since they are able to see a broader perspective and they have the resources to support these activities. Senge et al. (2000), described this role for the principal as "'lead teacher and lead learner,' and steward of the learning process as a whole" (p. 15). In addition, Ubben, Hughes, and Norris (2016) stressed, "Leaders are responsible for learning" (p. 26). In time, principals can step back as teacher leaders move beyond leadership in their classrooms or in small groups to working with the entire faculty. Teacher leaders in formal roles may experience whole-school-focused activities immediately. Again, whether individual or small-group professional learning, the success of these efforts depends on the principal's willingness to be closely involved and supportive with available resources.

## Professional Learning Design

Sometimes the design of professional learning is hastily planned because of the time pressures placed on the leaders responsible. Unfortunately, this can result in wasted resources and, most likely, limited or no transfer of knowledge and skills to classrooms. Rather than asking teachers to participate in these activities, principals can seek permission from central office leaders to develop school-site experiences that match the criteria for quality professional learning. This would not prevent individual teachers from attending external professional learning opportunities appropriate for their work, but it would allow the majority of the professional learning to take place at the school site. The following elements are essential for quality on-site professional learning programs:

### From the Field

All the classes are different . . . And the ones that are teaching you are teachers from the districts and they're just people who have done these things in the classroom—people that have experienced it. It's not outsiders teaching us, it's our own teachers teaching others.

Sharon Raye<br>
Elementary Teacher<br>
Harlingen, TX

- Analysis of student learning needs to determine the focus of the professional learning
- Involvement of teachers in decision-making regarding their own learning
- Design of the evaluation of the professional learning before it is implemented
- Use of research-based strategies for improved instruction
- Placement of responsibility on teacher learners to become "experts" in the instructional strategies so that they can help other teachers learn them
- Encouragement of teacher learners to become teacher leaders by demonstrating their new skills
- Scheduling of collaborative support groups for teacher inquiry into their practice

- Evaluation of the student learning outcomes as a result of the teacher learning

Principals are sometimes surprised at the level of support needed for teachers to transfer their professional learning to the classroom. A workshop alone is not sufficient. The research of Joyce and Showers (2002) demonstrated the percentage of teachers who actually transfer an instructional strategy from a workshop to skillfully using the strategy in their classrooms. This transfer depends on the teachers' participation in four components: 1) learning the theory supporting the instructional strategy; 2) watching a skillful demonstration of the instructional strategy; 3) practicing the strategy; and 4) finally, and most important, engaging in peer coaching at the school site to ensure the strategy is competently used in the classroom. If a group of teachers experiences only the first three components, as few as 5 percent of them transfer and master the strategy in their classrooms (2002, p. 78). If these same teachers also participate in substantive follow-up at the school site, such as the peer coaching, the prediction is 95 percent will transfer the professional learning to their classrooms. Even at this time, few professional learning activities intended to improve teaching address all four components, especially follow-up.

## From the Field

School-based learning teams would help to engage all staff and provide ongoing support, if done well. . . . I've experienced the following: A principal assigned a book, assigned the teams, and had us meet during the time available to us before the students got off the bus in the morning . . . this particular implementation of "learning teams" soured the staff on the whole process.

Anonymous by request

It is difficult to condone offering an isolated workshop that does not fit into the context of the school's professional learning goals or does not engage participants in the study of theory, demonstrations, skill practice, and follow-up with peer coaching. There has been substantial research over the last 20 years arguing for designing professional learning based on these conditions. This professional knowledge has been ignored for too long. According to Drago-Severson, Blum-DeStefano, and Asghar (2013), specific activities/strategies include:

- developing and agreeing upon concrete rules, routines, and structures;
- providing technical information about the tasks and responsibilities; and
- providing ample opportunities to engage in dialogue and reflection that may support adult development, which in turn helps build capacity of adults. (p. 150–152)

There are times when a presentation or workshop is the best tool to use. For example, if introducing a new technology that all teachers must use, an inquiry method to learn about the program would be inappropriate. Also, the school or district may have a reason to invite an inspirational speaker for a session to set a particular tone for the faculty. If professional learning is well thought out, there will be flexibility that acknowledges and utilizes alternative approaches. Principals should work with central office administrators to gain approval for recertification or licensure credits for unique types of professional learning. Figure 6.1 gives a more comprehensive list of professional learning models that are not "workshops."

Figure 6.1. **Options for Professional Learning Focused on Student Learning**

| *Options for Professional Learning Include:* |
|---|
| ♦ Enrolling in a webinar or online course |
| ♦ Joining or leading a study or support group |
| ♦ Engaging in classroom observations—scheduled and/or walk-throughs |
| ♦ Inviting someone to observe you in the classroom and offer feedback |
| ♦ Attending and/or delivering presentations at conferences |
| ♦ Serving on a district-, state-, or national-level task force |
| ♦ Joining online networks focused on professional topics of interest |
| ♦ Serving as a mentor to a new teacher or a coach for a verteran teacher or teacher in need |
| ♦ Leading a student data analysis session with grade-level or subject-level colleagues |
| ♦ Pursuing a specialized certification or recognition |
| ♦ Becoming a supervising teacher for clinical and practice teacher students from teacher education programs |
| ♦ Videotaping a lesson and doing your own performance analysis |
| ♦ Reading journals, educational magazines, books |
| ♦ Preparing and presenting project/program information sessions for community groups |
| ♦ Touring schools using programs or strategies being initiated at your campus |
| ♦ Participating in lesson study |
| ♦ Working on a strategic planning team for campus or district |
| ♦ Listening to audio recording and/or watching videos on specific topics |
| ♦ Joining and contributing to Pinterest, EL Education, Edutopia, and other professional learning blogs/websites |
| ♦ Participating in a videoconference or conference call with experts |
| ♦ Enrolling in a university credit or continuing education course |
| ♦ Maintaining a reflection journal and/or a professional portfolio |

Good judgment by school leaders is needed to determine what type of professional learning is appropriate, but each decision must be based on the school's shared vision for student learning and available student data. A structure that can be particularly helpful in assuring that professional development opportunities are directly linked to the school's shared vision and student learning data, as well as determined through various levels of shared decision-making, is the professional learning community (PLC). Cultivating the development of a PLC empowers continuous learning for teachers in order to increase learning for students. Moving toward a school-wide PLC is a transformational process for the organization. Hord's work in PLCs was among the first to appear and continues to be refined. Hord's (2004) early work identified five dimensions of a PLC: 1) shared values and vision, 2) intentional collective learning and its application, 3) supportive and shared leadership, 4) supportive conditions, and 5) shared personal practice. However, more recent work (Hall & Hord, 2015; Tobia & Hord, 2012) stressed the importance of separating supportive conditions into two separate elements resulting in six dimensions of a PLC:

1. Shared values and vision
2. Intentional collective learning and application
3. Supportive and shared leadership
4. Structural conditions
5. Relational conditions
6. Shared personal practice/peer-to-peer support (p. 164)

## Collective Learning

Many principals envision their schools as school-wide professional learning communities where everyone is involved in learning to improve student performance. Making this a reality can be stressful for principals. Examples where a school has been able to maintain the focus on professional learning remain somewhat limited. When schools are identified as professional learning communities, the strong leadership of a principal is always a primary factor. Sustaining the PLC as school leadership changes occur can be difficult. As more emphasis is placed on building teacher leadership, the possibility that school change can be sustained increases.

Forming collaborative learning teams and engaging in learning activities is at the heart of professional learning communities (Hord & Sommers, 2008). We recommend two frameworks. The first is taken from Hord and Sommers and encourages engagement in learning activities expressed as follows:

- What do you notice about the interactions with staff?
- Are the conversations more creative, with richer dialogue?
- What is the evidence that the conversations have changed?
- Is everyone getting a chance to speak?
- Is trust being built so that authentic issues are being expressed in the meeting?
- Are participants able to advocate for a position without degrading other ideas? (2008, p. 111)

A second framework adapted from Joyce and Showers (2002) uses four components that principals and teacher leaders can design to ensure needed support for collaboration:

### *Component 1: Time and Space*

Quality time and space for the collaboration is a prerequisite. Asking teachers to find their own time and space is unrealistic and sends a message that collaboration is only important if you can find time to work it in. Killion in *Learning Forward* recommended a teacher spend at "least three times per week for a total of three to four hours per week for collaborative learning" (2013, p. 47). Most schools are a long way from meeting this goal, but it is certainly worthy of pursuit. Targeting this percentage signals that professional learning is a part of the work of professionals not just a "catch-as-catch-can" phenomenon. Principals can use structures such as teaching schedules, substitute teacher teams, and room assignments to facilitate finding time and space to support collaboration.

### *Component 2: Start Early*

If teachers are going to learn together, their collaboration should begin as soon as they start working on a common program project. In the comprehensive model shared later in this chapter, these groups may form after a few teachers have gained the knowledge and skills to use a specific teaching strategy or with all teachers immediately. The decision on how and when groups form should be made in context, but principals should be attuned to providing different levels of support depending on where members of the team are in their personal contexts.

### *Component 3: Provide Guidelines*

Guidelines help teachers learn to collaborate with each other. Too many well-meaning efforts by principals result in teachers coming together without knowing what to do and how to do it. Engaging in substantive conversations about teaching and learning demands skills some teachers do not have. Additionally, other teachers have worked autonomously for so long that they may be reluctant to share. On the positive side, there are numerous resources for learning these skills.

### *Component 4: Accountability*

Professional learning, individually or collectively, demands accountability. If principals provide resources and teachers spend time working together, there should be improvements in students' learning. Persuading teachers to continue their work together requires a strategy of establishing and using measures to link professional learning to student success.

## A Comprehensive Professional Leading and Learning Model

Extensive literature exists on what quality professional learning is and numerous models exist to help implement what is currently known in this area. So, while the model here is not the only professional learning model, it does give principals examples of specific steps to follow in establishing the professional learning levels we have described. There are other models that may be more appropriate depending on the teaching culture and the designated purpose; however, this model demonstrates how teacher leadership and teacher learning can be aligned.

Where professional learning starts is unpredictable, because it depends on the human and social resources and the school's culture for professional learning. If when an invitation to learn is offered, only a few teachers accept then, this is where the professional learning community begins. There is a "ripple effect" that can move the learning beyond the group to reach most of the faculty. In every school there will be teachers who never join this learning community. If these individuals desire to remain in this particular school, then the principal will need to confront these reluctant learners. In other cases, some teachers will look for positions in schools, where they will not be expected to be a part of a professional learning community.

The work in this comprehensive model begins with small groups of teachers and then expands over time to include all teachers. The model includes five phases: gap analysis, development of a vision for desired outcomes, involvement of professionals in readiness experiences and decision-making, formation of a professional learning evaluation plan, and entry of the professional learning community in a continuous "learning and leading cycle." This cycle is based on strategies used by an exceptional middle-school principal that resulted in sustained teacher leading and learning (Gonzales, 2004).

## Phase 1: Gap Analysis

Today, learning for all students is an expectation, not an option. This requires an examination of the current level of student performance and comparing that to what we want students to achieve. The results of this gap analysis should be the driving force for decisions about quality professional learning. Without this student learning information, it is impossible to effectively determine the learning needs of teachers.

## Phase 2: Vision Development and Action Planning

From the data obtained in the gap analysis, the faculty and staff determine a vision and action plan. The vision influences where the investment of resources, both human and fiscal, should be made in professional learning in order to meet the expectation of learning for all students. Teachers are invited to help plan the professional learning and principals ensure that plans are based on student data. Professional learning should add value to the school's human and social capital, reflect teachers' individual differences, and still remain focused on the vision.

## Phase 3: Readiness

After a vision for student performance is established, the principal and teachers search for strategies to address the gap. There are countless ways this readiness phase could play out. The purpose is to find research-based information and best-practice strategies that address the students' learning needs. Listed below are a few suggestions to help principals and teachers jump-start the process:

- ♦ Form a task group to examine books, journal articles, and websites addressing the identified needs.

- Attend professional conferences and select relevant concurrent sessions.
- Visit schools with similar demographics where there is exemplary student performance in the area of concern.
- Search out and communicate with national networks where other educators are focused on the issue or issues the gap analysis has defined.

It is best not to spend too much time in this readiness phase. Decisions must be made to move quickly into action. Though now decades old, Fullan's (1993) claim that we spend too much time on planning before getting into the work remains worthy of consideration He suggests rather than using the process of "ready, aim, fire," we should consider using "ready, fire, aim" (p. 31), because moving into action allows us an opportunity to refine the plan while working on it.

## Phase 4: Evaluation Process

Whether the professional learning is worthwhile is measured in terms of student learning and performance. Before beginning professional learning, specific, measurable student learning goals must be established and a plan developed to determine how to evaluate the processes used to meet these goals. There is a tendency to rely too heavily on test data for evaluation. To counter this, the evaluation plan should include additional assessment methods to help determine needed adjustments to the plan.

## Phase 5: Learning and Leading

This constructivist phase exemplifies the use of existing resources in order to build human and social capital. If principals understand how to build positive relationships, as discussed in Chapter 4, this phase requires putting that information into action. This phase is to create social networks in which teachers develop

Figure 6.2. **Effect of Teacher Learning on Teacher Leadership and the School**

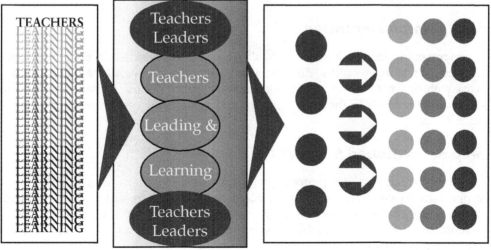

knowledge, beliefs, and skills for improved instruction. If organizational learning is desired, then learning as a social enterprise must be recognized. In order to transform teacher behaviors, professional learning must connect teachers' emotions with their intellect. The steps in the cycle below tap into knowledge, skills, and emotions through the "shared network of social situations" (Gonzales, 2004, p. 45). Figure 6.2 illustrates how teacher learning results in teacher leadership, which then can spread throughout the school.

## Step 1: Invitation

Invite teachers to participate in a study group focused on a selected teaching strategy from Phase 3. Extend the invitation to all teachers. Not all teachers will come, but the teachers who accept the invitation become the core group. At first, the principal is the person who identifies and secures materials for the study group, but as teacher leadership emerges, this responsibility will move to someone in the group.

## Step 2: Learning the Strategy

There are a variety of ways teachers can learn instructional strategies, such as attending a workshop, visiting a school to observe the strategies in action, or joining an external network of teacher leaders who are willing to share their struggles with the same issue. It is important to involve at least two teachers so they can reinforce each other in the learning process. Regardless of the source of the learning, in the beginning, principals should join teachers as co-learners. As this model is sustained, teacher leaders take the place of the principal as the support system for other teachers trying to find solutions to student learning problems.

## Step 3: Reassembling and Providing Support

Teachers from Step 2 who have accomplished this phase of their learning are too often left on their own. To avoid this, a system should be in place to bring the study group from Step 1 back together as a way to support the teachers as they begin using the new skills. Other teachers are not obligated to use the new skills, but they and the principal should nurture the teacher learners as they face the inevitable disappointments involved in implementing a new skill in the classroom.

## Step 4: Implementation

In too many schools, teachers are asked to learn a new skill and then teach other teachers. While this would seem to be a good use of resources, it generally does not work well. Teachers cannot teach a skill that they have not used. Teachers must use and refine the skills in their own classrooms before they can help other teachers learn them.

## Step 5: Continued Support

Continue support group meetings for the teacher learners. Membership in this support group may vary, but if the principal and a few interested teachers join with the teacher learners to reflect on their experiences, the importance of their work is reinforced. This ongoing, nurturing support is vital to the success of professional learning, especially early on.

### Step 6: Demonstration

Invite other teachers to observe teacher learners working with the new teaching strategy. Once the teacher learners are somewhat comfortable with the new strategy, an invitation to all teachers to learn can be extended. The teacher leaders may offer a workshop or open their classrooms for teacher observation. The teacher learners now become the teacher leaders.

### Step 7: Coaching

Ask teacher leaders to coach other teachers willing to try the new teaching strategy by modeling it. Teachers may invite a teacher leader to come into their classrooms while they experiment with the strategy. They may work as a team or the teacher leader can observe and provide feedback.

### Step 8: Ongoing Support

To sustain momentum in using new teaching strategies, teacher learners need to share what is happening in their classrooms and seek feedback to make adjustments. Teacher leaders can serve as facilitators of discussions, offer assistance through coaching, and identify needed resources. Principals must continue to maintain a connection to these groups to provide resources and reinforce continuous learning.

### Step 9: Evaluation

Evaluate both the process and student performance results. The evaluation plan developed during Phase 3 is used to collect data throughout the process for both making adjustments along the way and providing measures for a final determination regarding the achievement of student learning goals. This does not have to be a complicated process, but it is important to measure the success of the professional learning in terms of student outcomes.

## Reluctant Teacher Learners

Predictably, there will be teachers, especially at first, who will not want to participate in professional learning regardless of the incentives. These teachers are reluctant for a variety of reasons, including the personal context issues discussed in Chapter 3. Sometimes the most resistant teachers are those who in the past were strong advocates for innovations but became disillusioned. Then there are teachers who cherish their autonomy and feel that involvement in collaborative professional learning will reduce their independence and impinge on their time for working with students. Finally, there are teachers who are mediocre or incompetent, but do not perceive themselves as such.

### Disillusioned Teachers

Many teachers become enthusiastic about professional learning and spend valuable time learning and working to make a program succeed with their students. After the teachers are involved, the principal or the central office leaders drop the program and jump to a new initiative. Often these teachers face multiple new programs and their accompanying professional development within a short time frame. The result is experience overload with skepticism replacing enthusiasm.

Principals should acknowledge that the history these teachers have with change was likely unpleasant. Faculty and staff may need to revisit previous experiences, recognize the misuses of professional learning, and establish norms for how initiatives and professional learning will take place in the future. Making the past public gives the disillusioned teachers affirmation that their experiences were unfortunate, but in the future they will be supported in their learning.

## Teacher Individuality

Some individuals select teaching because they prefer not to work closely with other adults and can focus their energy on students. For whatever reasons, these individuals believe they can succeed by securing their own resources, inventing teaching strategies, and developing relationships with their students. Although most of these teachers are social in public areas of the school, they retreat to their classrooms as soon as possible to protect their time and space. Sadly, these teachers may even give up on the more challenging students (Talbert & McLaughlin, 2002), but a school with a vision of learning for all students cannot allow this.

The principal must clarify what is meant by *autonomy*. Social networks can be used to build authentic collaboration while still respecting teachers' individuality. This can help teachers see the benefits of collaboration for the students they are not able to reach, yet still maintain some individuality and autonomy.

## Teachers of Concern

There are teachers who do not see professional learning as part of their job responsibilities. These are the teachers who fulfill the minimum renewal requirements for licensure or attend professional learning without being truly engaged. Some of these teachers are able, but mediocre in their performance. Other teachers are incompetent, but not to the point that a principal can document and recommend their dismissal.

## Teachers in Need of Improvement

Mediocre teachers usually do not see or admit they have problems in their teaching. If problems are pointed out to them, they usually do not believe it is their problem and blame negative results on the students' backgrounds, lack of motivation, or lack of parent support. Parent complaints, poor student performance, and discipline problems are but a few of the outcomes resulting from the mediocre teacher's performance. Dealing with each of these demands an excessive amount of administrative attention. Principals should resist the temptation to avoid these teachers in the hopes that they will improve on their own. It will not happen.

In the traditional performance appraisal process, principals are often faced with an overload of teacher evaluations. Mediocre teachers may have previous positive evaluations on file, which can make it difficult to move them toward improved performance. Unfortunately, principals tend to identify professional learning, such as attending a workshop, observing another teacher, or reading an article, as an improvement goal. There are two reasons this approach is not effective. First, the performance problems may not be learning problems; instead, they may be based on something else, such as the teacher's personal situation or a long-held belief that teaching is a job fulfilled only to provide resources for participation in their personal activities outside the school. Second, if the performance problems are skill related, sending a teacher out alone to learn will rarely change teaching behaviors. Teachers may comply with the principal's mandate to participate in a professional learning experience, but their beliefs and teaching strategies will likely remain unchanged.

An alternative approach to working with weak teachers is to refrain from focusing on their deficits. To do this, leaders can build structures in which weak teachers work with other teachers to be accountable for student learning. So, in essence, a group of teachers are taking responsibility for helping each other learn and holding each member of the team accountable.

Most states and school systems have performance appraisal systems in place to evaluate teachers. These systems range from the once-a-year visit by the principal or another administrator to comprehensive clinical supervision models. In all these models, the legal responsibility for making judgments regarding teacher performance rests with the principal. There are efforts to improve the traditional teacher evaluation process, which most teachers know does not help them improve their teaching. Four possible strategies to increase the impact of teacher evaluation on teacher mediocrity are:

- *Peer assistance.* This process taps into competent teachers to help mediocre teachers. In many school systems, the peer assistance program is developed in collaboration with the teachers' union.

- *The standards movement.* The standards and their accompanying accountability put pressure on mediocre teachers to perform.

- *Teacher portfolios.* Teachers must present evidence of their performance over time in a portfolio.

- *Data about student performance.* The focus here is not on what the teacher is doing, but how the students are learning. Although high-stakes tests are often the source of these data, there are other authentic strategies to collect such data (adapted from Platt, Tripp, Ogden, & Fraser, 2000, pp. 181–191). More recently, Datnow and Park (2014) stressed that "the real power in data-informed decision-making is the ability to change classroom practice . . . thus teachers who are guided by data are better able to craft lessons to meet their students' needs" (p. 126).

Principals are obligated to work within the existing teacher evaluation process in their school systems, but, alternate structures in which teachers are responsible for the learning of all students, not just those students in their individual classrooms can be pursued; this is directly related to the collaborative culture of the PLC. With this focus, professional learning decisions to improve performance are based on student needs rather than a quick fix to make the mediocre teacher better.

## Incompetent Teachers

With mediocre teachers, there is at least hope they can improve their teaching. Incompetent teachers, however, are those who may exist in a deep phase of withdrawal; they simply show up to work but not teach (and in some cases they can't teach) or are emotionally unstable to the point that students are at risk in their classrooms. We might tolerate a mediocre teacher, but the incompetent teachers are the ones we would never allow to teach our own children. Principals know who these teachers are, dread the complicated process to remove them from the profession, and may want to shrink from addressing the problem. Helping these teachers goes way beyond professional learning, demanding a level of support that is not available in most school systems. When students are in danger intellectually, physically, or emotionally, intentional leaders have no choice but to put in the energy and time necessary to remove these teachers from the classroom. Principals faced with this situation should begin work with their supervisors and the school district's legal counsel; this is no effort to undertake without these supports.

## Summary

Intentionally leading professional learning is an important responsibility of the principal. Here is where teacher leaders emerge and work best. Rather than being tied down with operational concerns, teacher leaders want to learn in order to help others learn and, more importantly, to ensure that more students learn. Principals can use the Professional Learning Rubric (Figure 6.3) to self-assess professional learning in their schools.

**Figure 6.3. Professional Learning Rubric for Principals**

| Quality Teacher Leadership Requires Alignment of Teacher Leadership with Professional Learning ||
|---|---|
| Level | Outcome |
| Unsure and Unskilled | Professional learning opportunities are available, but may or may not be related to the school's vision or aligned with individual teacher needs. |
| Moving Along | A school vision has been developed and decisions regarding professional learning evolve from the vision. Teacher leaders are directly involved in determining what many of these learning opportunities will be. |
| Leading Teacher Leaders | All professional learning opportunities are aligned with the school's vision and the individuals' job needs; a variety of learning formats are employed for delivery of learning; everyone in the school is involved in continuous learning. Teacher leaders have improved their leadership skills through specific professional learning opportunities. |

The knowledge base regarding professional learning is highly developed, and we can no longer ignore what is known about this area. As teachers move into structures for collective learning within a comprehensive professional learning model, teacher leadership will grow. Even reluctant teacher learners must join in; no student should be in a classroom with a teacher who is not also a learner.

## Resources

6.1 Education Northwest—One of 10 regional educational research and development organizations funded by the U.S. Education Department, Institute of Education Sciences (IES). The site has information and services on a variety of topics relevant to teacher professional learning. Retrieved from http://educationnorthwest.org

6.2 Annenberg Media Learner.org—Videos on demand, credit and non-credit courses, and other resources provided for examining critical issues in school reform, such as *A Community of Learners.* Provides information on critical friends groups, looking at student work, and other practices that engage teachers in collaborative learning. Some items are no cost, while others are for purchase. Retrieved from www.learner.org

6.3 Sweeney, D. (2003). *Learning along the way: Professional development by and for teachers.* Portland, ME: Stenhouse—Provides practical suggestions on how to form study groups.

6.4 Jolly, A. (2005). *A facilitator's guide to professional learning teams.* Greensboro, NC: SERVE—Step-by-step process to teacher learning in teams. The site has a variety of resources in addition to the one listed here. The facilitator's guide aligns with the content of this chapter, but items on other topics are worthy of review. Retrieved from www.serve.org

6.5 GoENC.com—Previously known as ENC.com, this website for mathematics and science education was formerly funded by the U.S. Department of Education. Currently, the website is subscriber-based, but it contains excellent information on how to design professional learning. Retrieved from www.goenc.com/

6.6 ASCD: Professional Learning & Community Educators. This is the webpage for the professional association. Information on membership and items for purchase are provided here. Additionally, a number of brief articles on specific topics are available for reading on line or downloading for later. These articles will provide excellent information immediately and offer the reader a sense of the items produced by the association, help them decide if membership is desired. Retrieved from www.ascd.org

6.7 Action Research—emTech ConsultingAction—A listing of websites containing a variety of information regarding action research. Retrieved from www.emtech.net/actionresearch.htm

6.8 Easton, L.B. (2015). *Powerful designs for professional learning, Third edition.* Oxford, OH: Learning Forward—This book contains detailed information on 24 learning designs, 15 of which are new in this edition. Edited by Lois Brown Easton, the chapters are written by various experts in adult learning.

6.9 Center for Teacher Quality (formerly Teacher Leaders Network)—Professional Learning Communities: Entering this term in the search area on this website results in a long list of resources related to this topic. Their List of Resources has links to numerous resources related to professional learning communities. Retrieved from www.teachingquality.org

6.10 Barker, C.L., & Searchwell, C.J. (2010). *Writing meaningful teacher evaluations—right now!!!* Thousand Oaks, CA: Corwin Press—Featuring a time-saving CD-ROM with easily customizable forms, this resource provides a diverse bank of updated proficiency statements to clearly and comprehensively describe a teacher's performance.

# Part 3: Supporting and Sustaining Teacher Leadership

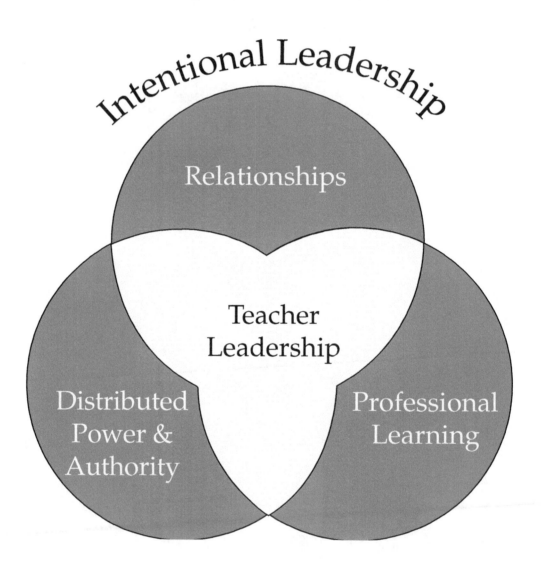

# Part 3: Supporting and Sustaining Teacher Leadership

Here, we return to the Framework for Intentional Leadership to look once again at all the components as the focus moves to continuing the work. Intentional leadership actions to build relationships, distribute power and authority, and align professional learning must continue in order to sustain emerging teacher leadership. In Chapter 7, "Creating a Context of Support for Teacher Leaders," we discuss the predictable tensions in the relationships between principals and teacher leaders. We acknowledge that informal leadership can be powerful and we advocate the enthusiastic development and utilization of this important resource. We also want to look more closely at formal teacher leader roles. With the increase in such leadership roles, we believe principals need strategies to support these teachers. Finally, we recommend leadership development skills teachers need.

An expanded description of Markham Middle School frames Chapter 8, "Sustaining Teacher Leading and Learning." This is followed by commentaries regarding how to sustain support for teacher leading and learning beyond the leadership of a single principal. Then we look at intentional leadership strategies in the larger context, beyond the school where predictable disruptors can cause a school to lose sight of the vision. Finally, we share a letter from Jay, the principal of Markham Middle School (with a P.S. from Theresa, MMS Dean of Instruction) to incumbent and potential principals regarding the work to be done and their role in making it happen.

# 7 Creating a Context of Support for Teacher Leaders

"What I get from teachers in the United States," Leena noted, "is that they are in a hurry all the time—and they are frustrated with what they have to do." "But teacher leadership is built into our day in Finland," Marianna said, "and we are educated to lead and have influence outside of our schools."
Berry, Byrd, & Wieder in *Teacherpreneurs*

*Theresa had a busy day scheduled but couldn't stop thinking about her role and work at MMS. She was excited about her new position. As Dean of Instruction, Theresa works collaboratively with faculty to get things done. She understands that a major advantage she brings to the position is her previous work experience with the faculty. Theresa wanted to stay at MMS and lead in a different way than she had previously. She didn't want to leave her middle school and the teachers she had grown to respect and love. Consequently, having worked with Theresa for some time now, MMS teachers have come to trust her. Theresa has been thinking that she wants to be more than just collaborative! How does she create real support for teachers every day so that MMS builds its own cadre of teacher leaders? How can the campus encourage more teachers to lead by example and not necessarily through a position? How will she maintain and sustain leaders over time? What daily actions and strategies should she adopt to create an environment that supports teacher leaders? Theresa has more questions than answers, but is eager to continue working with colleagues to generate answers to these questions and solutions to problems, create more and stronger levels of support, and ultimately provide increased quality learning for students.*

## From the Field

Principals want to create the conditions that enable teachers and learning teams to provide instructional leadership to one another—and by constantly sending the message that expertise around practice belongs to practitioners instead of principals, they leave their learning teams and teacher empowered to accept responsibility for finding ways to meet the needs of every learner.

Bill Ferriter
6th-grade Teacher, Author, Professional Developer
District near Raleigh, NC

Building relationships with teacher leaders is the first step to providing supportive conditions for them. Additionally, it is critical to the principal's success and the health of the school culture. A poor relationship with an informal or formal highly influential teacher leader may cause the principal stress, and even result in strain among the staff members. Distributing power and authority is critical if teachers are to be authentically involved in making decisions and accountable for results. Finally, aligning teacher leadership with professional learning is the core instructional leadership work of the principal. Promoting, building, and sustaining teacher leadership are aimed at improving student learning. If principals expect to reap the full benefits of teacher leadership, they must offer teachers leadership development opportunities, ensure they are coached in their work, and secure needed resources.

In the following section, we describe some of the predictable causes of tension between principals and teacher leaders. Next, we describe some of the various informal and formal teacher leader roles, with emphasis on the emerging formal instructional teacher leader role. Finally, we recommend some areas of skill development critical to teacher leader success.

## Tensions Between Principals and Teacher Leaders

The ways principals interact with teacher leaders will determine the effectiveness of this work. Frequently referenced in current literature are Anderson's (2004) three models of how these key leaders might work together. First, there is the "buffered principal" (p. 107), who is surrounded by a small group of teacher leaders but is mostly isolated from other teachers. Other teachers view these teacher leaders as an elitist group that may or may not allow others (even the principal) access to information and resources. The second model is "contested" (p. 109), where teacher leaders hold an unskilled principal hostage in order to maintain the status quo. These teachers believe they are guarding the school against attempts to damage what is good. Finally, there is the "interactive principal" (p. 108), who is inclusive in offering formal and informal leadership opportunities for all teachers based on teachers' interests. Similar to a food buffet, these principals lay out the issues that must be solved and engage teachers to choose freely from the options available. We believe principals from this model can develop skills and strategies to work interactively with teacher leaders in a productive way.

Both principals and teacher leaders come to their relationships with unique resources and needs. Principals' resources are housed within the formal power and authority of their positions; teacher leaders' resources are more intangible and based on their human and social capital. If principals and teacher leaders are to work together, their relationships must be reciprocal; each must be allowed to tap the resources of the other with the purpose of achieving the shared vision for student learning. Principals and teacher leaders have different needs, interests, and perceived role identities (Smylie & Brownlee-Conyers, 1992). Teacher leaders are concerned about their relationships with their students, colleagues, and the principal. If these relationships are put in danger, the teacher leader cannot work effectively. On the other hand, principals see their needs, interests, and perceived role identities as connected to the assignment of tasks, the budget, personnel evaluation, and interactions with internal and external publics. The principal's role is to build trust and openness with teacher leaders to focus on both their joint responsibilities and uniqueness. In order to build this trust, principals and teacher leaders must feel that the other person is not a threat. According to Theoharis's research on social justice and school reform (2009), "principals identified building relationships not only as an essential component to their leadership style, but also as a means to overcome the countervailing pressures they faced daily" (p. 121). Thus, building trust provides a strong foundation from which to negotiate positive and productive relationships.

The level of ambiguity in roles is dependent on the quality of the principal–teacher leader relationships. If a teacher assumes a single task and works relatively independently of the principal, there is less tension than when a teacher takes on a formal, full-time instructional leadership role. Both principals and teacher leaders must pay attention to building a relationship that moves beyond individuals' personal interests to focus on the tasks to be accomplished.

## Teacher Leader Roles and Functions

Teacher leaders assume their roles through countless pathways. Some emerge to informally take on responsibilities their colleagues do not want or simply do not see as problems. Others are selected, either by the principal or a leadership group, to take on formal managerial or leadership roles, such as department chair, dean of instruction, or assessment coordinator. Finally, with school reform initiatives, the number of teacher leaders taking on instructional leadership roles through a directive from either the central office or the school's leadership is increasing.

### Ubiquitous Teacher Leadership

Think of informal teacher leadership as a kaleidoscope, with teachers moving in and out of various leadership roles depending on need. These teacher leaders often take on responsibilities when they want to use their talents to address a problem they perceive as important. In most cases, they view themselves not as leaders but as people who see tasks that need to be done and do them.

Principals who build relationships with informal teacher leaders can set in motion incredible accomplishments, such as establishing safe school procedures, designing a tutoring program, or building parent-community programs. The opportunities for informal teacher leaders to take action are unlimited. Teacher leaders have creative and exciting ideas and principals should take advantage of the willingness and talents of these teachers.

Teams of teachers focused on student learning also need the principal's attention. In these teams, informal leadership emerges as teachers work collaboratively. Teachers take on leadership responsibilities as needed. If a team of teachers realizes their students are struggling with a particular skill, they look to their colleagues with expertise in this area. Through this sort of joint inquiry, teachers discover their strengths, build on them, and provide leadership to the team.

### Recognized Teacher Leader Functions

Most schools have formal teacher leaders who assume a variety of roles focused on governance, student activities, managerial or leadership tasks, or instructional leadership. The relationships between the principal and these teacher leaders may demand structure that is not necessary with informal teacher leaders.

## *Governance Leadership Roles*

Most schools have site-based governance structures. How elaborate these structures are depends on factors such as school size, state and local mandates for shared governance, maturity of the principal and staff in the distribution of power and authority, and the influence of teachers' professional organizations. Membership in governance structures places teachers in formal teacher leadership roles. Whether serving as a member or chair of a site-based leadership team, a behavior intervention council to assist classroom teachers, or a hearing committee to provide a forum for voicing faculty grievances and student appeals, teachers in these roles are formal leaders making decisions. Teacher leaders may also represent their school on governance entities at the district level.

## *Student Activities Leadership Roles*

Another category of essential leadership roles is focused on co-curricular or extracurricular activities. Teachers accept the formal responsibility for working with various student activities, including subject-area clubs, team and individual sports, honorary and scholastic organizations, and service clubs. Quite often one teacher serves as a formal coordinator to help an individual group in communicating with other groups, making sure efforts are not being duplicated, securing facilities, coordinating fund-raising activities, and publicizing events. In large high schools, this role may require release time from teaching responsibilities.

## *Managerial or Leadership Roles*

Countless teacher leaders take on managerial or leadership roles to keep the school functioning. These roles include positions such as team leader, union representative, mentor, or school improvement team chair. For most of these roles, teacher leaders serve as liaisons between classroom teachers and the administration, representing their team, department, or grade level in discussions about school-wide issues.

Working with these teacher leaders offers the principal an opportunity to put together a cadre of emissaries to build teacher leadership. In addition to handling the administrative tasks related to their jobs, these teachers interact with the teachers they represent. They are strategically placed to recognize, initiate, and support informal teacher leaders. Even when a school has a formal instructional teacher leader, one person cannot work with every member of the staff; therefore, principals rely on team leaders, department chairs, and others to develop their teams to improve student learning. The principal's task is to build relationships with these leaders and ensure they are skilled and willing to be inclusive in their work with others.

Team leaders and department chairs are increasingly being asked to become instructional leaders. If supportive structures are present, including time, space, and an expectation for collaboration, then powerful acquisition of knowledge can occur through collective learning, joint planning, and personal practice for increased student achievement. Principals should be sensitive to the needs of team leaders. For example, a teacher leader who has previously worked with a well-functioning team may move to another team that does not work as well together. The teacher leader may need the principal's coaching on building new relationships within this team. Another example is a teacher leader's need to engage in efforts that sustain the quality, collaborative functioning of a team. Principals can help by being sensitive to changing relationships and alert to needed skill development to address a variety of relationship issues.

## *Instructional Leadership Roles*

Teacher leaders who assume formal instructional leadership roles purposely work with teachers to improve student learning. Increasingly, schools and school systems are building internal structures to select teachers for roles such as staff developer, literacy coach, and lead teacher. Because formal instructional teacher leadership is often a relatively new concept, many principals do not always have experience in building relationships with a person in this position.

The relationships of principals and teacher leaders depend in part on their previous experience together. If teachers have previously assumed leadership roles within a school's supportive culture before moving into a more formal role, then the building of a positive relationship will be more rapid; if a new teacher leader is assigned to a school, relationship building will take more time. There are certainly other personal factors that can influence this process, some of which we described in Chapter 3.

## Principal Support of Instructional Teacher Leaders

Regardless of the path teacher leaders followed to their roles, their relationship with the principal is important. Simultaneously, teacher leaders must balance their relationships with their peers. The principal holds power and governs access to resources such as information, opportunities for professional learning, and fiscal support (Vandiver, 1996; Kochanek, 2005). In most situations, even when the relationships are positive, a distinct difference between the principal's role and the teacher leader's role still exists. Traditionally, the principal works with strategic and managerial issues, whereas the teachers focus primarily on teaching and student learning (Crowther, Kaagan, Ferguson, & Hann, 2002). However, in the twenty-first century, the role of principals and teacher leaders has evolved to include the "reimagining of instructional leadership of what teachers know and do as leadership" (Collay, 2011).

Examples of strategies principals can use to help build strong partnerships with formal teacher instructional leaders are:

- Maintain the focus on instructional leadership.
- Give them access to human and fiscal resources.
- Protect the teacher leader's relationships with peers.
- Collaboratively build and monitor action plans.

- Build a community of practice that encourages teacher leaders to discuss process and implementation.
- Assist in maintaining balance to avoid overload.
- Be available.

## Maintain the Focus on Instructional Leadership

Principals must avoid the temptation to ask instructional teacher leaders to take on administrative responsibilities. Such responsibilities distract teacher leaders from their focus on instructional responsibilities. Sometimes emergencies happen and teacher leaders must pick up duties critical to the management operations of the school, but this should not be the norm.

Teacher leader activities focused on instructional leadership are varied, but they usually include:

- Helping others see how a new approach relates to the shared vision for student learning
- Leading decision-making regarding the school's professional learning plan
- Designing and delivering professional learning experiences
- Facilitating groups to examine, design, and use appropriate teaching and learning strategies
- Being available to answer questions about teaching and learning
- Mentoring new teachers
- Working with individual teachers who request assistance
- Pulling together assessment data for teachers' use in their decision-making
- Seeking outside resources to support teachers
- Building relationships with parents and community members to support student learning
- Working with central office to align school goals with local, state, and national standards
- Advocating beyond the school for policies and resources that support the shared vision for student learning
- Seeking their own professional renewal to better serve teachers

### *Give Access to Human and Fiscal Resources*

Leaders cannot function without resources—teacher leaders included. As decisions are made about the teacher leader's responsibilities, principals should identify both human and fiscal resources they will need in their work. Individuals responsible for accounting for school funds should be informed about the teacher leader's decision-making power over any allocated resources. Ways must be found to assure autonomy to teacher leaders in seeking and accessing available resources while simultaneously maintaining fiscal responsibility.

## *Protect the Teacher Leader's Relationships with Peers*

According to Berry, Byrd, and Wieder (2013), building relational trust amongst teacher leaders strengthens and encourages teachers to be actively involved in making a difference. Consequently, teachers who learn and begin to lead often believe they are taking on these responsibilities to help their colleagues. Earlier, Cress and Miller (2003) found these teacher leaders "believe their own kinship with teachers—as teachers themselves—uniquely qualifies them to help. Second, their work is inspired by a sense of moral purpose" (p. 2). As a result, teacher leaders consider their relationships with colleagues of utmost importance, yet they are sometimes uneasy about them. Although teacher leaders may also have classroom responsibilities, their roles change in many ways. They frequently worry about how they are perceived by other teachers and actively try to avoid reprisals that can result when a teacher steps "out of the ranks." Even teachers who themselves are not interested in taking on leadership roles may express resentment that certain teachers are more empowered than others. Formal teacher leader roles are becoming more common, but many school cultures still support the view that all teachers should act and be treated the same.

Many teachers begin their leadership endeavors with facilitating professional learning activities. These are generally not particularly controversial, and other teachers would expect a teacher leader to take on such a responsibility. Eventually, as a teacher leader gains confidence and develops trust, he or she can work with teachers in other ways to improve instruction. The path, though, between where teacher leaders begin and the real work of influencing other teachers is littered with obstacles ensuring the ever-present possibility that other teachers can reject them. Cress and Miller (2003) described three strategies teacher leaders sometimes use to build relationships, note the disadvantages of each:

1. "Bearing gifts." These gifts, such as materials or other resources, are selected to appeal to other teachers. The disadvantage of this strategy is that once the teachers start receiving the gifts they want them to continue and teacher leaders do not have unlimited resources.

2. "Anything you need." The teacher leader may be drawn into the other teachers' agendas rather than promoting the desired instructional improvement when they promise "anything you need."

3. "Unfailing accepting and uncritical language." Not wanting to hurt teachers' feelings, teacher leaders sometimes couch their feedback in ways that result in teachers never receiving critical feedback. (pp. 3–4)

Helping teacher leaders understand these strategies are not productive is part of the coaching role for the principal. One way principals can do this is to ensure everyone knows he or she endorses the work of the teacher leader. Teacher leaders may not be taken seriously by other teachers unless there is a supportive school culture and an endorsement from formal leadership, such as the principal, central office leaders, and school district policies. If there is no support from the formal structure, teacher leaders will only work in isolation with individual teachers who agree to learn. Principals need to send the message to everyone that the teacher leaders' work is important and collaboration is expected.

## From the Field

If you let teachers, . . . come up with how to present curriculum, usually they're gonna get it right. So, as far as at this school, we are given a lot of freedom to do that. Our principal does not come and try to dictate how we do something; the systems do not either.

Mark Conway<br>
High School Science Department<br>
Harlingen ISD, Harlingen, TX

Most teachers do not see themselves as leaders and their socialization within the teaching culture may cause them to feel they have no right to lead colleagues even when they assume formal roles. While they agreed to accept these leadership responsibilities because they believe in the effort, they may still doubt their own knowledge and skills. Although these teachers may have taken on leadership roles in the past, this new role is different: They are not administrators, nor are they quite the same as the other classroom teachers. This hybrid leadership role can make for uneasy feelings. By predicting how these tenuous peer relationships may play out, principals can work to build teacher leaders' confidence through strategies such as:

- *Sharing information.* Teacher leaders need information to help in problem solving, explaining how to access internal and external information, and offering resources to gather data. If teacher leaders are well informed, they can make better decisions and help others do the same.

- *Starting with low-risk tasks that will ensure success.* Principals should recommend starting with assignments that are less threatening, such as meeting with grade-level teams already engaged in conversations about teaching and learning.

- *Celebrating successes, even the small ones.* When principals see positive results of the teacher leaders' actions, they should find appropriate ways to celebrate these successes. A private celebration may be best because many teacher leaders do not want attention drawn to their efforts, believing it may cause an even broader divide between themselves and other teachers.

- *Complimenting the teacher leader with specific, behavioral praise.* It is important to not only give praise but also be specific about what the teacher leader did. Principals can identify specific behaviors teacher leaders are carrying out and state how valuable these actions are to accomplishing the shared vision.

- *Finding opportunities for sharing.* As teacher leaders gain confidence in their work with other teachers, principals should seek opportunities for them to share. Examples of sharing opportunities include presentations to the school board, professional conferences, or community groups.

- *Stressing the importance of maintaining confidentiality.* When teachers take on formal roles, their perspectives broaden. Some may be surprised to find that not all teachers have the same work ethic or commitment they do. Teacher leaders will be privy to information they must not share with others. The principal and teacher leader must establish an agreement that confidentiality is critical to everyone's success.

## *Collaboratively Build and Monitor an Action Plan*

The school year moves by quickly, and teacher leaders, although well meaning, may not accomplish all they had hoped. To minimize this, the principal and teacher leader should meet to discuss the shared vision for the school's instructional needs and agree on how the teacher leader will respond. The plan should include short-term goals for the school year and long-term goals that encompass up to 5 years.

After the plan is developed, regularly scheduled meetings will provide principals and teacher leaders opportunities to keep updated on progress. The teacher leader will find it easier to stay focused if the action plan is centered on instructional leadership tasks with measures of accountability.

The principal and the teacher leader should keep each other informed about actions taken. Leaders hate surprises. Finding that a teacher leader has moved in a direction not complementary to the overall plan can be a problem; on the other hand, teacher leaders feel betrayed when principals intercede before communicating with them. Both leaders need autonomy to make decisions, but there must also be constant communication between them to make sure they are moving in tandem.

## *Assist in Maintaining Balance to Avoid Overload*

Teacher leaders, like principals, can become consumed by serving others. For many teacher leaders, their work fulfills a desire to leave a legacy by helping others work more effectively with students. To do this, they take on more and more work; this frequently results in overload that intrudes on their personal lives. Just as the principal must learn to break the bond of dependency, teacher leaders must also. They must learn how to work with other teachers to build their independence.

Principals sometimes contribute to teacher leaders' overload. When a teacher leader completes a task well, the tendency is to give them more tasks. In trying to meet the principal's expectations, the teacher leader may attempt to do everything and create a situation of too many demands in too little time. The traditional principal–teacher relationships in which most teachers are socialized prevent them from refusing this additional work; therefore, principals must protect teacher leaders by monitoring their own reliance on them. If not, teacher leaders will experience stress, become less effective, and possibly move away from leadership roles.

## *Be Available*

This final strategy is difficult for principals because they are pulled in so many directions during the school day. Still, the principal's availability is an important resource for teacher leaders. By regularly putting aside time to talk with teacher leaders, principals can avoid problems and build relationships with them.

To take full advantage of teacher leaders as a resource, principals must provide them support. As principals and teacher leaders become more familiar with each other's needs and interests, less time is spent on the relationship-building process and more time on the tasks related to instructional leadership.

## Teacher Leadership Skills Development

### From the Field

What makes an effective teacher leader? Personally, as a teacher leader, I have had opportunities to participate and be a part of many diverse learning and leadership opportunities over the last few years. Among our team, on the surface, it may not be readily evident how all these opportunities have dramatically shaped the type of leaders we have become.

Brad Hurst<br>
10th–12th-grade Science<br>
Grimes, IA

All informal and formal teacher leaders need support in building specific leadership skills. The assumption that because teachers are confident in leading students, they automatically know how to lead adults is naive. To address this, principals can help teacher leaders learn how to work with diverse teacher perspectives, make public presentations, and navigate relationships with reticent teachers.

Listed below are several strategies principals can use to help teachers learn skills for leading adults:

- Establish a study group on leadership or group facilitation.
- Arrange for them to attend workshops, conferences, or courses (in person or online) focused on leadership skills.
- Invite formal teacher leaders to "shadow" principals through a variety of interactions and, in turn, have principals "shadow" teacher leaders to provide feedback and clarify expectations.
- Encourage the district to establish system-wide networking groups for teacher leaders.
- Debrief difficult experiences with teacher leaders to discuss alternative approaches.
- Be open about your own learning about leadership.
- Build an electronic library of tutorials on leadership skills via DVDs, YouTube, websites, webinars, networks, TED, etc.

Principals must observe how the teacher leader interacts with others and find ways to help build skills for leading decision-making, professional learning, and continuous improvement.

## Teacher Leader Skills for Decision-Making

Most principals complete a graduate degree or certification program in order to be licensed/certified as an administrator. Teacher leaders need skills included in these preparation programs, but may not have been exposed to them. No assumptions should be made about individuals' proficiency in these skills or their ability to use them in settings outside classrooms. Principals can coach teacher leaders on how to work with others in decision-making. For example, when a project requires a far-reaching decision, the principal can advise the teacher leader to consult with those who will be affected by the decision rather than deciding alone or with just a few close colleagues. Openness when working with others builds relational trust, for both principals and teacher leaders. Principals will need to be staff developer and mentor in order to help teacher leaders learn these new skills. In fact, principals may discover they too need to develop or fine-tune some of these skills.

In this section, we describe three categories of skills needed for decision-making: 1) meeting leadership, 2) problem solving, and 3) consensus building.

### *Meeting Leadership*

Schools are replete with groups and meetings. Much of the operational and developmental work in schools is done this way. Teacher leaders have increased responsibility for organizing and conducting meetings with a variety of colleagues. According to Heathfield (2016) at TheBalance.com:

> The meeting leader is the employee [in this case, the teacher leader] who is responsible for planning, organizing, managing the details about, and inviting the participants to a meeting. He or she is the employee who is in charge of and responsible for the progress of the actual meeting.
>
> (para. 1)

Principals can help teacher leaders become aware of actions before, during, and after a meeting to increase the effectiveness of the group's work. Meetings are no longer limited to on-site, face-to-face, gather-in-the-same-room events. With technology have come possibilities for meetings with individuals and groups in remote locations. The following information applies specifically to traditional on-site meetings. However, we have inserted text that references technology when appropriate and have located a number of websites for additional information regarding online meeting protocols (see eResources for Chapter 7).

#### Meeting Preparations
1. *Determine whether a meeting is even necessary.* Many people claim at least half or more of the meetings they attend are not necessary and much of what was done or shared could have been done as well or better through other means such as memos, e-mail or e-meetings, telephone calls, or individual visits. So the first meetings leadership skill is a solid understanding of when a meeting is best or if other options are better. Current technology can be a real asset here in soliciting feedback on the need to meet.

2. *Decide the size of the group.* If the intent of the meeting is to have conversation, smaller groups are more likely to meet that purpose whether online or in person. The more people in the group, the less time there is for each person to contribute. Adding individuals to the group can provide benefits by increasing the number of perspectives; on the other hand, it may be less positive because of the decrease in time for each person to talk. So, careful consideration should be given to "how many is too many." Again, technology can help here; if a particular part of the meeting agenda needs involvement from someone outside the smaller group, that individual can be invited to be with the group electronically for only that portion of the meeting.

3. *Determine who should attend the meeting.* Perhaps the complaints about meetings are from people who were asked to attend meetings where they were not really needed. Determining who should be involved in a decision is important for many reasons, not the least of which is the productive use of time. (We offered some help on how to make these determinations in Chapter 5.)

4. *Secure an appropriate environment for the meeting.* Everything from the amount of space available, ventilation quality, adequacy of light sources, room temperature, comfort of the furniture, and noise level can influence the actions of meeting participants. Even with limited space in schools, every effort should be made to optimize comfort for meeting participants. The principal and teacher leader can walk through the building to identify available spaces and discuss the merits of each. Teacher leaders should know the procedures for scheduling meeting spaces; this will avoid the negative impact of scheduling conflicts for the same space and time. Securing an appropriate environment also has relevance to meetings via technology. The environment surrounding each participant will influence the quality of interactions with others—lighting, distractions, equipment for speaking to and hearing others, etc.

5. *Circulate a draft agenda and request additional agenda items.* Having the agenda in advance of the meeting helps individuals focus their thoughts, gather input from colleagues, offer additional items, and know what their responsibilities will be. With today's electronics this task is easily accomplished and should be done whether the meeting is on site or online. There are many ways to structure a meeting agenda. For example:

   - Assign estimated time allotments to each item.
   - Indicate the individual responsible for leading the work on each item.
   - Group items so that priority items are dealt with first.
   - List topics with annotation and objectives.

   Timing for distributing the agenda is also important. Distributing too early may result in it being forgotten or misplaced, whereas sending it too late will create confusion and limited time for individuals to prepare.

Receiving the draft agenda 5 to 7 days prior to the meeting usually allows group members time to offer suggestions for revisions and to prepare any needed materials.

6. *Prepare meeting room with materials needed before members arrive.* Attention to small details is a sign of caring about the attendees and is ultimately a time saver. These details might include:

   ♦ A sign saying, "Welcome to the Meeting of the____"
   ♦ Name cards (for online meetings, too)
   ♦ All materials at each participant's seat (pens, pencils, tablets, etc.)
   ♦ Markers for use on chart paper or a dry erase board
   ♦ Refreshments, even if only cool water

Preparing the room and materials is also essential for electronic meetings. Checking equipment at each participant's location is crucial to meeting success and making sure that materials have been sent to each participant prior to the start of the meeting are among the necessary preparations for electronic meetings.

### During the Meeting

1. *Create group norms for working together.* At the first group meeting, norms should be developed and then revisited and affirmed periodically as the group's work progresses. This recommendation serves well for both on-site and online meetings. Group norms are those agreed upon expectations for the behavior of the group members in their work together. Examples of group norms include "be on time," "phones off," and "no side conversations." Ideas should be generated by the group members themselves, edited, and finally agreed upon. The norms should be posted (in the room or online) at every meeting, referred to when needed to redirect behavior, and reaffirmed and edited periodically to assure their relevance for the group's work.

2. *Identify group member roles.* Specific roles facilitate the efficiency and productivity of a meeting. Among the most common roles are group leader, recorder (who records ideas and captures the minutes), and timekeeper.

3. *Formally bring the meeting to closure.* Even if the entire agenda is not covered, the discussion must finish at the designated ending time. This will avoid stopping in the middle of an important discussion or, perhaps even worse, losing first one member and then another as other obligations require them to leave. The meeting leader needs to monitor time and allow for closure to review the following:

   ♦ What was accomplished?
   ♦ What was agreed upon, such as who is to complete tasks, within what timeline, between this meeting and the next meeting?
   ♦ How well did the process go relative to group norms, the agenda structure, or role responsibilities?

*After the Meeting*

1. *Distribute minutes.* All members of the group as well as those who may be affected by decisions, such as the principal, another grade team, or others, should receive a copy of the minutes in either hardcopy, electronic version, or both. Keeping a file (electronic and/or hardcopy) of the minutes from the group is a good idea. With electronic storage options available, this is more possible today than ever before. Maintaining these records helps preserve the history of the school's story.

2. *Monitor steps agreed upon.* Based on the tasks and timelines agreed upon during the meeting, the teacher leader should make follow-up contact with group members who have responsibilities for actions between meetings. This will help determine their progress and provide support if needed. Again, with technology, this is much easier than ever before in terms of time, energy, and travel.

## *Problem Solving*

Closely related to meeting-leadership skills are skills in problem solving. Many groups are formed with the purpose of dealing with a problem or situation of concern. Teacher leaders usually have excellent problem-solving skills regarding issues in their classrooms, so some of these skills will transfer to their work with adults; others will need to be developed.

In 1997, Ubben and Hughes (1997) claimed that "something is a problem when there is a difference between what is currently occurring (the real situation) and what would desirably be happening (ideal situation)" (p. 30). Teacher leaders need skills in problem solving to achieve the ideal for student learning, program implementation, and policy development. More recently, Ubben, Hughes, and Norris (2016) added the following six considerations to bear in mind when guiding group behavior in the area of problem solving:

- Decide if the task force is to be advisory in nature. Are decisions to be suggestion only, or is the group to be charged with coming up with final decisions?
- Cooperatively set a realistic time line.
- Establish a tentative budget for the project phases.
- Review any district-wide policies or state laws that might impinge on the nature of any resolution scheme.
- Establish the "essential conditions" that any decision must fit in order to be acceptable.
- Set up regular interaction sessions about progress and findings. (p. 59)

It is helpful for teacher leaders to understand the commonly recommended steps in problem solving. They include:

- *Define the problem.* Be sure there is clarity regarding the issue to be addressed, because "there are few things as useless—if not as dangerous—as the right answer to the wrong question" (Drucker, 1966, p. 353). Time spent making sure everyone involved in the decision understands the problem will ultimately save time. Too often needless energy is spent working on a symptom rather than the problem. Use tools to help identify the problem—decision-making matrix, communication matrix, and scorecard to measure benchmarks.

- *Establish selection criteria.* The selection criteria should be developed before any discussion of possible actions begins, preferably immediately after clarifying the problem. By creating the criteria *before* the generation of alternatives, the criteria will be more objective.

- *Analyze the problem.* In the analysis phase, information is gathered about the situation. Everyone in the group should assist in gathering the information and then hold a discussion to share this information so that members of the group are well informed.

- *Develop alternative solutions.* Once the problem has been clearly defined and the analysis completed, group members can begin to generate possible solutions. Strategies such as brainstorming and nominal group technique should be used to generate solutions; however, the meeting leader must ensure that members are not evaluating or discussing alternatives during this phase, only generating them.

- *Determine the best solution.* This step of the process requires that the selected criteria be applied to each of the alternative solutions generated so that each can either be retained for further consideration or discarded if it does not meet the selected criteria or cannot be modified to meet them.

- *Assess alternative solutions.* Next, all alternative solutions that meet the criteria must then be assessed for the positive and negative consequences of their implementation and their likely outcome. This work requires group members to engage in systems thinking in order to produce information that will help the group either select a "best" solution or reject all choices and start over.

- *Implement the solution selected.* Once the solution that appears to have the highest impact and most positive value for the organization is selected, the appropriate actions to implement the selected solution must be taken. This might include changes in resource allocations or new behaviors for staff members and students.

- *Evaluate the results.* Important, but often forgotten is the evaluation of both processes and results. To continue to improve the quality of the problem-solving process, as well as the quality of decisions, time should be taken to evaluate whether or not the solutions achieved what was intended. Evaluation data may include attitude surveys from staff, students, and/or parents; discipline referrals; student achievement data; or accident reports. These data should relate directly to the comparison of the reality of the situation to the ideal sought. Changes in the process or the approach to the problem should be made based on these results.

Even though the decision maker(s) determined the solution to be "best," others will need to be convinced of that before implementation begins. For full implementation of identified solutions to occur, there must be advocacy—or at least acceptance—of the recommendations made. When solutions are selected because of law, policy, or safety issues, failure to implement is not an option. However, when the solution is one selected from among several alternatives, agreement by everyone involved must be secured prior to initiation. Teacher leaders should seek consensus from these individuals. Consensus building is another important leadership skill.

## *Consensus Building*

There are three ways to reach a group decision: consensus, compromise, or vote. Consensus occurs when "all members agree to accept a particular solution even though it may not have been their original choice" (Hamilton, with Parker, 2001, p. 303). Compromise results when everyone involved has to give up something to enable agreement in the group. Everyone loses something but still gets at least a portion of what they wanted. Voting is used when neither of the other strategies is attainable. Deciding based on a simple majority can leave many people feeling left out or unhappy about the decision. Majority rule is really a political governance process, not a participative decision-making process (Owens, 2001). Voting should be used rarely and only as a last resort.

Consensus building is a participative decision-making process that allows all members a right to be heard. After an open and complete discussion, the group identifies a decision. "If everyone can say, in effect, 'I don't agree with every detail but accept the broad thrust of the decision,' then a consensus has been achieved" (Smith, 2004, p. 119).

We caution principals and teacher leaders that while consensus may be the best process for decision-making, it requires trust before it can be fully implemented. However, even at the early stages of a group's work, the process should be the closest approximation to the ideal as possible. Building consensus takes longer than voting or making a decision unilaterally. Time is needed to make sure that all participants are heard and feel comfortable enough to share concerns openly. The increased time needed for consensus should be recognized from the beginning of the decision-making or problem-solving process; if this is unacceptable, another process should be used. Smith (2004) identified two advantages of consensus in decision-making. First, the decision made is likely to be better than any achieved by the other means because the group must fully explore every option as a part of the consensus-building process. Additionally, when consensus is achieved, the members of the group generally feel more committed to the selected solutions.

## **Teacher Leader Skills to Lead Professional Learning**

Teacher leaders emerge as job-embedded professional learning (individual and collective) spreads across the school. Although teacher leaders will be co-learners with other teachers, there also will be opportunities for them to provide leadership for professional learning. Too often teacher leaders are asked to teach other teachers without the support and resources needed to be effective. This is based on the assumption that an outstanding teacher of students will be a good teacher of teachers. Certainly, quality professional development should mirror the constructivist teaching that is occurring in classrooms. Yet, when teachers take on the role of staff developer or coach, they often forget these skills and revert to models they have seen in their own educational experience. Principals can provide teachers with opportunities to build their skills in at least three areas: professional learning design, presentation skills, and coaching.

## *Professional Learning Design Skills*

Teachers may know their previous professional learning experiences were inadequate, and may even be able to recognize why. Nevertheless, designing a substantive professional learning experience for other teachers requires skills beyond what many teacher leaders have. Without these skills they revert to the traditional workshop design they know. Principals may also lack the skills to design professional learning activities; if so, the task is to connect teacher leaders with resources to help them.

Listed below are a few strategies for principals to consider:

- Provide resources for teachers to attend regional or national conferences (on site or electronic) focused on professional learning.
- Invite expert instructional designers from regional service agencies, central office, or other organizations to coach teacher leaders.
- Link with school-reform efforts where teacher leaders participate in and are taught how to design collaborative learning, such as examination of student work.
- Form teacher leader teams to learn, facilitate, and debrief their experiences in designing and delivering professional learning.

## **From the Field**

Schools need the ability to be innovative and flexible in supporting their students.... If necessity is the mother of invention (or innovation), then we have to look at our students' needs for the incentive to innovate. Again, the people most closely connected to these needs are the teachers.

Jeff Austin
Economics and Government Coordinator and Design Team
Member for Social Justice Humanitas Academy
Los Angeles, CA

## *Presentation Skills*

Teacher leaders are perhaps the best resource for delivering professional learning activities. At times bringing in an external expert who can help teachers learn specific knowledge and skills is appropriate, but in most situations, principals can depend on internal teacher leaders. However, few things feel more risky for teacher leaders than presenting to their colleagues. Principals may need to encourage teacher leaders to present and nurture them as they ease into this stressful territory.

The focus of teacher-led professional learning can range in complexity from a single information-sharing session to complex skill development. Such activities are only one component of the professional learning. Most of these sessions are "just in time," or planned quickly, when the need arises.

The principal's roles in helping teachers design quality presentations for their peers involve:

- Modeling quality presentations through professional learning activities facilitated by the principal
- Offering teachers the opportunity to learn from other teachers who have a reputation for skillful presentations
- Inviting teachers to participate in local, state, and national organizations that address professional learning
- Meeting with the teacher leaders before professional learning events to ensure they have needed resources
- Debriefing with the teacher leaders after the presentations to discuss what went well and what to do differently the next time

There are few resources as valuable as teacher leaders who share their knowledge and skills with their peers. When a person who has successfully used a teaching strategy talks with other teachers, they listen.

## *Coaching*

Increasingly, school systems are establishing formal teacher leader roles that include an expectation for coaching other teachers. Whether focused on a school reform effort or a subject area, these teacher leaders are school based or move from school to school depending on the design of the coaching program. They bring their expertise to other teachers in a variety of venues.

Although teacher leaders have expertise in their area of focus, they may lack the skills to coach other teachers. They quickly learn how difficult it is to move into other teachers' classrooms. If giving feedback to other teachers is an expectation, then many of these "coaches" must learn skills that will help them build trust and allow them to move beyond the perception by other teachers that their feedback is evaluative.

Teacher leaders who take on the role of coach can be excellent support for principals who establish teaching and learning as their top priority. Teacher leaders can provide job-embedded professional development that can be difficult, if not impossible, for an administrator to do. Strategies principals can use to support these teacher leaders include the following:

- Encourage networking with coaches at the local, regional, state, or national level.
- Provide opportunities for professional learning experiences (on site or electronically) to address needed coaching skills.
- Be a coach to the teacher leader by modeling listening and questioning skills.
- Help teacher leader coaches understand when to support and when to push teachers to move instructional practice forward.

## *Writing for Reflecting and for Sharing*

Teacher leaders often find that writing about their practice helps them to reflect on what is happening with their students and how they may change their teaching to better meet students' needs. Their writing can be private, such as through a journal, or more public, through blogs or formal publications. Encouraging teacher leaders to expand the audience for their writing can help increase their influence. With today's technology, publishing goes beyond the printed page. Numerous blogs, network discussions, and other online publications are readily available for expression.

Writing for publication (paper or electronic) may seem overwhelming, but there are strategies principals can use to support this effort:

- Encourage teacher leaders to begin their writing through private reflections via journaling.

- Link teacher leaders with websites, networks, bloggers, local university or college teachers, and others who have similar interests. Many individuals in higher education are anxious to be published or operate blogs or networks and look for practitioners who can provide school-based perspectives to enrich their work.

- Provide time for a team of teachers to write collaboratively in a common area of interest. This would be a great beginning for a blogging situation—independent or as contributors to existing sites.

- Share journal articles, blog entries, news editorials, opinion pieces, and the like that are similar to the type teacher leaders might write.

- Ensure that teacher leaders have access to a variety of databases to provide professional literature to support their writing.

## *Advocacy Skills*

There are few educational advocates who are taken as seriously by policymakers as teacher leaders. Unfortunately, teacher leaders often do not see their role as reaching beyond the school to influence policy. Teacher leaders can be encouraged to advocate for what they know is best for students.

Helping teachers learn how to advocate effectively is worth the principal's time. Caution is needed to avoid promoting actions that go against the school system's goals, thereby provoking animosity from principals' supervisors. This is especially important in today's Twitter-, Facebook-, Instagram-reactionary world. Strategies to help with advocacy skills may include:

- Solicit opportunities for teacher leaders to represent the school on system-wide task groups.

- Invite teacher leaders to attend school board meetings with the principal.

- Engage teacher leaders in conversations with senior-level administrators and/or policymakers.

- Provide assistance for effectively communicating with legislators about issues of concern.
- Link teacher leaders' advocacy interests with their efforts in writing via blogging, networking, journal publications, etc.

## Summary

Previously, principals who did not understand the potential for teacher leadership simply delegated responsibilities and expected teachers to follow through. In this chapter, we place the responsibility for the success of teacher leaders primarily with the principal; this demands purposeful attention to the needs of these teachers. First, principals must recognize the powerful potential of teacher leadership in both informal and formal roles. Additionally, they must build relationships with teacher leaders through ongoing support for their unique roles. Finally, principals must be deliberate in providing the knowledge and skills teacher leaders need to be effective in their roles.

Over time, the phenomenon of teacher leadership will lose its newness, especially if the principal and teacher leaders work to build relationships, distribute power and authority, and align teacher leadership with professional learning. At first, these efforts take a large amount of the principal's time and energy, but as teacher leaders take on more responsibilities, the tasks become less overwhelming for both the teacher leaders and the principal. Simultaneously, an intentional plan to sustain teacher leadership over time despite any leadership changes and teacher turnover should be developed. Actions that can be taken to sustain teacher leadership are the focus of Chapter 8.

## Resources

7.1 Brock, B. L., & Grady, M. L. (2002). *Avoiding burnout: A principal's guide to keeping the fire alive.* Thousand Oaks, CA: Corwin—Although this book was written for principals, the strategies suggested are helpful for teacher leaders seeking to find balance in their lives.

7.2 ManagementHelp.org—One of many websites offering information on conducting meetings. This particular website reinforces much of the information provided in this chapter from selecting the participants to closing the meeting. Additional information on the types of groups and meeting evaluations are also included. Retrieved from http://managementhelp.org/misc/meeting-management.htm

7.3 CreatingMinds.org—This website gives specific directions on how to effectively facilitate brainstorming and brainwriting, as well as other group process strategies. Retrieved from http://creatingminds.org/tools/brainstorming.htm

7.4 University of Wisconsin–Extension Program Development and Evaluation—This section of the website would be worth checking when designing programs and the evaluation of those programs. The website has many other sections on a variety of topic of interest to educators. Retrieved from http://fyi.uwex.edu/programdevelopment

7.5 Christensen, C., Aaron, S., & Clark, W. (2005). Can schools improve? *Phi Delta Kappan, 86*(7), 545–550—A grid titled "Degrees of Consensus and Tools to Create Agreement" helps readers select the appropriate tool to create agreement in various situations.

7.6 Kushner, M. (2004). *Successful presentations for dummies.* Forest City, CA: IDG Books—Information on such important issues as establishing credibility, using multimedia techniques, organizing presentations, getting the room right, handling questions, and the 10 biggest mistakes presenters make. This is only one of several of the "Dummies" series that might be helpful for teacher leaders; the books on public speaking and effective communication would also be worth looking into.

7.7 Neufeld, B., & Roper, D. (2003). *Coaching: A strategy for developing instruction capacity.* Washington, D.C.: The Aspen Institute Program on Education and The Annenberg Institute for School Reform—A 46-page guide to prepare coaches for instructional leadership. Retrieved from www.annenberginstitute.org/sites/default/files/product/268/files/Coaching.pdf

7.8 Center for Teaching Quality—This is a wonderful website for many reasons. Numerous resources are available here, excellent blogs by educators and an opportunity to join a community of educators on a variety of subjects. This would be a good place for teachers to begin sharing their reflections in a more public setting. Retrieved from www.teachingquality.org/

7.9 The Mentoring Leadership & Resource Network (MLRN)—Website designed to assist mentors of new teachers. Retrieved from www.mentors.net

# 8 Sustaining Teacher Leading and Learning

"Without substantial participation by practitioners in the design and adoption of reforms, most plans for improvements in teaching and learning—and the effects of those plans on what occurs in classrooms—will fall apart."

Larry Cuban in *The Blackboard and The Bottom Line*

"[T]here is one absolutely necessary, if not sufficient, condition for reform to work—the substantial broadening of teacher leadership until it embodies the majority of teachers in a given school, a given district, a given state, a given profession."

Michael G. Fullan in *Broadening the Concept of Teacher Leadership*

The extent and quality of teacher leadership comes and goes depending on the teachers, the current principal, and the demands of the school system. The only factor principals can control is their own leadership behavior; however, most principals hope that if they leave the school, the work they started will continue. Most leaders want to leave a tangible legacy from their work, and rather than depending on "hope," effective principals take actions to sustain teacher leadership and, in turn, school improvement efforts, long after their departure.

In this chapter, we return to Markham Middle School as Jay is beginning his last few years before retirement. He has served for 12 years as the school's principal; he wants to work 3 more years and then retire. His focus during these next 3 years will be to assess what has been done and what still needs to be done to sustain the positive changes made during the first 12. The material offered in this chapter attempts to reveal the processes Jay reviewed as well as describe his thinking and planning for the future. Sustainability is his focus; some wonderful work for student learning has been accomplished at MMS and Jay does not want any of this to be lost.

We will see how teacher leadership has evolved in the years since our first visit to MMS in Chapter 2. The entire MMS story serves to identify the intentional actions that Jay and the teachers took to ensure teacher leading and learning is sustained. In addition, there were disruptors that might have caused the school to stray from its intended purposes. We use the most common ones as organizers to offer a few strategies to minimize negative effects of these disruptors and lead to a self-sustaining system. We also use Theresa's work in her new position as an example of Jay's forward thinking about sustainability through a process of leadership succession. Finally, we offer a few words from both Jay and Theresa as encouragement to current principals, aspiring principals and teacher leaders in their work to promote, build, and sustain teacher leading and learning.

## Markham Middle School Revisited

With retirement approaching in 3 years, Jay walks through the hallways of Markham Middle School (MMS) and remembers the first day of school after his appointment as principal. There were the typical classrooms with bulletin boards and teachers who greeted the students and other teachers in congenial ways. Identifying anything wrong from a cursory walk through was difficult, but Jay knew MMS was not a professional learning community and that the assessment of student learning reflected a lack of teacher leading and learning. Now, as Jay walks around the school knowing his time as MMS principal is coming to an end, he decides his major purpose during these last years will be securing the school's improvement trajectory for the future. Sustainability is the next and final step.

He has spent many hours reflecting on the various relationships between and among staff members. Their collaboration now generates a sense of professionalism and enthusiasm based on teachers working together in order to improve student learning. During the summer before Jay began his work at MMS, he wrote a personal vision statement setting this level of collaboration as his goal. As a leader, Jay knew he needed to have clarity about his own vision before he could authentically work with others in developing a vision for themselves and the organization. Jay knows that when he cleans out his top desk drawer on the last day at this school, he will find his personal vision statement, written and rewritten over the years. The same has been true for the vision for the school; meeting minutes chronicle the transmutations of this statement and the changing culture at MMS. Both visions have driven Jay's efforts to push the MMS staff toward increasingly high expectations for all students.

During Jay's 12 years at MMS, building a strong foundation for teacher leadership has been a major achievement. Although Jay's vision for a professional learning community was the structure for teacher collaboration, he had a purpose greater than merely bringing teachers together. He saw this structure as a tool for relentlessly pushing for improved pedagogy across all grade levels. And he believed the structure gave teachers an opportunity to learn from and communicate with each other in ways that empowered all staff to lead by example and not by position. Jay saw his responsibility as providing assistance and resources with the expectations that teachers would lead and learn. With his time at MMS growing short, he needs and wants to spend some time thinking deeply about the pathways available and those that can be created to build on the good work attained thus far.

Over the 12 years, the differences in instructional approaches in response to the changing student population are easily recognized by anyone with a long-term connection to the school. Each new school year, Jay and the school's teacher leaders collaboratively designed a retreat for the entire staff. It was during this time they revisited the school's shared vision for student learning. The retreat setting allowed staff to work together in identifying gaps in student learning; everyone spent time analyzing assessment data, examining current teaching strategies, and recommending future teacher learning and related instructional practices. Also, the annual retreat encouraged staff to reexamine the culture and climate at MMS. Thus, student and organizational data drive decisions about the use of resources and the most effective campus-embedded professional learning; and strategic teaching assignments that put the needs of students first are addressed.

Teachers have learned to work collaboratively in various groups to tap their strengths. For example, Jaime, who still teaches eighth grade, continues to lead a group of Language Arts teachers representing each grade level. This group works to address standards and align curriculum, instruction, and assessment throughout the school. Other groups of teachers work on this same task for different content areas. Theresa was originally a member of one of these groups; now, as Dean of Instruction, she works with every existing group and is constantly listening, observing, and assessing the need for new ad hoc or continuing groups based on both teacher and student needs.

Jay has worked hard to minimize the administrative tasks required of Theresa in order to keep her focused on instruction. This has also helped teachers view Theresa not as an administrator, but as a mentor/coach/facilitator—someone who still "works in the trenches." In addition to her work with individual teachers, specialized faculty, and teacher leaders, she serves as a member of the leadership team.

The leadership team has evolved from a typical site-based decision-making body to an instructional leadership team, and now functions as a professional learning community. The teacher leaders who serve on this team are considered competent, credible, and approachable by other teachers, so they have not only the power to make decisions, but also the ability to influence the implementation of those decisions. More importantly, the team believes in shared and supportive leadership. Membership terms on the leadership team are structured so that new members come on each year to replace those veteran members who are rotating off. Members of this team have emerged as stronger leaders as a result of having been provided professional time to learn and implement successful teaching strategies and then coach other teachers to gain and apply these skills. Jay wants to be sure that over the next three years, he does everything possible to ensure the leadership team continues to function as a true representation of teachers learning together and sharing leadership at MMS. The structure of the team has provided a level of fluidity for encouraging and supporting teacher leadership; the school would suffer a major setback if the team was eliminated or diminished in any way. Teacher leadership is now embedded in the school culture at MMS.

Several years ago, Jay reconfigured the formal leadership team (with approval from central office leaders, of course). Instead of two assistant principals, Jay enlisted the help of a teacher leader who was respected by the students to take over the role of handling student discipline. Then he recruited Yolanda, the lead teacher, to take the role of curriculum assistant principal. In this position, Yolanda became the chief executive for teaching and learning. At that time, Yolanda collaborated with Theresa, who then served as a lead teacher, and Leticia, a part-time lead teacher and member of the leadership team, to ensure that the school's vision for student learning was achieved. Additionally, Yolanda, Theresa, and Leticia formed a three-member teaching team responsible for three classes each day. Jay remained as a member of the leadership team and often attended and participated in professional learning activities, but he delegated the instructional leadership to Yolanda and the other teacher leaders. Over time, Jay was able to establish Yolanda's presence as the same as his; teachers knew that if Yolanda attended professional learning activities with them, it had Jay's endorsement.

The school district formalized the instructional leadership position in each of the middle schools, calling it Dean of Instruction. Theresa is in her first year as Dean of Instruction at MMS. Yolanda has gone on to a specialty position at central office. She has been a wonderful mentor to Theresa this first year. Jay has provided support, but having Yolanda's guidance and support has been invaluable to Theresa's success. Again, as Jay contemplates the future, he acknowledges the need to determine what actions he and others should take to assure this level of supportive and welcomed leadership succession continues after his retirement.

The progress in MMS has not been without conflict. As teachers examined their practice compared to student achievement data, there were often intense conversations about how best to deliver more effective instruction. Although teacher individuality was encouraged, Jay remembers the challenge of remaining firm about the expectations for collaboration, especially when teachers wanted to revert to the old way of working, such as returning to their classrooms to avoid conflict. Jay continually facilitated the discussions and decision-making in ways that brought the focus back on the shared vision for student learning. This took courage and he suffered disappointments, but with perseverance, teachers finally began to see how working together could make a difference for both the students and themselves. A few teachers were never comfortable with their instructional practices being publicly examined, so they left the school. New teachers and the teachers who remained worked through tough discussions and learned to collaborate, and as a result, saw significant student growth. This new culture of collaboration must be continued, but will need continuous nurturing. Jay makes a mental note to bring this up at future leadership meetings. He has a couple of ideas, but knows that thinking with the leadership group will bring more, and better, ideas to the round table at MMS.

Professional learning is now campus embedded, which allows teachers to learn while they are using new strategies. Yolanda, Theresa, Leticia, and other teacher leaders presented numerous workshops, modeled lessons in classrooms, and facilitated team meetings. They continue to frequently be invited to provide feedback while observing other teachers even though they hold different positions across the campus and district. Breaking the norm of closed and isolated classrooms was one of the most difficult challenges for Jay and the teachers. At first, there were few teachers who purposefully learned from other teachers, but currently there are structures in place to provide resources and recognition for all teachers who learn from each other and transfer the new practices to their classrooms. This seems to have become second nature to nearly everyone at MMS. Sometimes when things become second nature, we forget how they came to be. We also make the assumptions that this is the way it will always be and do not take the actions necessary to maintain this way of doing things. Jay wanted to be sure this did not happen at MMS.

Teacher leaders no longer see the role of the principal as a job they do not want to pursue. In fact, several teacher leaders from MMS have moved on to principalships in other schools within the system. These new principals are using the same model Jay used at MMS, with their own twists, of course. At central office meetings, Jay often chuckles to himself about how many new principals and central office leaders came from MMS. Now, when conversations are held at the central office principals' meetings, there is a focus on student learning rather than only the typical administrative responsibilities. Recently, the current associate superintendent asked Jay to lead a study group for principals focused on a new state mandate in reading; there was little hesitation from the principals to participate. A critical mass of principals with a new view of leading is growing within the school system. Jay sees this as among his greatest accomplishments; he recalls a quote he read from Michael Fullan some years ago (2007):

> The main mark of an effective leader at the end of his or her tenure is not so much his impact on the bottom line (of profits or student achievement), but rather how many good leaders he or she leaves behind who can go even further.
>
> (p. 98)

Jay is not waiting until his last year at MMS to plan for sustaining teacher leading and learning. When he came to MMS, he started building relationships with external audiences, such as parents, central office leaders, and members of the teachers' organization. There has been turnover of superintendents and other senior-level leaders over the years, but Jay continues to build relationships with the new leaders and share his vision with them. He has repeatedly communicated the importance of sustaining effective school change. Working first with Yolanda and now Theresa to guide them in developing skills to work with and build trust with their colleagues has been one strategy Jay has used in sustaining this teacher leading and learning culture. It won't be long until the search for the next principal will begin. Certainly, central office and ultimately the school board will have the final say, but it might be appropriate to initiate some conversations with faculty, staff, and community regarding the type of leader they believe is needed based on this school's emergence as a maturing professional learning community. Given that the current superintendent has developed plans to pilot a process where there will be parent and teacher representatives from the school on the principal selection committee, it probably would be good to get people focused on the future.

Yolanda and others who have moved on to other positions built the capacity for continued teacher leadership during their time at MMS and are now doing the same in their new work situations. Team leaders, lead teachers, and other teachers identify and provide opportunities for potential leaders starting as early as a new teacher's first year. Their vision is to see the school in a continuous cycle of improvement, no matter who the leaders are. There are no guarantees of success, but Jay and other leaders at MMS are being intentional in their leadership rather than depending on chance to achieve their goal.

Figure 8.1. **Evolution of Teacher Leadership and Learning at MMS**

## Jay's Intentional Leadership: Connecting to the Framework for Intentional Leadership

From the start, Jay's purposeful actions to bring teachers together for leading and learning contributed to his plan for leadership succession at MMS. He used specific strategies to build positive relationships, distribute power and authority, and align teacher leadership with teacher learning. Jay also paid attention to the level of support provided for teacher leaders. Throughout these 12 years, Jay has focused on creating the current culture in which a high level of leadership density exists at MMS. Along the way, Jay was also sensitive to the need for preparing the system for the school's self-perpetuation. In this section, we pull strategies from the MMS story and add some strategies Jay and MMS teacher leaders can consider for long-term sustainability.

### Building Relationships

When Jay was assigned to MMS, he knew there were both positive and negative social networks, so he took time to assess existing and potential knowledge, skill, and relationship resources in order to increase both human and social capital. Here are strategies he used:

- Encouraged positive teacher-with-teacher relationships by establishing structures that tapped into existing healthy social networks and available teacher resources
- Invited teams of teachers to participate in external professional learning experiences

- Established teaching schedules based on student needs and linked to existing or potential teacher social networks
- Used traditional meetings, such as faculty meetings, for teacher dialogue and learning
- Set aside his time to learn with the teachers as often as possible
- Matched individual teacher interests with organizational needs and opportunities
- Attended teacher meetings to keep informed and encourage cross-communications
- Followed through on commitments to teachers
- Provided appropriate public and private recognition of teacher leaders
- Learned with the teachers how to better manage conflict
- Encouraged teachers who sought new challenges both within and outside the school
- Developed and nurtured relationships with external audiences such as parents, central office personnel, and leaders of the teachers' organization

Because relationships are crucial to the success of an organization, strategies to ensure that trusting, positive relationships are built and sustained at MMS are needed. As personnel changes occur over time, relationships and the dynamics among them change as well; no assumptions can or should be made. Building and maintaining relationships with organizational colleagues should be considered a constant work in progress; this job is never complete. Knowing this, Jay, along with others at MMS, needs to find ways to continue the strategies they have been using and consider others such as:

- Build a strong mentoring and coaching program for new teachers and veteran teachers new to the school.
- Structure candidate interviews for faculty and formal leadership positions that involve representatives from across the school in a range of both formal and informal settings.
- Give careful consideration to applicants' résumés to determine special interests and/or talents that might match well with current or future MMS projects.
- Maintain and sustain communities of practice (COP) to continue the dialogue and build relational trust across the campus.
- Codify school and team structures in written form and have the document(s) (electronic or hardcopy) reviewed and ratified annually by faculty.

## Distributing Power and Authority

In Jay's previous experience as a principal in other schools, he learned retaining control of power and authority only resulted in limited benefits to the school.

He came to realize he could actually increase power and authority throughout the school by distributing it to others. These are strategies Jay used to distribute power and authority when he came to MMS:

- Wrote and revisited his personal vision statement describing his goals for achieving improved student learning through teacher leading and learning
- Worked with faculty and staff to develop a shared vision for student learning
- Maintained control of decision-making authority upon arrival at the school, but gradually distributed this to the leadership team, and then to other teacher leaders
- Established parameters for decision-making authority
- Restructured and refocused the leadership team to become an instructional leadership team
- Made certain that delegated leadership responsibilities were supported with resources and monitored for accountability
- Created structures and operational procedures that assured governance, managerial, instructional, and other leadership opportunities were open to all teachers
- Set up structures to empower existing staff in selecting and inducting new staff
- Ensured teaching and student placements were driven by student data
- Obtained permission to restructure the traditional administrative roles so teacher leaders had power and authority to focus on student learning and classroom instruction

As Jay looks to the time when he will no longer be at MMS, he knows the importance of finding ways to sustain distributed power and authority. Some of these might be:

- Meet with central office supervisors annually to reaffirm the power and authority philosophy and structure operating in the school. Having the understanding and empowerment of supervisors can provide a powerful context of support for continuation.
- Conduct school orientation meetings and workshops with individuals new to the school. This can be done at both the school-wide and team/department levels. The purpose can be to explain authority and responsibilities, go over practices in the school, and address questions. Invite teacher leaders to assist with these meetings and in some cases take full responsibility for them.
- Work with central office to arrange for selection of the new principal 1 year prior to Jay's retirement. Encourage the design of a profile specific to the needs of MMS and its sustainability. This allows Jay and his replacement to work for a year in a mentor–mentee relationship in learning about the school, building relationships with faculty and

staff, learning about school operations, and observing some of Jay's unique administrative practices on a daily basis as he or she considers strategies for taking the school to the next level.

## Aligning Teacher Leadership and Teachers' Professional Learning

To improve student learning at MMS, Jay knew the teachers must be involved in substantive, ongoing professional learning. The purpose of building relationships and distributing power and authority was primarily to establish a school culture in which teachers learned continuously. Strategies Jay used to confront and nurture teachers in their learning included:

- Participated with teachers as co-learner and partner
- Supported unique, individual teacher learning, but required the vast majority of professional learning resources be focused on teacher learning to address student learning needs
- Worked with teacher leaders to set up an evaluation plan of professional learning that reflected student outcomes' and teachers' learning needs
- Created job-embedded professional learning with the support of lead teachers and others to work directly with classroom teachers
- Provided resources and held teachers accountable for transferring new instructional strategies to classrooms
- Used student work as a measure of teaching effectiveness
- Made time available for teachers to share personal practice and learn from others
- Accessed a variety of technologies for use in learning for both adults and students at MMS
- Confronted reluctant teacher learners with support, remediation, documentation for dismissal or some combination of these

Looking ahead, Jay must give careful consideration to ways in which the great strides in aligning teacher leadership with teachers' professional development can be sustained. So much has been accomplished in terms of moving from centralized, workshop-only professional development during these last several years. Sustaining and even improving these levels of alignment will not easily be done. Some strategies that could assist in these efforts include:

- Establish a plan for continuous updating of equipment and training with the latest technology.
- Continue to build time into the schedule for teachers and work groups to meet, discuss, plan, and resolve issues via a community of practitioners.
- Establish campus-embedded professional development focused on the specific learning needs of all teachers.

- Work to secure resources for hiring instructional coaches either full or part time to work specifically with helping teachers implement instructional strategies in classrooms.
- Create, implement, and monitor a campus-wide process to measure teacher learning to teacher leader effectiveness.

## Support of Teacher Leaders

As Yolanda and others took on formal leadership roles, Jay knew they would need unique types of support to work effectively with their peers. Strategies he used included:

- Avoided asking teacher leaders to take on administrative duties
- Provided training for and coached teacher leaders in decision-making skills and professional learning skills
- Protected teacher leaders in their relationships with colleagues
- Held teacher leaders accountable for expected outcomes

Two dimensions need to be considered in sustaining the advances made in providing support for teacher leaders at MMS. The first dimension should be strategies focused on updating and renewing the training and skill development of individuals currently serving in formal and informal leadership roles. Unless a conscious effort is made to keep current in acquiring new skills and keeping acquired skills sharp with regular use, most of us tend to regress a bit. So, it will be important to draft a schedule to ensure planned maintenance and updated training for current teacher leaders. The second and perhaps more obvious dimension is the need to induct leaders new to these positions. Certainly a mentoring program is one option for assuring induction. Another might be to identify or create a professional learning opportunity for training and developing basic teacher leadership skills that all new personnel must complete, and that perhaps can be delivered, in many instances, by individuals already in these roles. This strategy would assure not only professional learning but also support continued reculturing of the school as a professional learning community.

# Theresa's Intentional Leadership: Connecting to the Framework for Intentional Leadership

Theresa has more than gotten her feet wet this first year in her new job as Dean of Instruction at MMS! The year has been filled with events ranging from wonderful to not so wonderful. She has to admit that the majority of events are bunched toward the wonderful end of the continuum, but still it seems sometimes the few not-so-wonderful ones overpower her thinking. The good part of that is when things don't go well, her reflection and analysis senses kick into high gear. It is interesting how we bask in our successes, but analyze our mistakes or wrong turns. What a gift that Jay has always been available to help her process the events and learn from them. Theresa couldn't be more thankful for Jay's support over their years together at MMS and especially this year in their new working relationship.

She also is thankful for her colleague Yolanda. As a friend, colleague, and mentor, Yolanda has been a wonderful sounding board for Theresa for many years, but especially this one. Yolanda knows most all of the MMS faculty members and works with many of them through her central office responsibilities. So, Yolanda has provided Theresa with an interesting balance of simultaneous familiarity and distance in their conversations about Theresa's first-year adventures in a formal leadership position.

One of Theresa's big surprises in her new role was the change in her relationships with individuals who had been her teaching colleagues for years. The changes were almost instantaneous. Once-close colleagues seemed more reserved in their interactions with her; in some instances, Theresa saw individuals not avoid her exactly, but they certainly did not seek interactions with her. Following Jay and Yolanda's advice, Theresa took a big, deep breath and purposefully engaged with MMS faculty in every setting available and as much as 24 hours a day allowed. Little by little, interactions became more comfortable and soon faculty members were seeking her out to inform, ask questions, and invite. Without question, Theresa was convinced the initial change was normal and the bounce back was due to the strong relational trust she had built at MMS over the years.

Another surprise for Theresa was the new insights she gained about MMS when she saw all, not just her portion, of the school operations. In her teacher leader work prior to this year, the team functioned well and she worked well with the other team leaders. In her new role, she learned of some less-than-optimal situations in other areas of the school that she had not ever known about before. This was a big change for her; she marveled that had been so naïve about what Jay and some of the other team leaders were working with. Wow! Now these issues were her issues too. Others were looking to her for help. This was new; it was challenging; and, sometimes, it was stressful. Still it was part of the job. Information gathering was the first step in addressing these situations. Theresa needed to know more and she discovered that everyone involved needed to know more too. In a way, her ignorance of the situations let her engage without a lot of assumptions. This turned out to be a wonderful circumstance for everyone. She was able to ask questions, observe, and analyze with a unique level of objectivity. Early on her questions were pretty scattered, but as her experience with gathering information increased, so did her skills as a questioner.

Another "Ah-ha! moment" for Theresa came when she realized "not everyone was like her." In her own work as a teacher, she was anxious to implement the new things she learned. This, she learned, was not true of everyone; some teachers worked to implement new teaching strategies, but most gave up after a try or two, and a few didn't even try! While the learning opportunities were available, the knowledge was not converted to changed actions in all classrooms. Once over the surprise, Theresa set herself a goal of working to change this.

Theresa has worked as MMS Dean of Instruction for only 1 year. However, even during this short time period, she has accomplished a lot and learned a great deal. Using the three principles from the framework, we have identified some strategies Theresa employed in her new formal teacher leadership role.

## Building Relationships

Because of Theresa's work history in the school, she might have taken this area for granted. Fortunately, she followed Jay's advice and her own common sense and implemented some intentional actions to build relationships. Here are strategies she used:

- Placed this effort as a priority in her first weeks and months on the job
- Put people first and paperwork second
- Balanced her interactions in ways that allowed her to be visible school wide and offered appropriate attention to everyone
- Learned the importance of follow-up with promises and requests, taking advantage of technologies to help her with this
- Realized the need to develop new relationships with members of the leadership and administrative teams
- Allowed time for both her colleagues and herself to become comfortable with their relationships within the context of her new position

This first year in the new role was critical for Theresa in establishing new relationships with people, most of whom she had worked with for years. Still, her new role responsibilities required significant changes in her actions and reactions that in turn required similar changes by others. These changes were needed whether with classroom teachers with whom she worked side-by-side or with administrative team members to whom she used to report and is now a peer.

## Distributing Power and Authority

Theresa's experience with distributing power and authority prior to this new role was mostly within her own teaching team. As team leader, she had confidence in her teammates to move forward with the various assignments with which the team was charged. In her new role, she was responsible for empowering and entrusting individuals she knows, but with whom she has not worked closely. This created a level of risk that was new for Theresa. Her intentional actions here were limited this first year; she wanted to solidify a greater degree of relational trust before making many changes for herself or others. Some initial actions she did take included:

- Keeping Jay informed of what she was doing and how things were going.
- Accepting and sometimes even requesting Jay's support in establishing the power and authority of this new role with a variety of individuals and groups. When Jay introduced her, gave an overview of her assignments and then took his leave, Theresa felt and was seen by others as empowered to do the work.
- Recognizing that her power and authority sources were Referent and Expert. Jay's work to introduce her and her new role resulted in others seeing her as associated with Jay and his power and authority. However, Theresa soon discovered that her power associated with Jay would last only so long. Her long-term source of power was her own expertise. As she interacted with others, they came to see her as someone who actually seemed to know what she was doing; as a result, individuals came to admire, respect, and respond to her knowledge and skills, which in turn influenced them to follow her directions and advice.

Another year in the job and Theresa's relational trust levels will be more fully developed. She will have greater trust in herself and her colleagues, as well as they with her. Staying relationally connected and continuing to enhance her knowledge and skills will serve her well in the year to come.

## Aligning Teacher Leadership and Professional Learning

This principle provides so much of the basis for Theresa's work. As Dean of Instruction, her major responsibilities lie with making sure teachers have the knowledge and skills they need to succeed with students in their classrooms. While she did well with this within her own team as team leader, now her perspective must encompass all teachers, subjects, and school-wide issues of curriculum and instruction. This area required numerous intentional leadership actions even in this first year. Theresa was able to use a lot of her knowledge and skills this first year; however, one of the most important results of her work was recognizing how much she still had to learn and what important learning must be provided to MMS teachers if the vision was to be achieved. Some of the actions Theresa took and others she plans to take include:

- Discovered her need for additional professional learning in the areas of working with groups and conflict management. If she was to continue growing as a leader she needed this professional learning to align with her new job responsibilities.

- Identified coaching knowledge and skills as professional learning needed for all teachers as well as herself. Theresa realized coaching would be essential in moving MMS to a more mature PLC. Training is one thing, while implementation is another.

- Asked more questions rather than providing answers. Theresa soon realized that questions help people provide their own answers and solve their own problems. She viewed this learning as a new strategy through which she could help in distributing power and authority to those with whom she worked. She thought it was odd that she knew this as a strategy for working with students to solve problems, but had to learn it again in her new role working with adults!

- Acknowledged that her general knowledge of curriculum and instruction issues was good, but specific knowledge about issues within specific subject areas was less than optimal. She had a lot of learning to do. Among the learning strategies she plans are visiting with and listening to the subject specialists in her own school and district, reading some of the more recent reports from subject matter associations and task forces, visiting websites and blogs hosted by subject matter specialists, and watching for opportunities to attend subject matter workshops with MMS teachers.

## Markham Middle School and Predictable Disruptors

The Markham Middle School story, if not carefully read, can appear to be an ideal creation, set apart from the realities of the world in which the rest of us live.

Not so. MMS experienced the typical external and internal troubles that all schools face—turnover at the system level; teacher attrition; federal, state, and school-system mandates; shifting student and community demographics; and now, an imminent change in the principalship. All schools experience such disruptions at one time or another, temporarily taking time and energy from the normal routine. Sadly, dealing with disruptions has become the focus of many school principals, leaving little time or energy to attend to the school's primary mission—teaching and learning. How is it possible that MMS experienced the same disruptions but was able to minimize the negative impacts and remain focused on the school vision?

We can assume from the MMS story that there were defensive strategies Jay and the teacher leaders used to prevent these disruptors from becoming detractors from the school's mission. These strategies are described below. Jay must share these with key teacher leaders who will be remaining in the school following his departure; additionally, these strategies should be a major component in Jay's mentoring agenda with his replacement. Increasing the awareness of the teacher leaders will embed this knowledge widely in the school providing a foundation for continuation. Alerting the new principal to the ups and downs of the school's development over the long term will broaden this individual's historical perspective of the school.

## Turnover at Central Office and School Board Levels: Lead in Spite of Changes

When there is a change in the superintendency or school board membership, many principals are hesitant to make major decisions until the new formal leadership is in place. Taking time to wait for this type of direction wastes time at the school level and discourages teacher leaders. Jay maintained support of continuous improvement in spite of these changes by:

- Sharing the school's vision with central office leaders and continuing to do so even as the individuals occupying these positions changed

- Creating school-system capacity to support the school's vision by nurturing and promoting individuals to assume leadership positions throughout the system

- Teaching and learning with peers and supervisors at every opportunity

- Cultivating strong relationships with parents and others in the school's community

## Faculty and Staff Attrition

Faculty and staff members leave schools for various reasons, such as retirement, family moves, or health concerns. These factors are out of the control of principals, so they must plan each year to proactively ensure that replacement faculty and staff members are aligned philosophically with the concept of teachers leading and learning together. Listed here are strategies Jay used to maintain a quality staff:

- Established a system led by teachers for recruiting, selecting, inducting, and retaining quality staff members and assigned Theresa a project of making the system even stronger

- Invited current staff to participate in the hiring of new staff members

- Was explicit during interviews with potential staff members that they would be expected to share their practice, collaborate, and commit to a vision focused on students' learning
- Embedded rituals into the school culture, such as MMS's annual faculty and staff retreat, where everyone recommitted to the school's vision

## Shifting Demographics of Students and Community

With increased population diversity in all parts of the country, few schools are untouched by shifting demographics. Most of the MMS teaching staff began their careers working with middle-class, English-speaking students, but then needed to adjust their practice to address a more diverse student population. Here are strategies MMS faculty and staff used to reduce this disruption to achieving the school's mission:

- Established a system for identifying teacher learning needs based on student learning data
- Offered varied approaches to professional learning, relying on expertise from within the school as well as from external sources
- Created structures that required communication focused on sharing practices for effective instruction for all students
- Built strong relationships with parents and other community members, including inviting them to be represented in decision-making structures

## Federal, State, and Local Mandates

Mandates from outside the school are uncontrollable factors that MMS faculty and staff faced. Jay had to effectively communicate these changes to teachers in a positive way so that solutions could be developed without dwelling on what could be perceived as unfair or inappropriate policies. Here are strategies Jay used:

- Established a system of governance structures that can adapt as necessary to accommodate external mandates within existing operations
- Used the school's shared vision as the framework for assessing how mandates can support the focus on student learning
- Kept staff fully informed regarding the mandates, both as they developed and when they were to be implemented
- Invited teachers to assist in determining ways to meet the requirements of the mandates with the least disruption possible to the instructional programming

## Changing Principal Leadership

At MMS, the new disruptor is a change in the principalship. However, given the actions that Jay and the teacher leaders have taken over 12 years, the likelihood of a change in principal disrupting the school's operations is reduced. The system has been created to be self-sustaining; because of this, the new principal at MMS can work with the teachers to continue making improvements. The senior-level leaders must now assume the responsibility for ensuring a good match between the new principal and MMS.

## Theresa Manages Her Disruptors

Interestingly, because this is Theresa's first year in a newly established position, some of her reality issues are easier to see as disruptors of her work than the 12-year history of Jay's MMS principalship. While everyone has some level of impact from the disruptors described above, some of those experienced by Theresa may be more familiar to most of us, especially those of us moving into school-wide leadership positions for the first time. Some of her disruptors and her strategies for dealing with them included:

- Mistakes, which she analyzed, often with Jay's help. Now she wonders why not analyze her successes too; perhaps she can learn from those as well.

- Relationships took one step back before they moved forward. Theresa was initially surprised when she realized that her relationships with people she had worked with for years changed as soon as she accepted the new position. Shortly, the new relationships became more comfortable and initial posturing was slowly replaced with trust.

- Relationships need to function within parameters/boundaries. This disruptor is closely related to the previous one. People with whom Theresa had worked for years and considered as her friends remained so, but within limits. Her new role put her in a position of needing a new level of objectivity, especially helping with conflicts and sensitive issues. Theresa learned that she still needed to be caring, but also to curb her emotions.

- Caution—you can't share everything you know! More than ever before, Theresa realized she had information about people and situations that at one time she might have thought worthy of sharing with colleagues to demonstrate being "in the know." Now, she really was "in the know," however, her hard-earned trust would vanish in an instant if she were thought to be sharing this information outside specific parameters. Sometimes this was a heavy burden for her, especially when she had information that might soothe the angry, calm the anxious, or relieve the pressure for a colleague. Jay would know what to share, when, and with whom. It was her responsibility to keep the confidences with which she was entrusted.

- Everything is great, right? Wrong! When Theresa was team leader, most everything was copacetic. She quickly learned that was not necessarily the case school wide; while things on the surface seemed calm and peaceful, in reality numerous issues were bubbling below the surface in various parts of the school. This connects directly with her realization of needing to keep confidences with the information to which she was privy. There were lots of things happening in the school that only a few individuals knew about; Theresa decided that in many instances not knowing was a good thing—in fact, sometimes she wished she didn't know either. Still, knowing the whole school was a part of her new job; she really couldn't do it well without this knowledge.

Theresa was quickly learning that her view of MMS before becoming Dean of Instruction was very different than after working in the position for a year. This very realization was probably the most significant disruptor for Theresa. She had changed because her perspective had changed. Fortunately, she had great mentors, especially Jay and Yolanda, and she was quick to analyze and learn from her mistakes. In many ways, the disruptors in Theresa's first year in her new role at MMS helped her grow into it. After this first year, she was feeling more confident and definitely more aware of her needs and those of the people she serves. Last year was good; this coming year would be great!

## Summary

As Gandhi once shared, "You must be the change you wish to see in the world." *Lead with Me* advocates that intentional leadership is the change we wish to see across schools. That change comes in the form of teacher leaders and principals playing major roles in the implementing and supporting of teacher leadership. The importance of sustaining teacher leading and learning while addressing the disruptors that affect all schools at one time or another will likely become even more imperative as pressures intensify to improve schools. Creating strong systems in a school through building relationships, distributing power and authority, and aligning teacher leadership with professional learning will be the key factors in sustaining that leading and learning and enabling the school's continued improvement.

As we have emphasized throughout this book, these are continuing endeavors that are accomplished only through intentional leadership. As teacher learning and leading emerges and increases throughout the school, the responsibility of intentional leadership permeates all levels of the organization. Intentionally leading and learning must become ubiquitous.

We realize some schools are in the early phases of putting this new view of leading and learning into practice, and there are still relatively few schools where this is the norm. Even so, the proliferation of literature about teacher leadership, teacher leader roles, and interest in sustainability of school improvement encourages us to believe teacher leadership is expanding and that it holds the potential for significant changes in education. Principals who take advantage of this resource can reap the benefits for both themselves, the individuals they support, the school, and, most importantly, the students. To support this premise, we have asked both Jay and Theresa to close this work with some words of inspiration and encouragement for incumbent and aspiring principals and emerging teacher leaders.

# Afterword

Dear current and potential principals,

If you have read this far, you are very near the end of the book. I have no illusions that you have a fail-safe recipe in your hands that will magically transform you, your school, its staff, its students, and its community into a utopian type of educational Camelot. What you do have is a template that can guide you in developing a school and staff that most surely can become and endure as an authentic community of learners. Take a moment or two and contemplate that as a real possibility.

1. Could it really happen? Absolutely!

2. Can you do it without changing yourself and influencing others to change to greater or lesser degrees? Probably not!

3. Does this book identify the behavioral changes and their concomitant philosophical and psychological orientations that are essential to achieving the desired outcome—the school's vision for student learning? Yes!

4. Are these required changes achievable? Yes!

5. Easily? No!

6. With commitment, perseverance, and patience? Yes!

7. Have any other schools done it? A few have been successful.

Don't hesitate to begin your new adventure. The twenty-first-century school needs you now—even more so as the years go by. I wish you the very best as you strive to give life to the ideas described in this book.

Sincerely,

*Jay*

P.S.

This is Theresa! I just want to echo Jay's comments and encouragement. We educators love talking about the importance of nurturing every child's full potential; so, why wouldn't we also want to do that for the professionals who work with these children? That can and will happen if school leaders intentionally employ the principles in this book. Imagine schools in which teachers are operating at their full potential and nurturing students to reach their full potential! It can be done, but not without principals working to make it happen. What a powerful path to achieve the vision of improving student learning—take it, please!

# Bibliography

Abrego, C., & Pankake. A. (February 2011). The district-wide sustainability of a professional learning community during leadership changes at the superintendency level. *Administrative issues journal: Education, practice, and research. 1*(1), p. 3–13.

Ackerman, R. H., & Mackenzie, S. V. (2007). *Uncovering teacher leadership: Essays and voices from the field*. Thousand Oaks, CA: Corwin Press.

Anderson, K. D. (2004). The nature of teacher leadership in schools as reciprocal influences between teacher leaders and principals. *School Effectiveness and School Improvement, 15*(1), 97–113.

The ASCD Whole Child Symposium, 2014, Fall 2014 Teacher Leadership www.ascd.org/WholeChild

Barth, R. S. (2001). *Learning by heart*. San Francisco: Jossey-Bass.

Barth, R. S. (2007). The teacher leader. In R. H. Ackerman & S. V. Mackenzie (Eds.), *Uncovering teacher leadership: Essays and voices from the field* (p. 10). Thousand Oaks, CA: Corwin Press.

Berry, B., Byrd, A., & Wieder, A. (2013). *Teacherpreneurs: Innovative teachers who lead but don't leave*. San Francisco, CA: Jossey-Bass.

Blasé, J., & Blasé, J. (2006). *Teachers bringing out the best in teachers: A guide to peer consultation for administrators and teachers*. Thousand Oaks, CA: Corwin Press.

Blasé, J., & Kirby, P. C. (1992). *Bringing out the best in teachers: What effective principals do*. Newbury Park, CA: Corwin Press.

Blasé, J., & Kirby, P. C. (2009). *Bringing out the best in teachers: What effective principals do* (3rd ed.). Thousand Oaks, CA: Corwin Press.

Boles, K., & Troen, V. (2003, September/October). Mamas, don't let your babies grow up to be teachers. *The Harvard Education Letter*.

Bolman, L. G., & Deal, T. E. (2003). *Reframing organizations: Artistry, choice, and leadership* (3rd ed.). San Francisco: Jossey-Bass.

Bowman, R. F. (2004). Teachers as leaders. *The Clearing House, 77*, 187–189.

Bridges, E. (1967). A model for shared decision-making in the school principalship. *Educational Administration Quarterly, 3*, 49–61.

Bridges, W. (1991). *Managing transitions: Making the most of change*. Reading, MA: Addison-Wesley.

Bridges, W. (2004). *Transitions: Making sense of life's changes* (2nd ed.). Cambridge, MA: Da Capo Press.

Bryk, A. S., & Schneider, B. (2002). *Trust in schools: A core resource for improvement*. New York, NY: Russell Sage.

Coleman, J. S. (1988). Social capital in the creation of human capital. *The American Journal of Sociology, 94*, Supplement: Organizations and Institutions: Sociological and Economic Approaches to the Analysis of Social Structure, 95–120.

Collay, M. (2011). *Everyday teacher leadership: Taking actions where you are*. San Francisco, CA: Jossey-Bass.

Collay, M., Dunlap, D., Enloe, W., & Gagnon, G. W. (1998). *Learning circles: Creating conditions for professional development*. Thousand Oaks, CA: Corwin Press.

Collins, J. (2001). *Good to great: Why some companies make the leap . . . and others don't.* New York, NY: HarperCollins.

Copland, M. (2001a). *Accelerated Schools Leadership to Learning Conference.* Presentation at Accelerated Schools Leadership to Learning Conference, Storrs, CT.

Copland, M. (2001b). The myth of the superprincipal. *Phi Delta Kappan, 82*(7), 528–532.

Cotton, K. (2003). *Principals and student achievement: What the research says.* Alexandria, VA: Association for Supervision and Curriculum Development.

Cress, K., & Miller, B. (2003). *Understanding limits in teacher leaders' relationships with teachers.* Newton, MA: Education Development Center. Retrieved from http://cllc.edc.org/docs/UnderstandingLimitsinRelationships.pdf

Crowther, F., Kaagan, S.S., Ferguson, M., & Hann, L. (2002). *Developing teacher leaders: How teacher leadership enhances school success.* Thousand Oaks, CA: Corwin Press.

Cuban, L. (2004). *The blackboard and the bottom line: Why schools can't be businesses.* Cambridge, MA: Harvard University Press.

Cunniff, D., Elder, D., & Padover, W. (2013). *Innovative educational leadership through the cycle of change.* Dubuque, IA: Kendall Hunt.

Danielson, C. (2006). *Teacher leadership that strengthens professional practice.* Alexandria, VA: LASCD.

Darling-Hammond, L. (2007). Teacher learning that supports student learning. In B.Z. Presseisen (Ed.), *Teaching for intelligence* (2nd ed.). Thousand Oaks, CA: Corwin Press.

Datnow, A., & Park, V. (2014). *Data-driven leadership.* San Francisco, CA: Jossey-Bass.

Donaldson, G.A. (2001). *Cultivating leadership in schools: Connecting people, purpose, and practice.* New York, NY: Teachers College Press.

Drago-Severson, E. (2004). *Helping teachers learn: Principal leadership for adult growth and development.* Thousand Oaks, CA: Corwin Press.

Drago-Severson, E., Blum-DeStefano, J., & Asghar, A. (2013). *Learning for leadership: Developmental strategies for building capacity in our schools.* Thousand Oaks, CA: Corwin Press.

Drucker, P.F. (1966). *The effective executive.* New York, NY: Harper & Row.

DuFour, R. (2003). Leading edge: 'Collaboration lite' puts student achievement on a starvation diet. *Journal of Staff Development, 24*(3). Retrieved from www.nsdc.org/library/publications/jsd/dufour244.cfm

DuFour, R., DuFour, R., Eaker, R., & Many, T. (2010). *Learning by doing: A handbook for professional learning communities at work* (2nd ed.). Bloomington, IN: Solution Tree.

DuFour, R., Eaker, R., & DuFour, R. (2005). *On common ground: The power of professional learning communities.* Bloomington, IN: Solution Tree.

DuFour, R., & Marzano, R.J. (2011). *Leaders of learning: How district, school, and classroom leaders improve student achievement.* Bloomington, IN: Solution Tree Press.

Elmore, R.F. (2002). *Bridging the gap between standards and achievement: The imperative for professional development in education.* Washington, DC: Albert Shanker Institute. Retrieved from www.shankerinstitute.org/Downloads/Bridging_Gap.pdf

Eros, J. (2011). *The career cycle and the second stage of teaching: Implications for policy and professional development.* Arts Education Policy Review, 112: 65–70, Milton Park, Abingdon, UK: Taylor & Francis Group. doi: 10.1080/10632913.2011.546683

Fishbein, S., & Osterman, K. (2001). *Crossing over: Learning the roles and rules of the teacher-administrator relationship.* Paper presented at the annual meeting of the American Educational Research Association, Seattle (April 10–14, 2001). ERIC Number: ED463276 Retrieved from http://eric.ed.gov/?id=ED463276

Fullan, M. (1993). *Change forces: Probing the depths of educational reform.* New York, NY: Falmer Press.

Fullan, M. (1997). Broadening the concept of teacher leadership. In S. D. Caldwell (Ed.), *Professional development in learning-centered schools* (pp. 34–48). Oxford, OH: National Staff Development Council. Retrieved from http://files.eric.ed.gov/fulltext/ED470231.pdf#page=41

Fullan, M. (2001). *Leading in a culture of change.* San Francisco, CA: Jossey-Bass.

Fullan, M. (2003). *The new meaning of educational change* (3rd ed.). New York, NY: Teachers College Press.

Fullan, M. (2005). *Leadership & sustainability: System thinkers in action.* Thousand Oaks, CA: Corwin Press.

Fullan, M. (2007). Leadership to the fore. In R. H. Ackerman & S. V. Mackenzie (Eds.), *Uncovering teacher leadership: Essays and voices from the field* (pp. 93–106). Thousand Oaks, CA: Corwin Press.

Fullan, M. (2016). *The new meaning of educational change* (5th ed.). New York, NY: Teachers College Press.

Fullan, M., with Ballew, A. C. (2004). *Leading in a culture of change personal action guide and workbook.* San Francisco, CA: Jossey-Bass.

Gandhi, Mahatma, Retrieved from Brainy Quotes at www.brainyquote.com/search_results.html?q=

Garet, M. S., Porter, A. C., Desimone, L., Birman, B. F., & Yoon, K. S. (2001). What makes professional development effective: Results from a national sample of teachers. *American Educational Research Journal, 38*(4), 915–945.

Glazerman S., Dolfin, S., Bleeker, M., Johnson, A., Isenberg, E. Lugo-Gil, J., Grider, M., . . . Ali, M., (2008). *Impacts of comprehensive teacher induction: Result from the first year of a randomized controlled study.* National Center for Education and Regional Assistance, Institute of Education Science. Washington, DC: U.S. Department of Education. Retrieved from http://files.eric.ed.gov/fulltext/ED503061.pdf

Gonzales, L. D. (2004). *Sustaining teacher leadership: Beyond the boundaries of an enabling school culture.* Lanham, MD: University Press of America.

Goodbread, M. (2000). 'Be friendly, fervent, firm.' *Journal of Staff Development, 21*(3). Retrieved from www.nsdc.org/library/publications/jsd/voices213.cfm

Grogan, M. (2013). *The Jossey-Bass Reader on Educational Leadership* (3rd ed.). San Francisco, CA: Jossey-Bass.

Hall, D. J., Gunter, H., & Bragg, J. (2013). The strange case of the emergence of distributed leadership in schools in England. *Educational Review, 65*(4), 467–487. doi: 10.1080/00131911.2012.718257. Publication link: 3dfad8d8-8be1-48c6-879b-19dfc295d3f0

Hall, G. E., & Hord, S. M. (2001). *Implementing change: Patterns, principles and potholes.* Boston, MA: Allyn & Bacon.

Hall, G. E., & Hord, S. M. (2015). *Implementing change: Patterns, principles and potholes* (4th ed.). Boston, MA: Pearson.

Hamilton, C., with Parker, C. (2001). *Communicating for results: A guide for business and the professions* (6th ed.). Belmont, CA: Wadsworth.

Hamilton, K. (2015, November/December). The teacher as professional learner: what the National Board Standards say. *Techniques,* 14–18. Retrieved from www.acteonline.org

Hargreaves, A. (2005). Leadership succession. *The Educational Forum, 69*(2), 163–173.

Hargreaves, A., & Fink, D. (2004). The seven principles of sustainable leadership. *Educational Leadership, 61*(7), 8–15.

Hargreaves, A., & Fullan, M. (2009). *Change wars.* Bloomington, IN: Solution Tree.

Harrison, C., & Killion, J. (2007). Ten roles for teacher leaders. *Educational Leadership, 65*(1), 74–77.

Heathfield, S. M. (2016, July). *Meeting leader: Roles and responsibilities.* Retrieved from www.thebalance.com/meeting-leader-roles-and responsibilities-1918732

Heifetz, R. A., & Linsky, M. (2002). *Leadership on the line: Staying alive through the dangers of leading.* Boston, MA: Harvard Business School Press.

Hess, R. M. (2015). *The cage-busting teacher.* Boston, MA: Harvard Press.

Hirsh, S. A., & Hord, S. M., (2012). A context for developing social justice for staff and students: Communities of professional learners. In E. Murakami-Ramalho & A. Pankake (Eds.), *Educational leaders encouraging the intellectual and professional capacity of others: A social justice agenda* (pp. 25–43). Charlotte, NC: Information Age.

Hord, S. M. (Ed.). (2004). *Learning together, leading together: Changing schools through professional learning communities.* New York, NY: Teachers College Press.

Hord, S. M., & Sommers, W. A. (2008). *Leading professional learning communities: Voices from research and practice.* In R. H. Ackerman & S. V. Mackenzie (Eds.), *Uncovering teacher leadership: Essays and voices from the field.* Thousand Oaks, CA: Corwin Press.

Howard, L. (2016). *Supporting new teachers: A how-to guide for leaders.* Thousand Oaks, CA: Corwin.

Huffman, J. B., & Hipp, K. K. (2003). *Reculturing schools as professional learning communities.* Lanham, MD: Scarecrow Education.

Hughes, W. H., & Pickeral, T. (2013). School climate and shared leadership. In T. Dary & T. Pickeral (Eds.), *School climate practices for implementation and sustainability: A school climate practice brief* (Number 1). New York, NY: National School Climate Center. www.ijvs.org/files/Publications/School-Climate-Practice-Briefs-for-Implementation-and-Sustainability-2013.pdf#page=26

Ingersoll, R. M. (2001). Teacher turnover and teacher shortages: An organizational analysis. *American Educational Research Journal, 38*(3), 499–534.

Ingersoll, R. M., & Smith, T. M. (2003). The wrong solution to the teacher shortage. *Educational Leadership, 60*(8), 30–33.

Ingersoll, R. M., & Smith, T. M. (2004). Do teacher induction and mentoring matter? *NASSP Bulletin, 88*(638), 28–34.

Institute for Educational Leadership Task Force on Teacher Leadership. (2001). *Leadership for student learning: Redefining the teacher as leader.* Washington, DC: Author. Retrieved from www.iel.org/pubs/s121ci.html

Joyce, B., Mueller, L., Hrycauk, M., & Hrycauk, W. (2005). Cadres help to create competence: Literacy-oriented school improvement program in Alberta, Canada, boosts teacher leadership and improves abilities. *Journal of Staff Development, 26*(3).

Joyce, B., & Showers, B. (2002). *Student achievement through staff development* (3rd ed.). Alexandria, VA: Association for Supervision and Curriculum Development.

Katzenmeyer, M., & Moller, G. (2001). *Awakening the sleeping giant: Helping teachers develop as leaders* (2nd ed.). Thousand Oaks, CA: Corwin Press.

Katzenmeyer, M., & Moller, G. (2009). *Awakening the sleeping giant: Helping teachers develop as leaders* (3rd ed.). Thousand Oaks, CA: Corwin Press.

Kegan, R. (1994). *In over our heads: The mental demands of modern life.* Cambridge, MA: Harvard University Press.

Killion, J. (2002). *What works in the elementary school: Results-based staff development.* Oxford, OH: National Staff Development Council.

Killion, J. (2013). *Establishing time for professional learning.* Oxford, OH: Learning Forward. Retrieved from www.literacyinlearningexchange.org/sites/default/files/establishing-time-for-professional-learning.pdf

Kochanek, J. R. (2005). *Building trust for better schools: Research-based practices*. Thousand Oaks, CA: Crowin Press.

Kouzes, J., & Posner, B. (2012). *The leadership challenge: How to make extraordinary things happen in organizations* (5th ed.). San Francisco, CA: Jossey-Bass.

Lambert, L. (2002). Toward a deepened theory of constructivist leadership. In L. Lambert, D., Walker, D. P., Zimmerman, J. E., Cooper, M. D., Lambert, Gardner, M. E., & Szabo, M. (Eds.), *The constructivist leader* (pp. 34–62). New York, NY: Teachers College Press.

Lambert, L. (2003). *Leadership capacity for lasting school improvement*. Alexandria, VA: Association for Supervision and Curriculum Development.

Lambert, L. (2005). Leadership for lasting reform. *Educational Leadership, 62*(5), 62–65.

Leeds, D. (2000). *The 7 powers of questions*. New York, NY: Berkley.

Leithwood, K., & Seashore Louis, K. (2012). *Linking leadership to student learning*. San Francisco, CA: Jossey-Bass.

Levenson, M. R. (2014). *Pathways to teacher leadership: Emerging models, changing roles*. Cambridge, MA: Harvard Education Press.

Lewin, R., & Regine, B. (2000). *The soul at work*. New York, NY: Simon & Schuster.

Lieberman, A., & Miller, L. (2004). *Teacher leadership*. San Francisco, CA: Jossey-Bass.

Louis, K. S., & Wahlstrom, K. (2011). Principals as cultural leaders. *Phi Delta Kappan, 92*(5), 52–56.

Lovely, S. D. (2005). Making the leap to shared leadership. *The Journal of Staff Development, 26*(2), 16–21.

Lumpkin, A., Claxton, H., & Wilson, A. (2014). Key characteristics of teacher leaders in schools. *Administrative Issues Journal: Connecting Education, Practice and Research, 4*(2), 59–67. doi:10.5929/2014.4.2.8

Marshall, K. (2005). It's time to rethink teacher supervision and evaluation. *Phi Delta Kappan, 86*(10), 727–744.

Maxwell, J. C. (2004). The 17 indisputable laws of teamwork. Dallas, TX: Thomas Nelson.

Maxwell, J. C. (2011). *The 5 levels of leadership: Proven steps to maximize your potential*. New York, NY: Center Street.

Maxwell, J. C. (2014). *Good leaders ask great questions: Your foundation for successful leadership*. New York, NY: Center Street.

Meehan, R. J. *Treasury of quotes for teachers*. Retrieved from https://sites.google.com/site/treasuryofquotesforteachers/

MetLife. (2012). *Survey of the American teacher: Challenges for school leadership*, 2012. (Survey conducted by Harris Interactive.) Retrieved from www.metlife.com/teachersurvey

Mid-continent Research for Education & Learning (McREL). (2000). *Principles in action: Stories of award-winning professional development*. Aurora, CO: McREL.

Miller, B., Moon, J., & Elko, S. (2000). *Teacher leadership in mathematics and science*. Portsmouth, NH: Heinemann.

Moller, G., & Pankake, A. (2006). *Lead with me: A principal's guide to teacher leadership*. Larchmont, NY: Eye on Education.

Moller, G., Pankake, A., Huffman, J. B., Hipp, K. A., Cowan, D., & Olivier, D. (2000). *Teacher leadership: A product of supportive and shared leadership within professional learning communities.* Paper presented at the annual meeting of the American Educational Research Association, New Orleans, LA.

Muijs, D., & Harris, A. (2003). Teacher leadership—Improvement through empowerment? An overview of the literature. *Educational Management and Administration, 31*, 437–448.

Murphy, J. (2005). *Connecting teacher leadership and school improvement*. Thousand Oaks, CA: Corwin Press.

Nappi, J. S. (November 2014). The teacher leader: Improving schools by building social capital through shared leadership. *Principal's Research Review, 80*(4), 29.

National Staff Development Council. (2005). E-X-P-A-N-D-I-N-G your vision of professional development. *The Learning System, 1*(1), 5.

Nelson, T. H. (2008). Teachers' collaborative inquiry and professional growth: Should we be optimistic? *Science Teacher Education, 93*(3), 548–580.

Northouse, P. G. (2013). *Leadership: Theory and practice* (6th ed.). Thousand Oaks, CA: Sage.

Norton, J. (2004). Today's effective schools have high-capacity leadership. *Working Toward Excellence: The Journal of the Alabama Best Practices Center, 4*(1), 1–2, 8.

Owens, R. G. (2001). *Organizational behavior in education: Instructional leadership and school reform* (7th ed.). Needham Heights, MA: Allyn and Bacon.

Pankake, A. M. (1998). *Implementation: Making things happen.* Larchmont, NY: Eye on Education.

Pankake, A. M., & Abrego, J. (2012). Building capacity: The foundation of developing others. In E. Murakami-Ramalho & A. Pankake (Eds.), *Educational leaders encouraging the intellectual and professional capacity of others: A social justice agenda* (pp. 3–23). Charlotte, NC: Information Age.

Perkins, D. (2003). *King Arthur's round table: How collaborative conversations create smart organizations.* Hoboken, NJ: John Wiley & Sons.

Peterkin, C. (2003). *Writing your personal vision/mission statement.* Retrieved from http:www.eyekai.tv/Articles/writing_your_personal_vision.htm

Phillips-Jones, L. (n.d.). *Writing a personal vision statement.* Retrieved from www.mentoringgroup.com/html/articles/mentee_2.html

Piercey, D. (2010, September). Why don't teachers collaborate? A leadership conundrum. *The Phi Delta Kappan, 92*(1), 54–56.

Platt, A. D., Tripp, C. E., Ogden, W. R., & Fraser, R. G. (2000). *The skillful leader: Confronting mediocre teaching.* Action, MA: Research for Better Teaching.

Quaglia, R. J. (1991). The nature of change. *Journal of Maine Education. 7*(1), 13–16.

Reason, C., & Reason, C. (2011). *Mirror images: New reflections on teacher leadership.* Thousand Oaks, CA: Corwin Press.

Roberts, M. B., & Pankake, A. (2012). Teacher induction: A process for advancing social justice. In E. Murakami-Ramalho & A. Pankake (Eds.), *Educational leaders encouraging the intellectual and professional capacity of others: A social justice agenda* (pp. 99–116). Charlotte, NC: Information Age.

Rogers, E. M. (2003). *Diffusion of innovations* (5th ed.). London, UK: Simon & Schuster.

Rubin, R., Abrego, M. H., & Sutterby, J. A. (2015). *Less is more in elementary school: Strategies for thriving in a high-stakes environment.* New York, NY: Routledge, Taylor & Francis Group.

Rushfeldt, J. (n.d.). *Write powerful mission and vision statements.* Retrieved from www.lifetoolsforwomen.com/p/write-mission-vision.htm

Sanders, W. L. (1998). Value-added assessment. *School Administrator, 55*(11). Retrieved from www.aasa.org/publications/sa/1998_12/sanders.htm

Schechter, C., & Tischler, I. (2007). Organizational learning mechanisms and leadership succession: Key elements of planned school change. *Educational Planning, 16*(2), 1–7.

Schein, E. H. (2013). *Humble inquiry: The gentle art of asking instead of telling.* Oakland, CA: Berrett-Koehler.

Scherer, M. (2002). A soccer game world. *Educational Leadership, 59*(8), 5.

Schlechty, P. (1993). On the frontier of school reform with trailblazers, pioneers, and settlers. *Journal of Staff Development, 14*(4), 46–51.

Schlechty, P. (1997). *Inventing better schools.* San Francisco, CA: Jossey-Bass.

Senge, P., Cambron-McCabe, N., Lucas, T., Smith, B., Dutton, J., & Kleiner, A. (2000). *Schools that learn: A fifth discipline fieldbook for educators, parents, and everyone who cares about education.* New York, NY: Doubleday.

Sergiovanni, T. J. (2000). Leadership as stewardship: "Who's serving who?" In Jossey-Bass (Eds.), *The Jossey-Bass reader on educational leadership* (pp. 269–286). San Francisco, CA: Jossey-Bass.

Silva, D. Y., Gimbert, B., & Nolan, J. (2000). Sliding the doors: Locking and unlocking possibilities for teacher leadership. *Teachers College Record, 102*(4), 779–806.

Smith, G. (2004). *Leading the professionals: How to inspire and motivate professional service teams.* Sterling, VA: Kogan Page.

Smith, J. V. (2003). *Key skills for coaching.* Bristol, England: Anaptys Ltd. Retrieved from www.uwe.ac.uk/hsc/learn teach/pec/keycoachingskills.doc

Smylie, M. A., & Brownlee-Conyers, J. (1992). Teacher leaders and their principals: Exploring the development of new working relationships. *Educational Administration Quarterly, 28*(2), 150–184.

Sparks, D. (2005). The final 2%: What it takes to create profound change in leaders. *Journal of Staff Development, 26*(2), 8–15.

Spillane, J. P. (2005). Distributed leadership. *The Educational Forum, 69,* 143–150.

Spillane, J. P. (2006). *Distributed leadership.* San Francisco, CA: Jossey-Bass.

Spillane, J. P., Hallett, T., & Diamond, J. B. (2003). Forms of capital and the construction of leadership: Instructional leadership in urban elementary schools. *Sociology of Education, 76*(1), 1–17.

Spillane, J. P., Halverson, R., & Diamond, J. B. (2001). Investigating school leadership practice: A distributed perspective. *Educational Researcher,* 23–28. Retrieved from www.education.wisc.edu/elpa/people/faculty/halverson/JamesSpillaneDistributed Leadership.pdf.

Spillane, J. P., Halverson, R., & Diamond, J. B. (2004). Towards a theory of leadership practice: A distributed perspective. *Journal of Curriculum Studies, 36*(1), 3–28.

Steffy, B. E., Wolfe, M. P., Pasch, S. H., & Enz, B. J. (Eds.). (1999). *Life cycle of the career teacher.* Thousand Oaks, CA: Corwin Press.

Sullivan, S., & Glanz, J. (2013). Supervision that improves teaching and learning: Strategies and techniques (4th ed.). Thousand Oaks, CA: Corwin Press.

Sykes, G. (1999). Introduction: Teaching as the learning profession. In L. Darling-Hammond & G. Sykes (Eds.), *Teaching as the learning profession: Handbook of policy and practice* (pp. xv–xxiii). San Francisco, CA: Jossey-Bass.

Talbert, J. E., & McLaughlin, M. W. (2002). Professional communities and the artisan model of teaching. *Teachers and teaching: Theory and practice, 8*(3/4), 325–344.

Teach Plus National Headquarters. (2015). The decade-plus teaching career: How to retain effective teachers through teacher leadership. (February 6, 2015). Boston, MA: Teach Plus. Retrieved from: http://www.teachplus.org/sites/default/files/publication/pdf/decade-plus_final.pdf

Teacher Leadership Exploratory Consortium. (2011). *Teacher leader model standards.* Carrboro, NC: Author. Retrieved from www.teacherleaderstandards.org

Theoharis, G. (2009). *The school leaders our children deserve: Seven keys to equity, social justice, and school reform.* New York, NY: Teachers College.

Tobia, E., & Hord, S. M. (2012). I am a professional: Learning communities elevate teachers' knowledge, skills, and identity. *Journal of Staff Development, 33*(3), 16, 18, 20, 26.

Ubben, G. C., & Hughes, L. W. (1997). *The principal: Creative leadership for effective schools.* Needham Heights, MA: Allyn and Bacon.

Ubben, G. C., Hughes, L. W., & Norris, C. J. (2016). *The principal: Creative leadership for effective schools* (8th ed.). Boston, MA: Pearson.

Vandiver, F. M. (1996). The identification and characteristics of teacher leaders within a selected elementary school. (Doctoral dissertation, University of Miami, 1996). *Dissertation Abstracts International, 57* (12A), 5122.

Wahlstrom, K. L., & Seashore Louis, K. (2008). How teachers experience principal leadership: The roles of professional community, trust, efficacy, and shared responsibility. *Educational Administration Quarterly, 44*(4), 458–495.

Ward, M. E., & Wilcox, B. M. (1999). *Delegation & empowerment*. Larchmont, NY: Eye on Education.

Weiner, J. M. (2016). Principals' difficulty releasing decision-making to their instructional leadership team. *Journal of School Leadership, 26*(2), 149–180.

Whitaker, T. (1995). Informal teacher leadership: The key to successful changes in middle level school. *NASSP Bulletin, 79*(567), 76–81.

Whitaker, T. (2002). *Dealing with difficult teachers*. Larchmont, NY: Eye on Education.

Wiseman, L. (2010). *Multipliers: How the best leaders make everyone smarter*. New York: NY: HarperCollins.

Woodcock, M. (1989). *Team development manual* (2nd ed.). Aldershot, England: Gower.

Woolcock, M. (1998). Social capital and economic development: Toward a theoretical synthesis and policy framework. *Journal Theory and Society, 27*(2), 151–208.

Yoon K. S., Duncan, T., Lee, S. W., Scarloss, B., & Shapley, K. L. (2007). *Reviewing the evidence on how teacher professional development affects student achievement*. Institutes for Research, Retrieved from http://ies.ed.gov/ncee/edlabs REL Southwest, Regional Educational Laboratory AT EDvance Research, Inc. American /regions/southwest/pdf/rel_2007033_sum.pdf

York-Barr, J., & Duke, K. (2004). What do we know about teacher leadership? Findings from two decades of scholarship. *Review of Educational Research, 74*(3), 255–316.

Zinn, L. (1997). *Support and barrier to teacher leadership: Reports of teacher leaders*. Paper presented at the annual meeting of the American Educational Research Association, Chicago, IL.

 Taylor & Francis eBooks

## Helping you to choose the right eBooks for your Library

Add Routledge titles to your library's digital collection today. Taylor and Francis ebooks contains over 50,000 titles in the Humanities, Social Sciences, Behavioural Sciences, Built Environment and Law.

Choose from a range of subject packages or create your own!

**Benefits for you**
- Free MARC records
- COUNTER-compliant usage statistics
- Flexible purchase and pricing options
- All titles DRM-free.

**Benefits for your user**
- Off-site, anytime access via Athens or referring URL
- Print or copy pages or chapters
- Full content search
- Bookmark, highlight and annotate text
- Access to thousands of pages of quality research at the click of a button.

**REQUEST YOUR FREE INSTITUTIONAL TRIAL TODAY** | **Free Trials Available** We offer free trials to qualifying academic, corporate and government customers.

## eCollections – Choose from over 30 subject eCollections, including:

| | |
|---|---|
| Archaeology | Language Learning |
| Architecture | Law |
| Asian Studies | Literature |
| Business & Management | Media & Communication |
| Classical Studies | Middle East Studies |
| Construction | Music |
| Creative & Media Arts | Philosophy |
| Criminology & Criminal Justice | Planning |
| Economics | Politics |
| Education | Psychology & Mental Health |
| Energy | Religion |
| Engineering | Security |
| English Language & Linguistics | Social Work |
| Environment & Sustainability | Sociology |
| Geography | Sport |
| Health Studies | Theatre & Performance |
| History | Tourism, Hospitality & Events |

For more information, pricing enquiries or to order a free trial, please contact your local sales team:
**www.tandfebooks.com/page/sales**

 **Routledge** Taylor & Francis Group | The home of Routledge books

**www.tandfebooks.com**